of the Night

(4)

KOTOYAMA

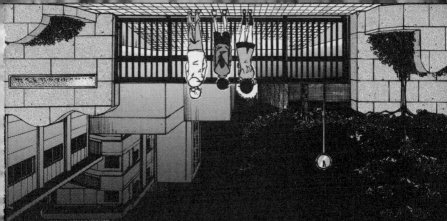

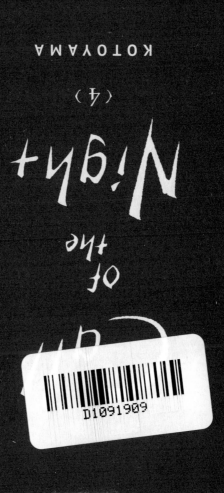

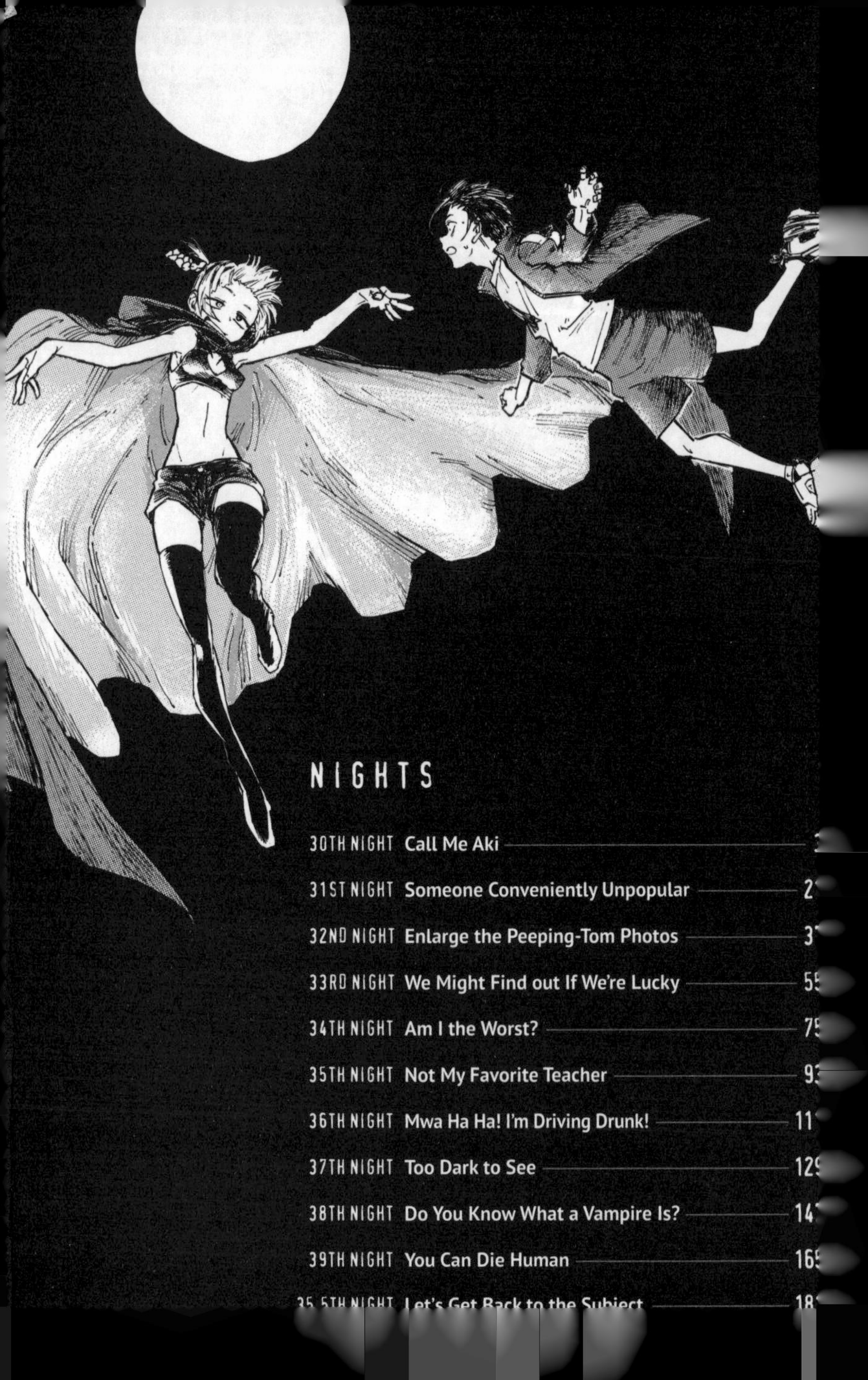

NIGHTS

NIGHT 30: CALL ME AKI

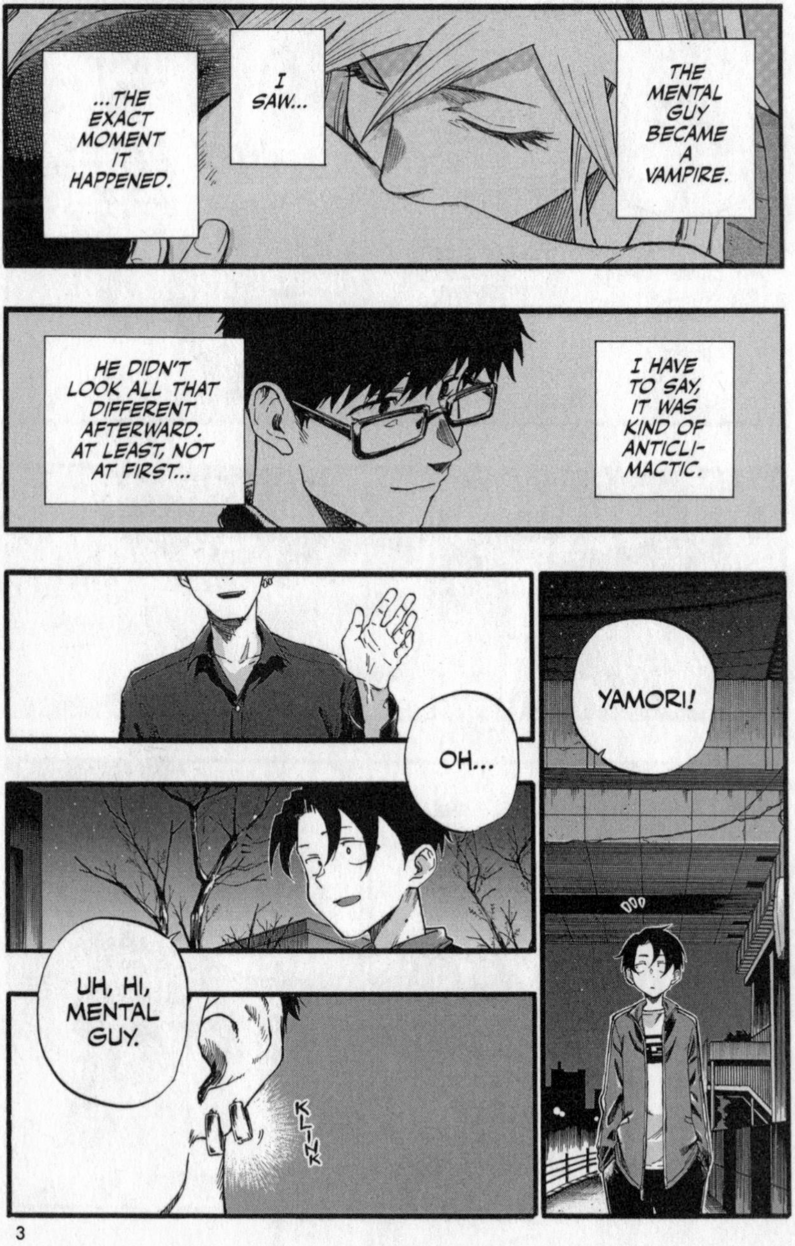
THE MENTAL GUY BECAME A VAMPIRE.
I SAW...
...THE EXACT MOMENT IT HAPPENED.
I HAVE TO SAY, IT WAS KIND OF ANTICLI-MACTIC.
HE DIDN'T LOOK ALL THAT DIFFERENT AFTERWARD. AT LEAST, NOT AT FIRST...
YAMORI!
OH...
UH, HI, MENTAL GUY.
KLINK

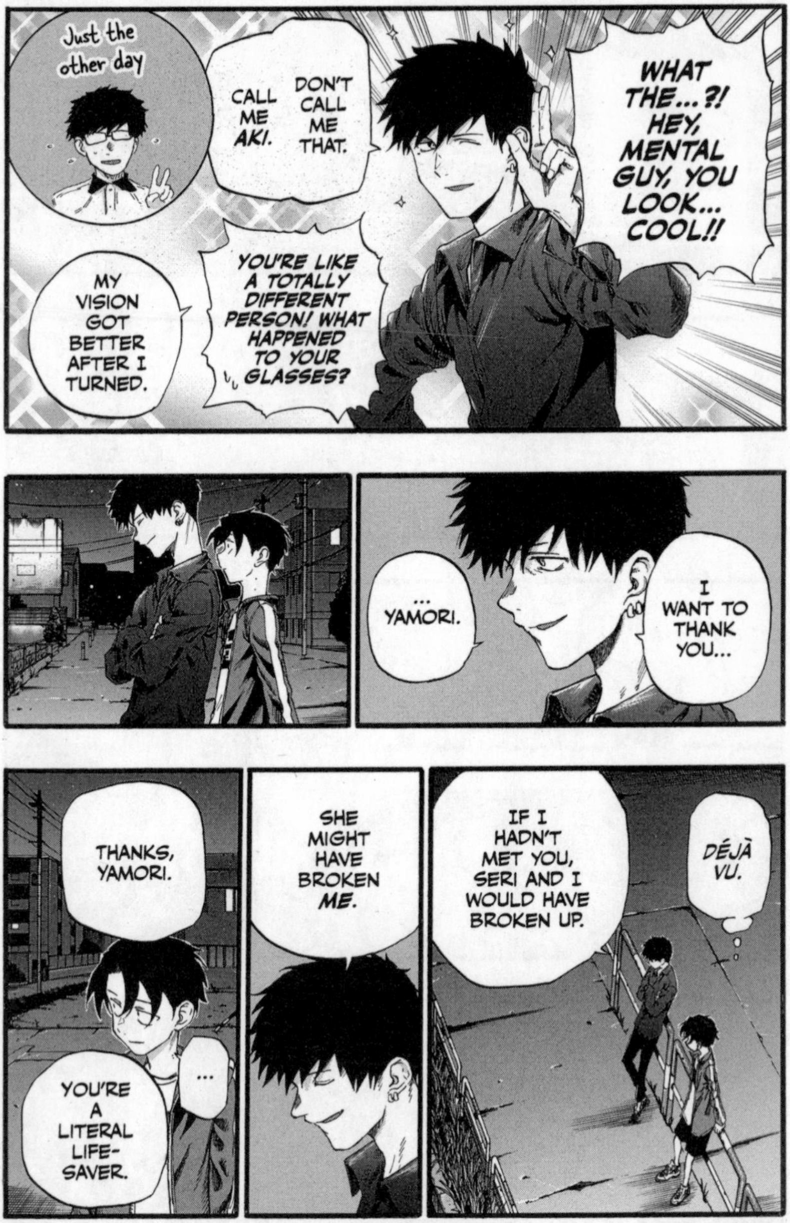
WHAT THE...?! HEY, MENTAL GUY, YOU LOOK... COOL!!
DON'T CALL ME THAT.
CALL ME AKI.
Just the other day
YOU'RE LIKE A TOTALLY DIFFERENT PERSON! WHAT HAPPENED TO YOUR GLASSES?
MY VISION GOT BETTER AFTER I TURNED.
I WANT TO THANK YOU...
... YAMORI.
IF I HADN'T MET YOU, SERI AND I WOULD HAVE BROKEN UP.
DÉJÀ VU.
SHE MIGHT HAVE BROKEN ME.
THANKS, YAMORI.
YOU'RE A LITERAL LIFE-SAVER.
...

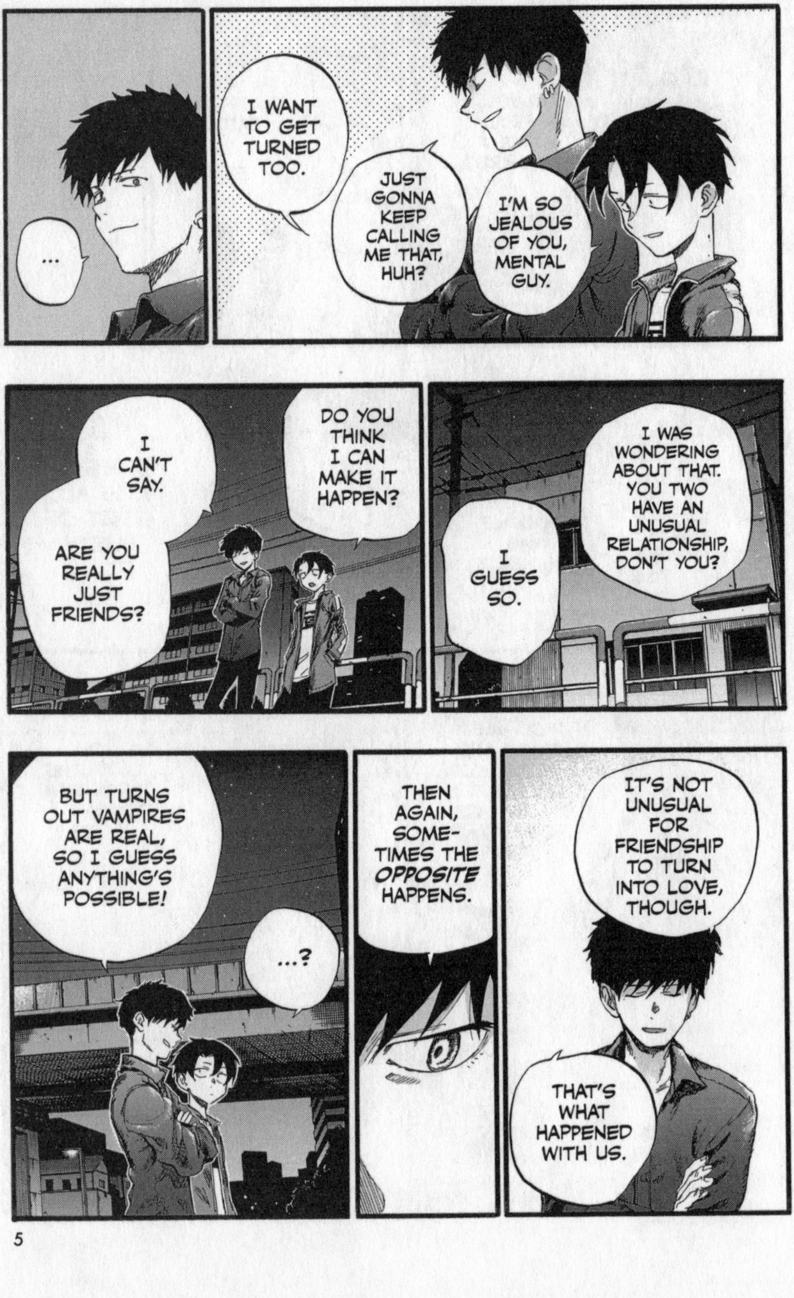
I'M SO JEALOUS OF YOU, MENTAL GUY.
JUST GONNA KEEP CALLING ME THAT, HUH?
I WANT TO GET TURNED TOO.
...
I WAS WONDERING ABOUT THAT. YOU TWO HAVE AN UNUSUAL RELATIONSHIP, DON'T YOU?
I GUESS SO.
DO YOU THINK I CAN MAKE IT HAPPEN?
I CAN'T SAY.
ARE YOU REALLY JUST FRIENDS?
IT'S NOT UNUSUAL FOR FRIENDSHIP TO TURN INTO LOVE, THOUGH.
THAT'S WHAT HAPPENED WITH US.
THEN AGAIN, SOME-TIMES THE *OPPOSITE* HAPPENS.
BUT TURNS OUT VAMPIRES ARE REAL, SO I GUESS ANYTHING'S POSSIBLE!
...?

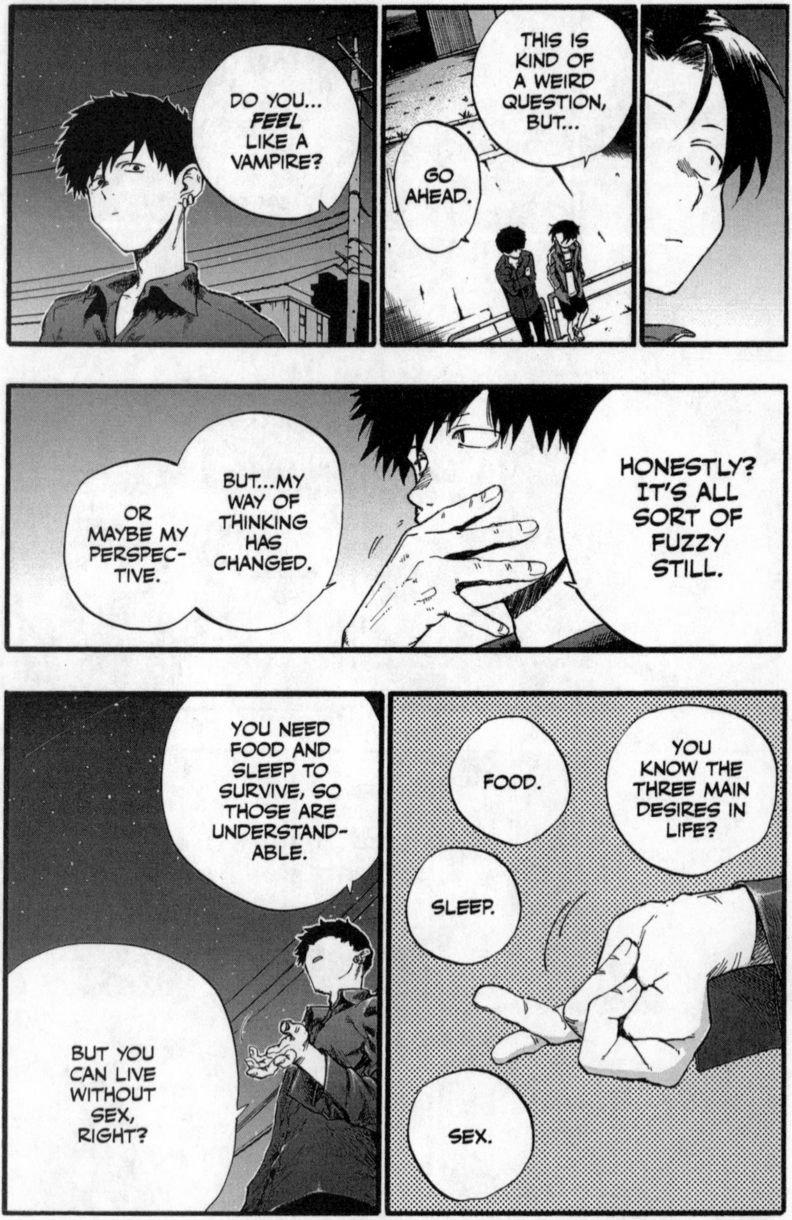
THIS IS KIND OF A WEIRD QUESTION, BUT...
GO AHEAD.
DO YOU... FEEL LIKE A VAMPIRE?
HONESTLY? IT'S ALL SORT OF FUZZY STILL.
BUT...MY WAY OF THINKING HAS CHANGED.
OR MAYBE MY PERSPEC-TIVE.
YOU KNOW THE THREE MAIN DESIRES IN LIFE?
FOOD.
SLEEP.
SEX.
YOU NEED FOOD AND SLEEP TO SURVIVE, SO THOSE ARE UNDERSTAND-ABLE.
BUT YOU CAN LIVE WITHOUT SEX, RIGHT?

THAT'S THE WAY I THOUGHT WHEN I WAS HUMAN.
...?
THOSE THREE DESIRES AREN'T ABOUT *THE SELF,* THOUGH.
THEY'RE ABOUT SURVIVAL OF YOUR SPECIES.
IF YOU DON'T EAT OR SLEEP...
...AND DON'T HAVE SEX...
...YOUR SPECIES WILL GO EXTINCT.

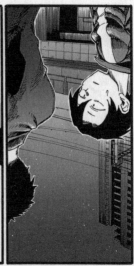

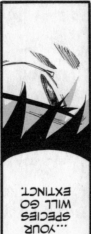

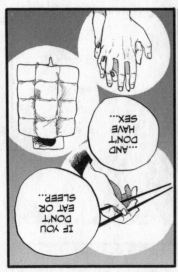

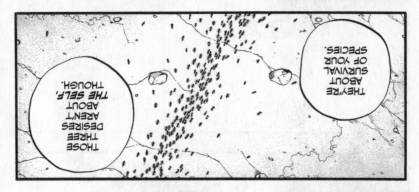

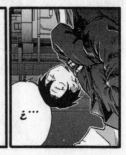

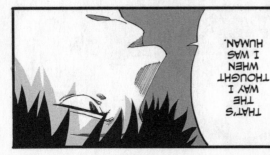

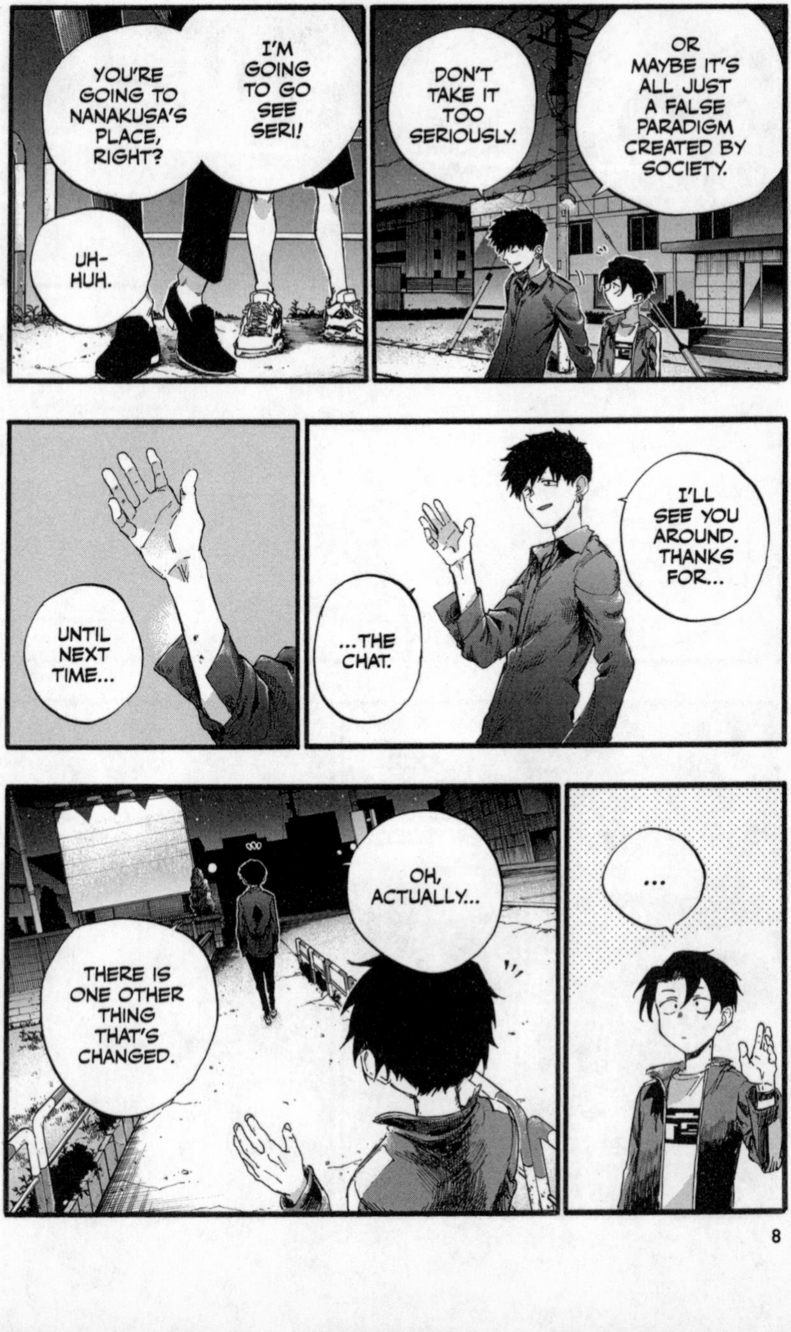
OR MAYBE IT'S ALL JUST A FALSE PARADIGM CREATED BY SOCIETY.
DON'T TAKE IT TOO SERIOUSLY.
I'M GOING TO GO SEE SERI!
YOU'RE GOING TO NANAKUSA'S PLACE, RIGHT?
UH-HUH.
I'LL SEE YOU AROUND. THANKS FOR...
...THE CHAT.
UNTIL NEXT TIME...
...
OH, ACTUALLY...
THERE IS ONE OTHER THING THAT'S CHANGED.

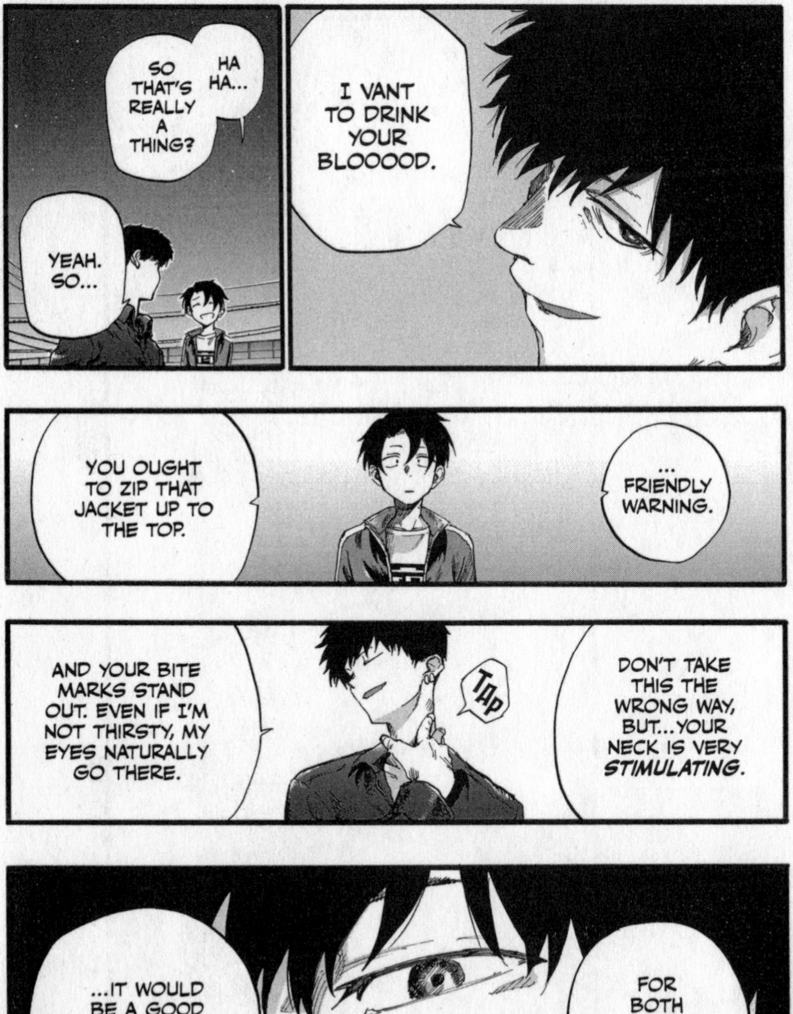
I VANT TO DRINK YOUR BLOOOOD.
HA HA...
SO THAT'S REALLY A THING?
YEAH. SO...
... FRIENDLY WARNING.
YOU OUGHT TO ZIP THAT JACKET UP TO THE TOP.
DON'T TAKE THIS THE WRONG WAY, BUT...YOUR NECK IS VERY *STIMULATING*.
TAP
AND YOUR BITE MARKS STAND OUT. EVEN IF I'M NOT THIRSTY, MY EYES NATURALLY GO THERE.
FOR BOTH OUR SAKES...
...IT WOULD BE A GOOD IDEA FOR YOU TO COVER THAT UP.

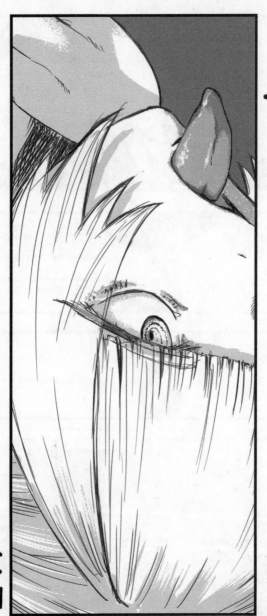

NIGHT 30:
CALL
ME
AKI

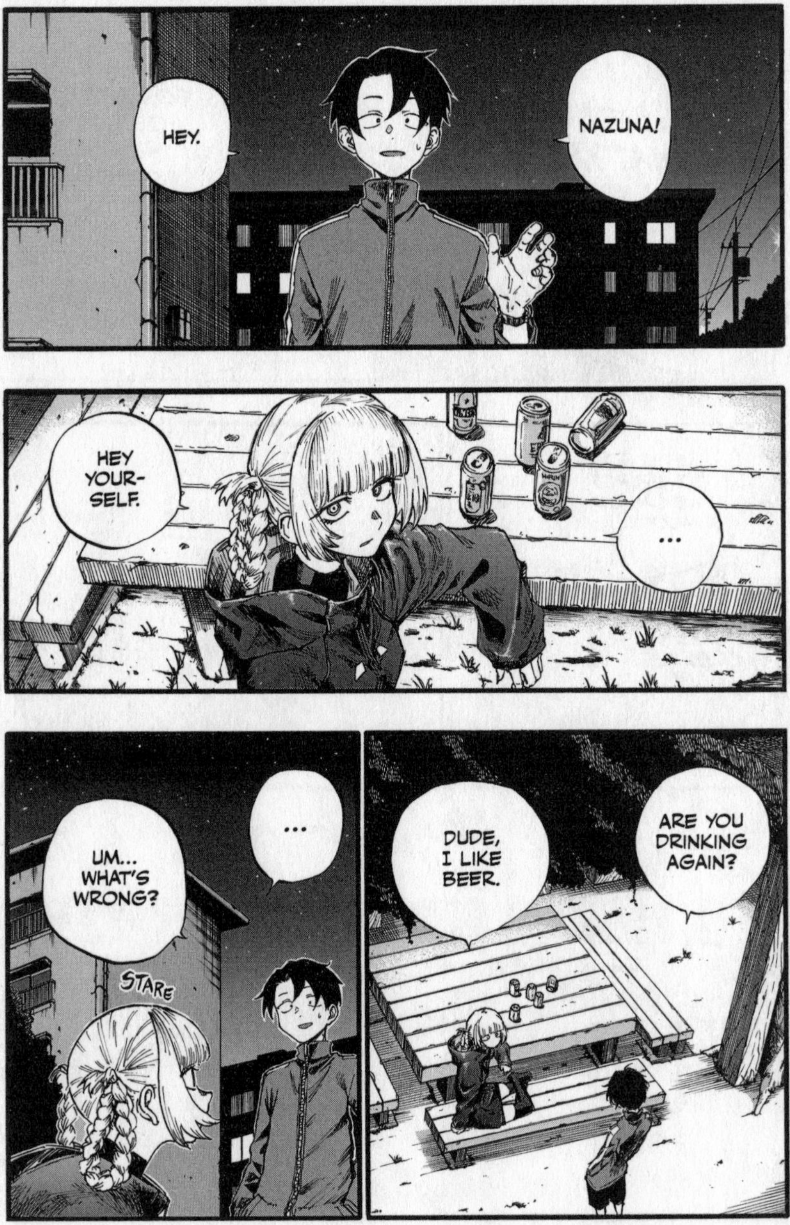
NAZUNA!
HEY.
...
HEY YOUR-SELF.
ARE YOU DRINKING AGAIN?
DUDE, I LIKE BEER.
...
UM... WHAT'S WRONG?
STARE

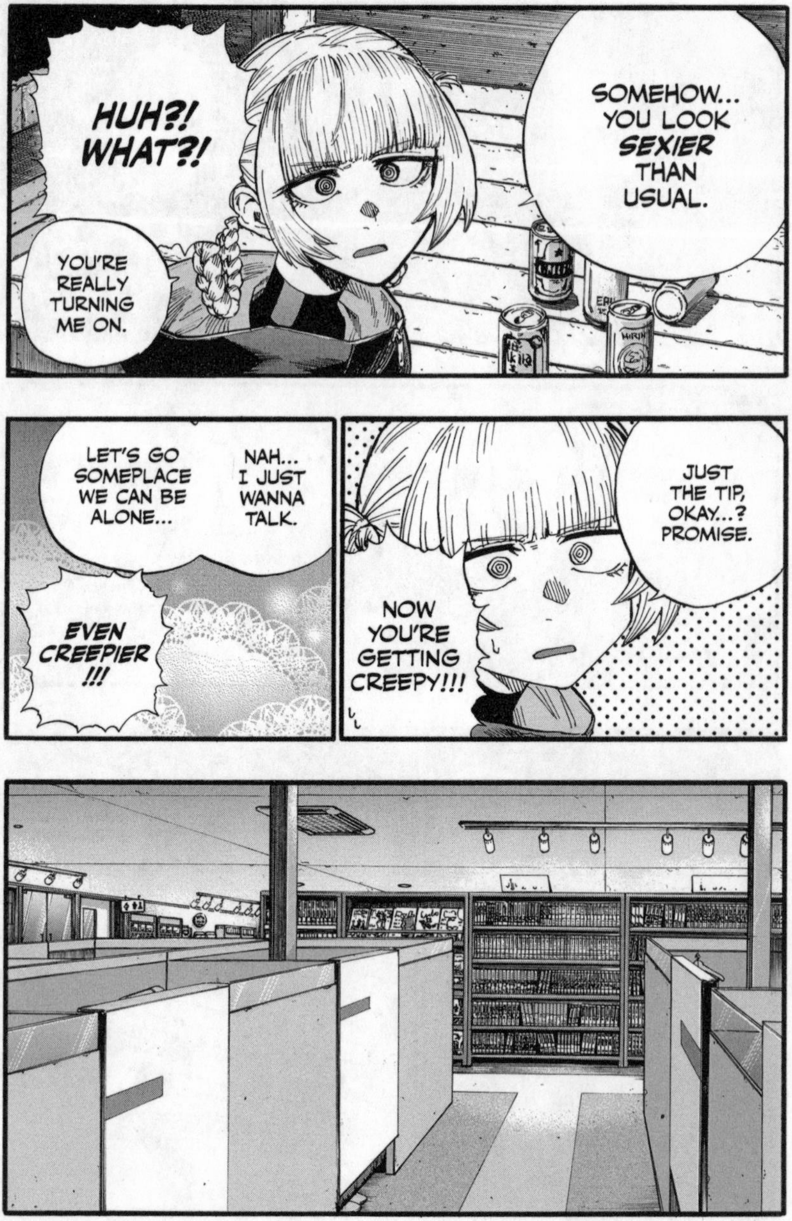
SOMEHOW... YOU LOOK SEXIER THAN USUAL.
HUH?! WHAT?!
YOU'RE REALLY TURNING ME ON.
JUST THE TIP, OKAY...? PROMISE.
NOW YOU'RE GETTING CREEPY!!!
NAH... I JUST WANNA TALK.
LET'S GO SOMEPLACE WE CAN BE ALONE...
EVEN CREEPIER!!!

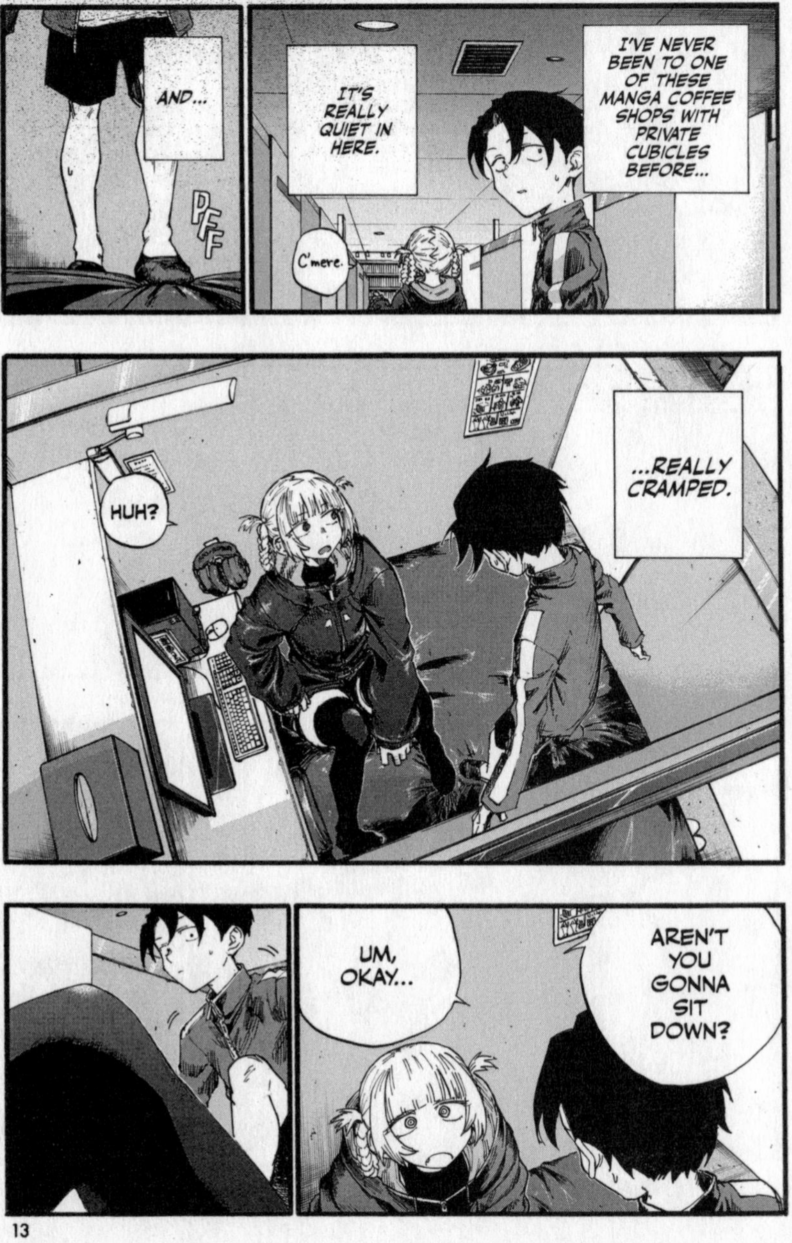

I'VE NEVER BEEN TO ONE OF THESE MANGA COFFEE SHOPS WITH PRIVATE CUBICLES BEFORE...
IT'S REALLY QUIET IN HERE.
C'mere.
AND...
PFF
...REALLY CRAMPED.
HUH?
AREN'T YOU GONNA SIT DOWN?
UM, OKAY...

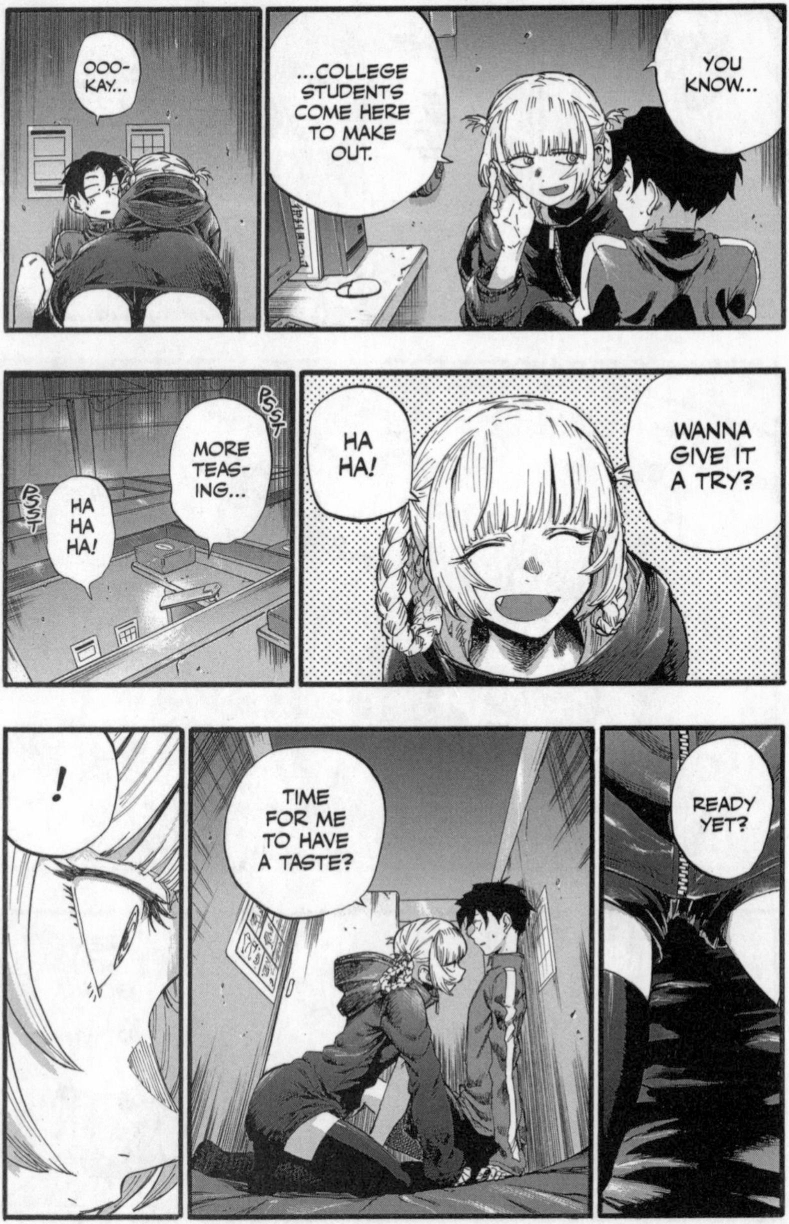
YOU KNOW...
...COLLEGE STUDENTS COME HERE TO MAKE OUT.
OOO-KAY...
WANNA GIVE IT A TRY?
HA HA!
PSST
MORE TEAS-ING...
PSST
HA HA HA!
READY YET?
TIME FOR ME TO HAVE A TASTE?
!

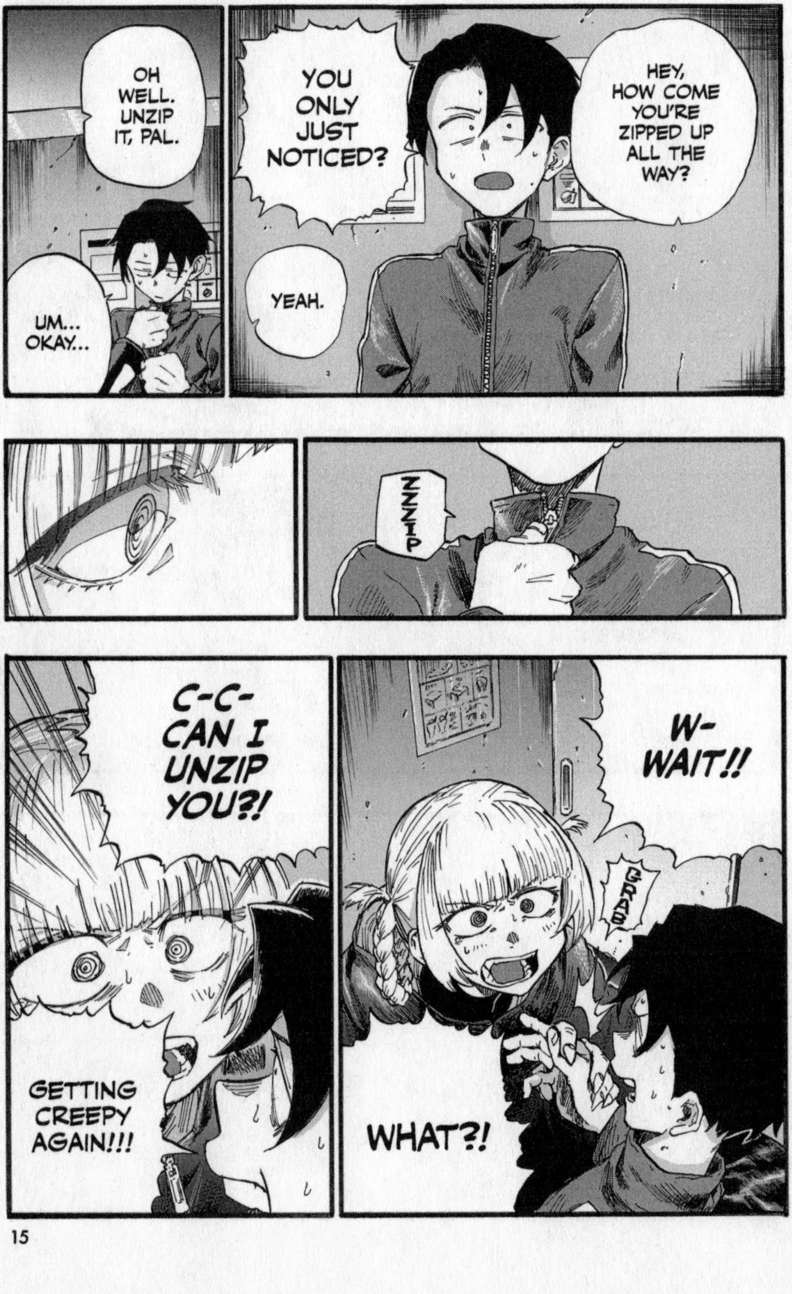
HEY, HOW COME YOU'RE ZIPPED UP ALL THE WAY?
YOU ONLY JUST NOTICED?
YEAH.
OH WELL. UNZIP IT, PAL.
UM... OKAY...
ZZZIP
W- WAIT!!
GRAB
WHAT?!
C-C- CAN I UNZIP YOU?!
GETTING CREEPY AGAIN!!!

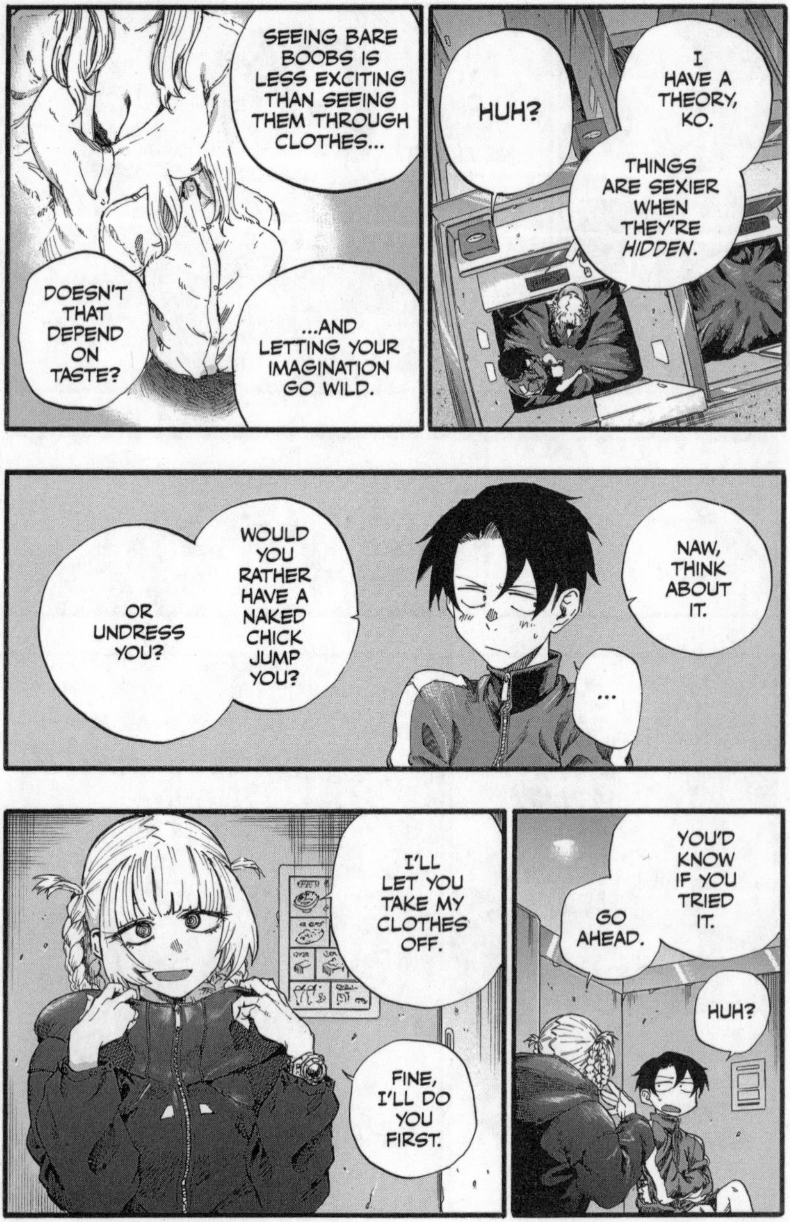
I HAVE A THEORY, KO.
THINGS ARE SEXIER WHEN THEY'RE *HIDDEN*.
HUH?
SEEING BARE BOOBS IS LESS EXCITING THAN SEEING THEM THROUGH CLOTHES...
...AND LETTING YOUR IMAGINATION GO WILD.
DOESN'T THAT DEPEND ON TASTE?
NAW, THINK ABOUT IT.
...
WOULD YOU RATHER HAVE A NAKED CHICK JUMP YOU?
OR UNDRESS YOU?
YOU'D KNOW IF YOU TRIED IT.
GO AHEAD.
HUH?
I'LL LET YOU TAKE MY CLOTHES OFF.
FINE, I'LL DO YOU FIRST.

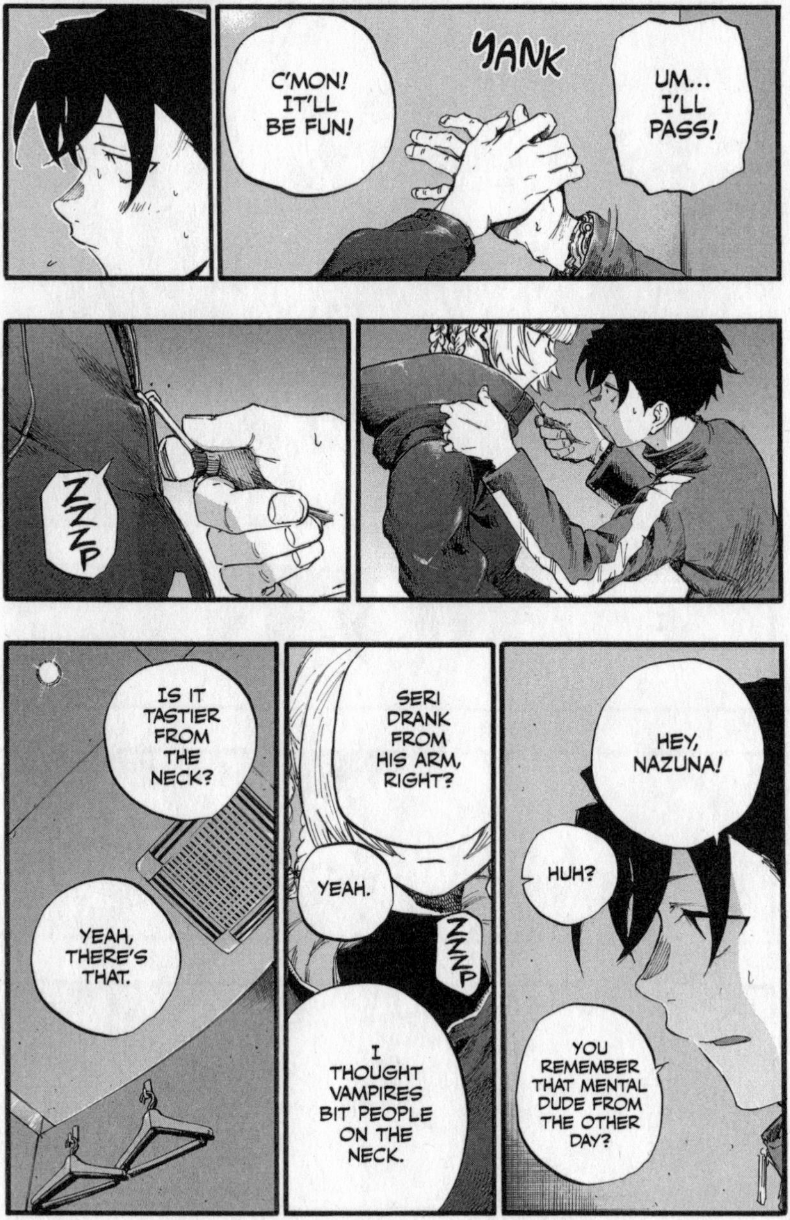
UM... I'LL PASS!
YANK
C'MON! IT'LL BE FUN!
ZZZP
HEY, NAZUNA!
HUH?
YOU REMEMBER THAT MENTAL DUDE FROM THE OTHER DAY?
SERI DRANK FROM HIS ARM, RIGHT?
YEAH.
ZZZP
I THOUGHT VAMPIRES BIT PEOPLE ON THE NECK.
IS IT TASTIER FROM THE NECK?
YEAH, THERE'S THAT.

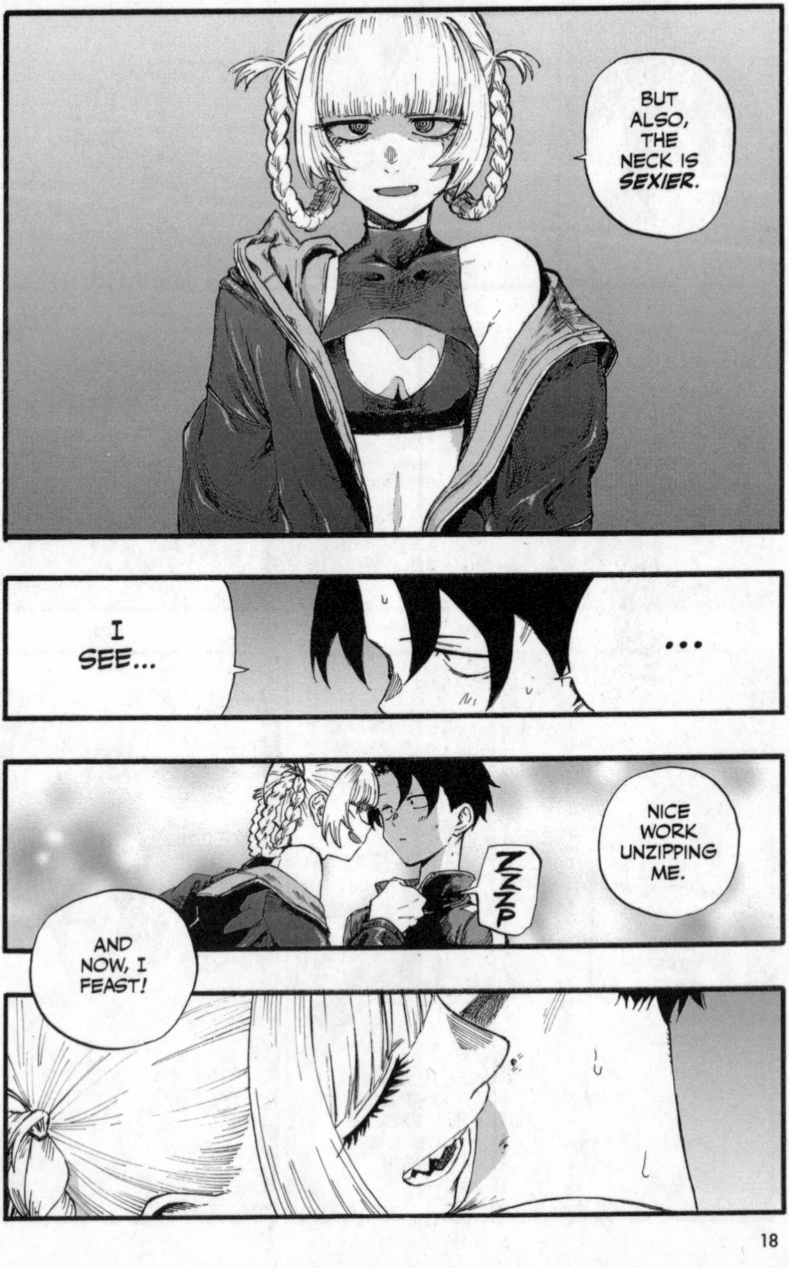
BUT ALSO, THE NECK IS SEXIER.
...
I SEE...
NICE WORK UNZIPPING ME.
ZZZP
AND NOW, I FEAST!

Call of the Night

Call of the Night

NIGHT 31: SOMEONE CONVENIENTLY UNPOPULAR

STOP BY ANYTIME!
Café Vamp!
WE'RE CAFÉ VAMP!
WHAT'S A CONVENIENT WAY FOR A BUSY VAMPIRE GIRL...
Um...
BING
!
...TO LURE MEN INTO HER CLUTCHES?
THANKS!
Sorry! Something came up last minute and I can't work today.

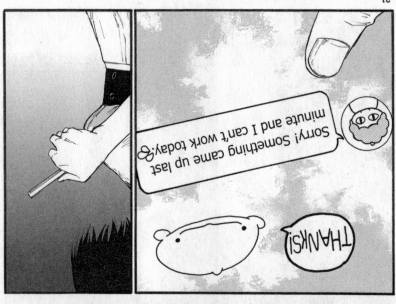

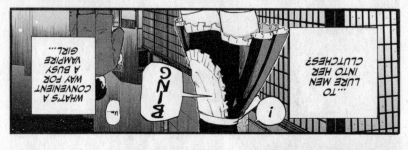

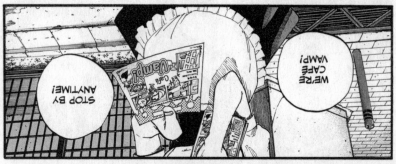

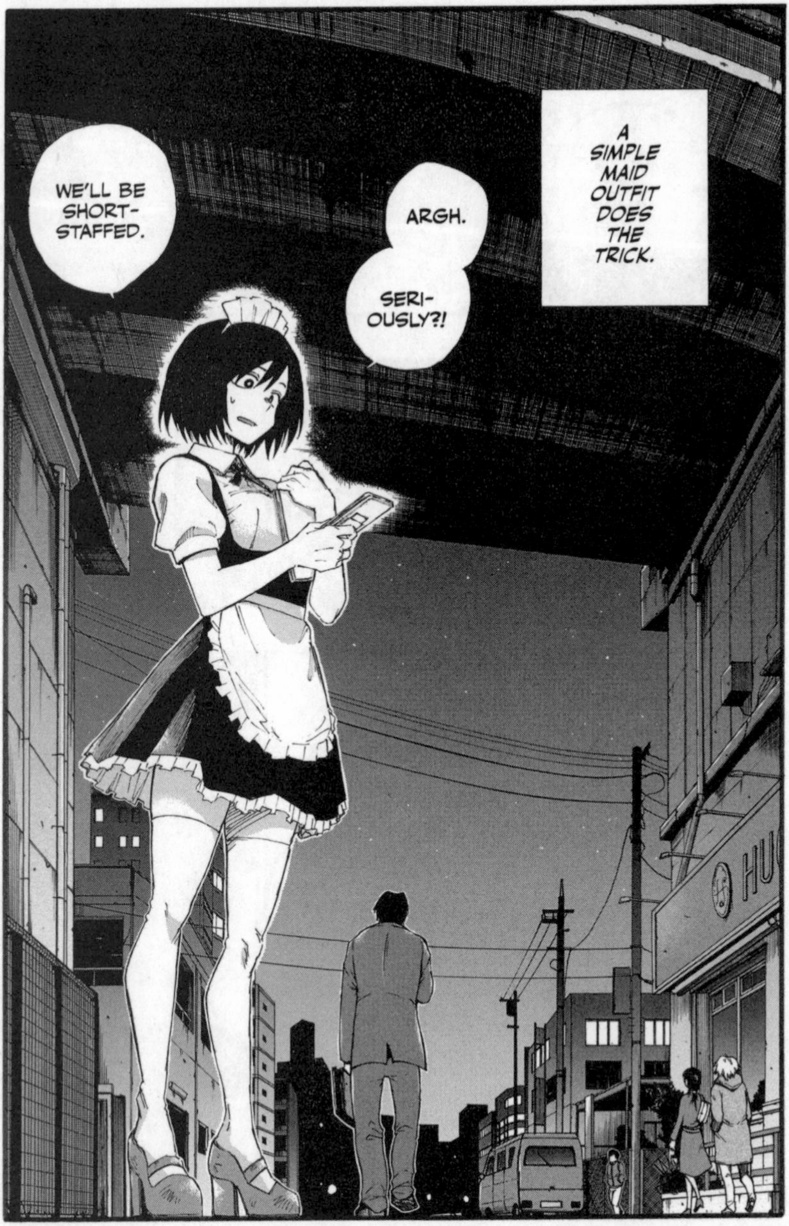
A SIMPLE MAID OUTFIT DOES THE TRICK.
ARGH.
SERI-OUSLY?!
WE'LL BE SHORT-STAFFED.
HU

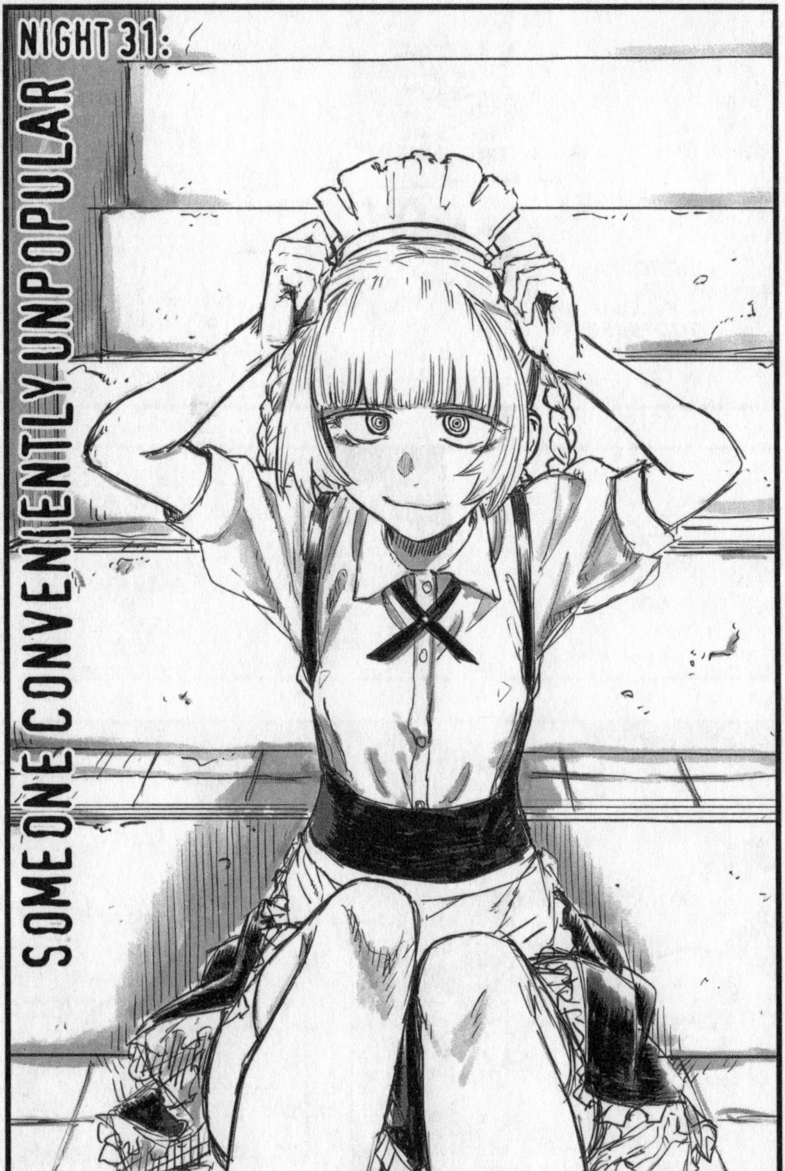
NIGHT 31:
SOMEONE CONVENIENTLY UNPOPULAR

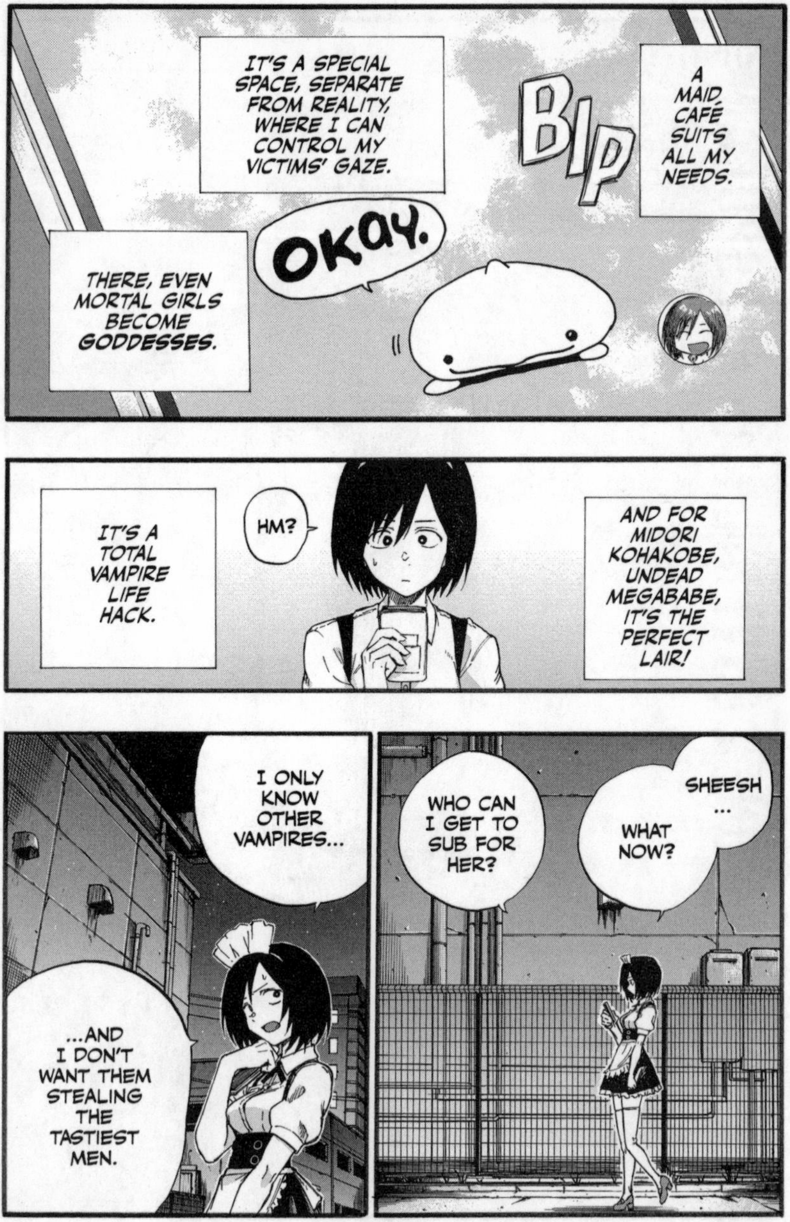
A MAID CAFÉ SUITS ALL MY NEEDS.
BIP
IT'S A SPECIAL SPACE, SEPARATE FROM REALITY, WHERE I CAN CONTROL MY VICTIMS' GAZE.
OKAY.
THERE, EVEN MORTAL GIRLS BECOME GODDESSES.
AND FOR MIDORI KOHAKOBE, UNDEAD MEGABABE, IT'S THE PERFECT LAIR!
HM?
IT'S A TOTAL VAMPIRE LIFE HACK.
SHEESH ...
WHAT NOW?
WHO CAN I GET TO SUB FOR HER?
I ONLY KNOW OTHER VAMPIRES...
...AND I DON'T WANT THEM STEALING THE TASTIEST MEN.

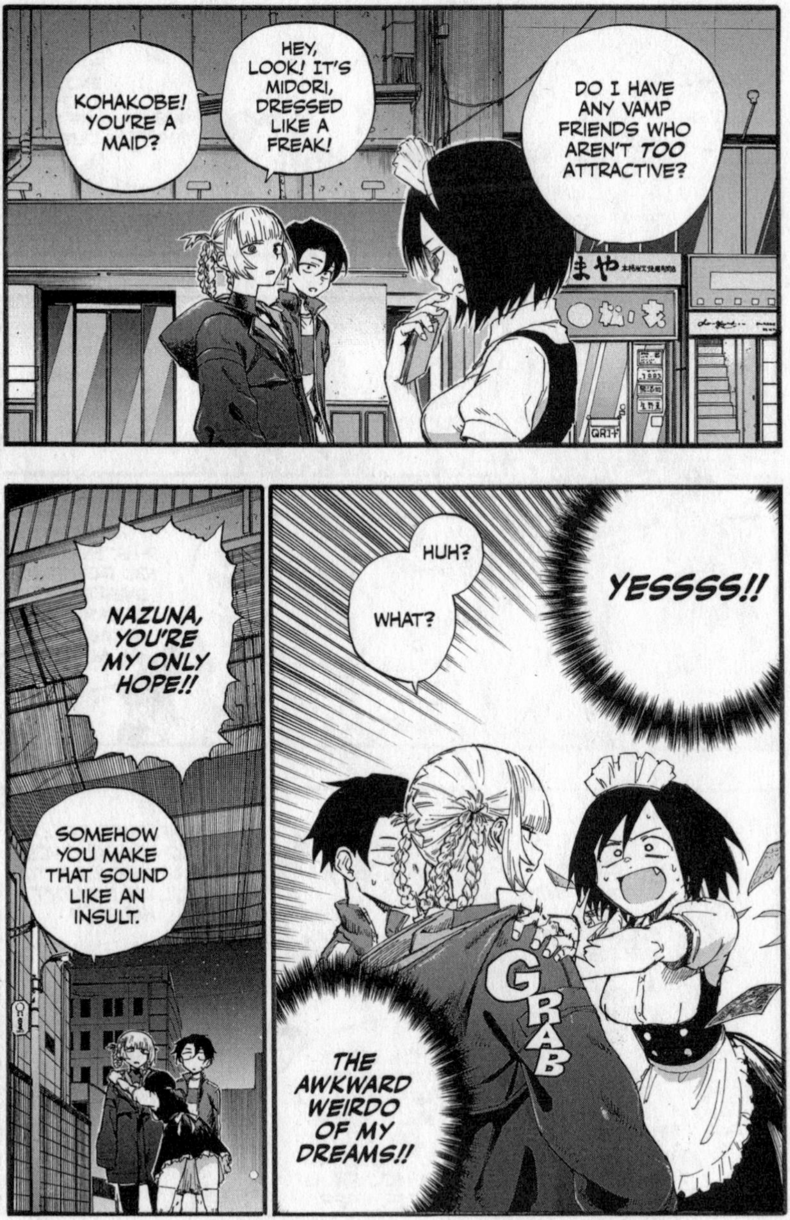
DO I HAVE ANY VAMP FRIENDS WHO AREN'T *TOO* ATTRACTIVE?
HEY, LOOK! IT'S MIDORI, DRESSED LIKE A FREAK!
KOHAKOBE! YOU'RE A MAID?
YESSSS!!
HUH?
WHAT?
GRAB
THE AWKWARD WEIRDO OF MY DREAMS!!
NAZUNA, YOU'RE MY ONLY HOPE!!
SOMEHOW YOU MAKE THAT SOUND LIKE AN INSULT.

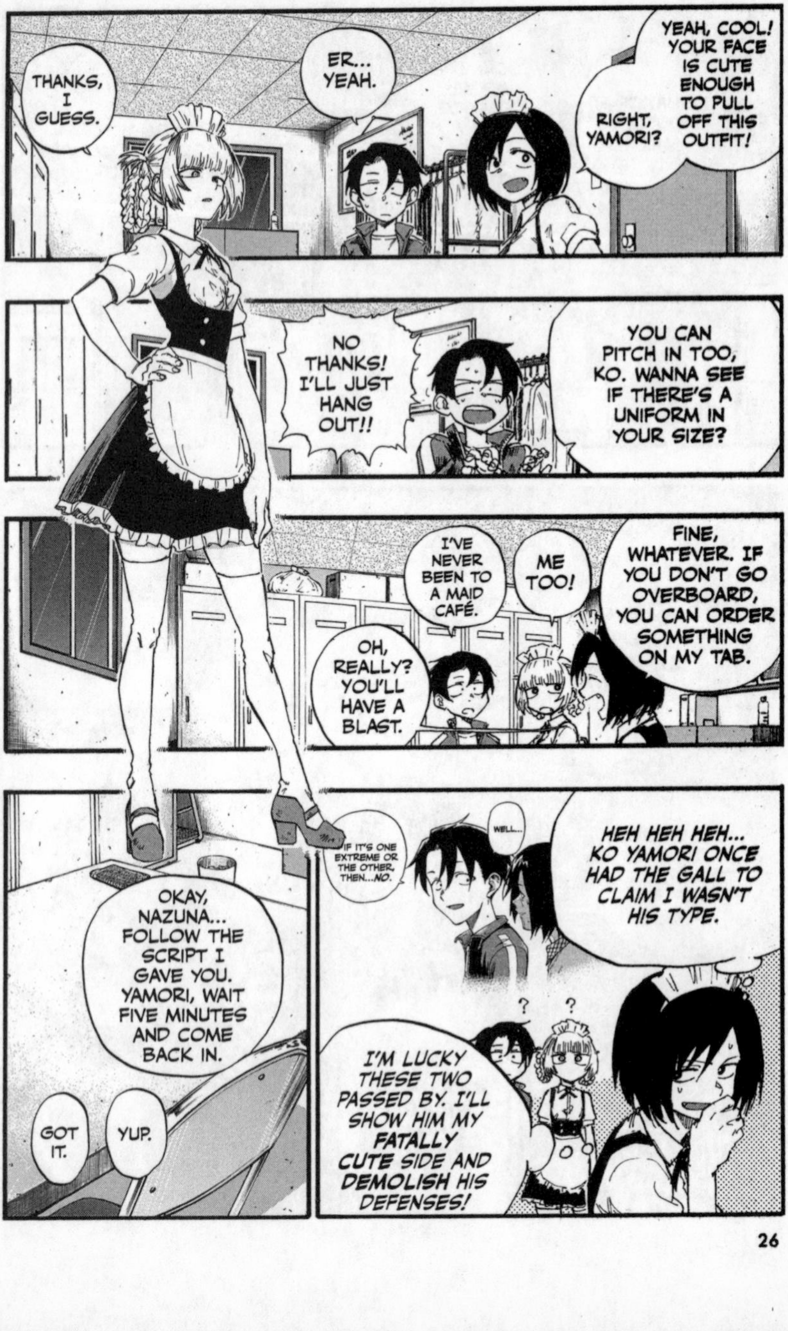
YEAH, COOL! YOUR FACE IS CUTE ENOUGH TO PULL OFF THIS OUTFIT!
RIGHT, YAMORI?
ER... YEAH.
THANKS, I GUESS.
YOU CAN PITCH IN TOO, KO. WANNA SEE IF THERE'S A UNIFORM IN YOUR SIZE?
NO THANKS! I'LL JUST HANG OUT!!
FINE, WHATEVER. IF YOU DON'T GO OVERBOARD, YOU CAN ORDER SOMETHING ON MY TAB.
ME TOO!
I'VE NEVER BEEN TO A MAID CAFÉ.
OH, REALLY? YOU'LL HAVE A BLAST.
HEH HEH HEH... KO YAMORI ONCE HAD THE GALL TO CLAIM I WASN'T HIS TYPE.
WELL...
IF IT'S ONE EXTREME OR THE OTHER, THEN...NO.
?
?
I'M LUCKY THESE TWO PASSED BY. I'LL SHOW HIM MY FATALLY CUTE SIDE AND DEMOLISH HIS DEFENSES!
OKAY, NAZUNA... FOLLOW THE SCRIPT I GAVE YOU. YAMORI, WAIT FIVE MINUTES AND COME BACK IN.
YUP.
GOT IT.

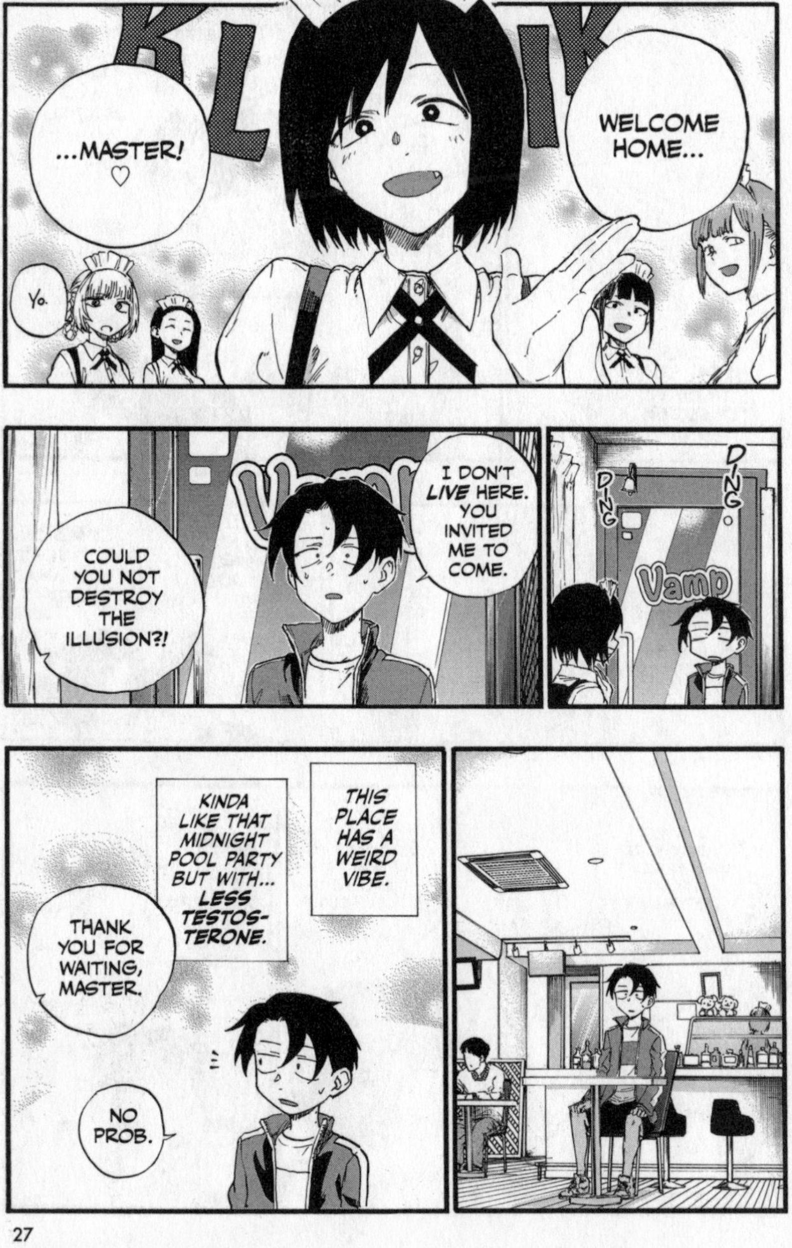
KLIK
WELCOME HOME...
...MASTER! ♡
Yo.
DING DING
Vamp
I DON'T LIVE HERE. YOU INVITED ME TO COME.
COULD YOU NOT DESTROY THE ILLUSION?!
THIS PLACE HAS A WEIRD VIBE.
KINDA LIKE THAT MIDNIGHT POOL PARTY BUT WITH... LESS TESTOS-TERONE.
THANK YOU FOR WAITING, MASTER.
NO PROB.

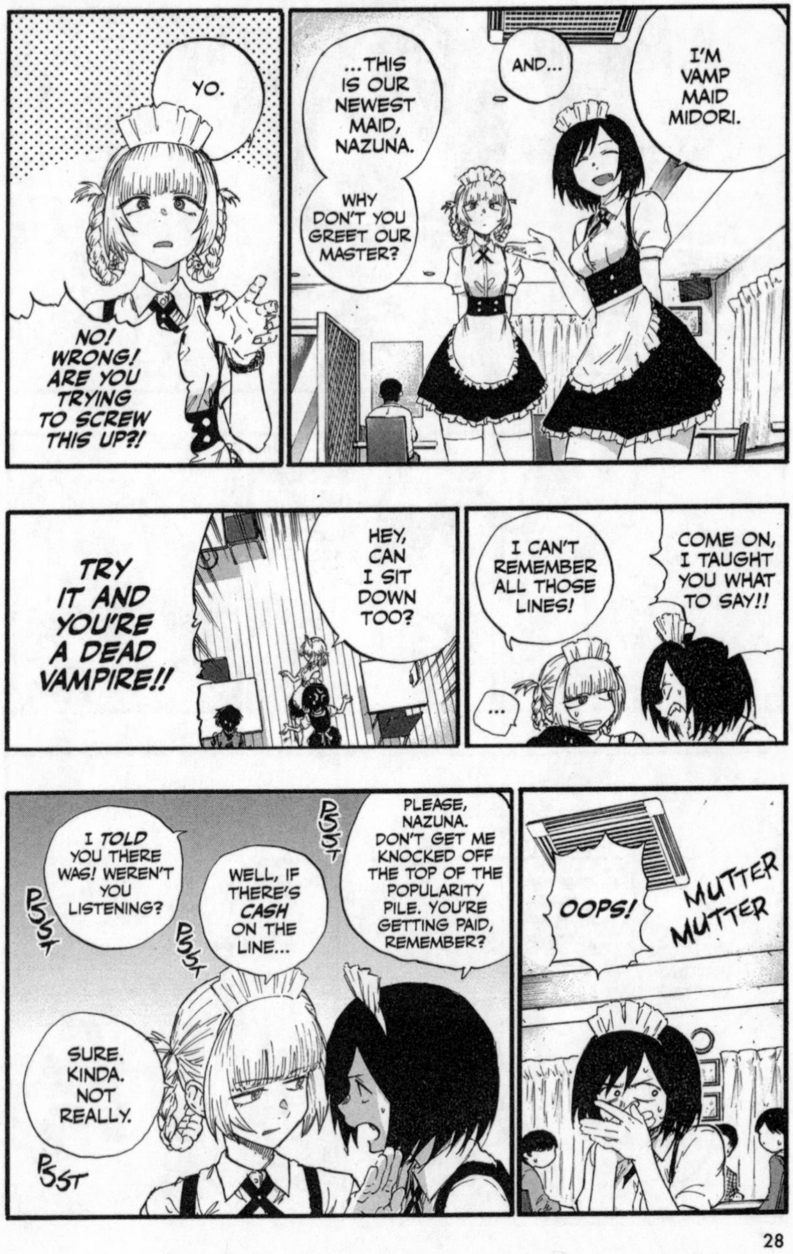
I'M VAMP MAID MIDORI.
AND...
...THIS IS OUR NEWEST MAID, NAZUNA.
WHY DON'T YOU GREET OUR MASTER?
YO.
NO! WRONG! ARE YOU TRYING TO SCREW THIS UP?!
COME ON, I TAUGHT YOU WHAT TO SAY!!
I CAN'T REMEMBER ALL THOSE LINES!
...
HEY, CAN I SIT DOWN TOO?
TRY IT AND YOU'RE A DEAD VAMPIRE!!
OOPS!
MUTTER MUTTER
PLEASE, NAZUNA. DON'T GET ME KNOCKED OFF THE TOP OF THE POPULARITY PILE. YOU'RE GETTING PAID, REMEMBER?
PSST
WELL, IF THERE'S CASH ON THE LINE...
PSST
I TOLD YOU THERE WAS! WEREN'T YOU LISTENING?
PSST
SURE. KINDA. NOT REALLY.
PSST

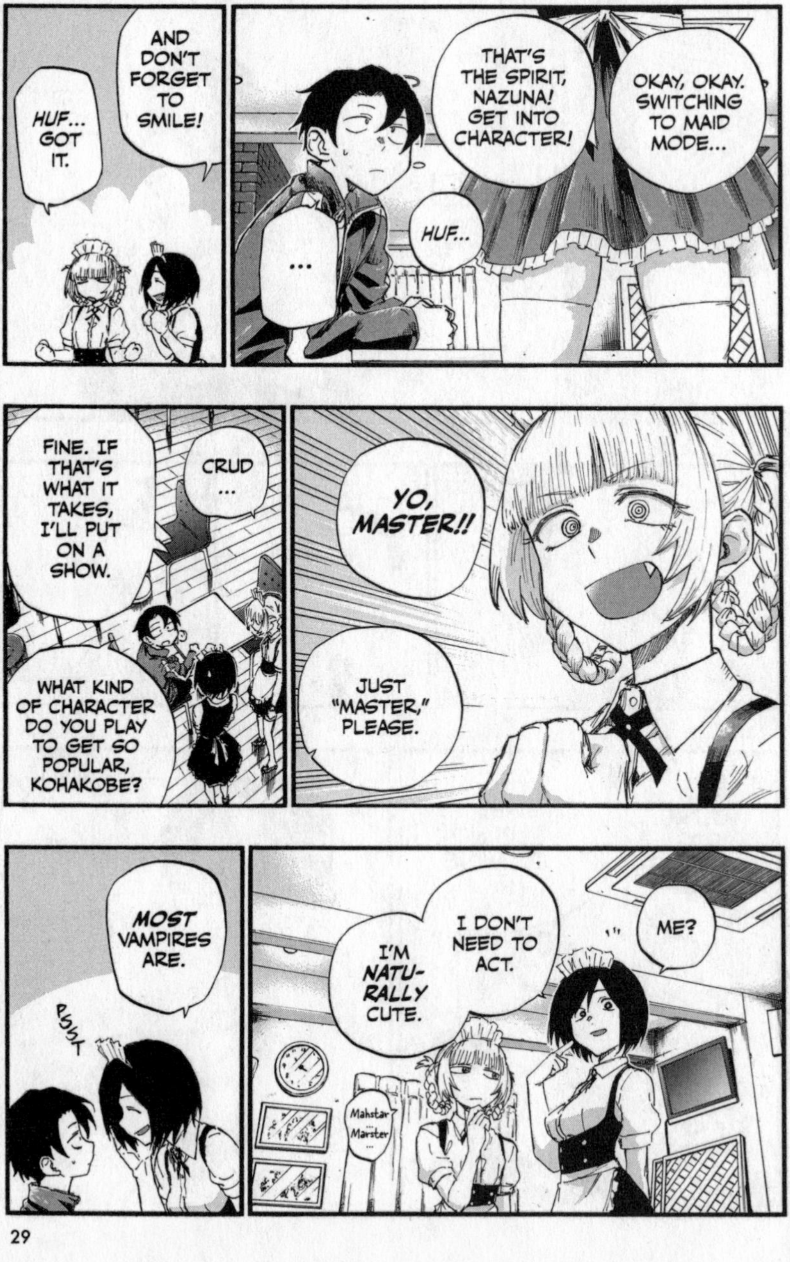
OKAY, OKAY. SWITCHING TO MAID MODE...
THAT'S THE SPIRIT, NAZUNA! GET INTO CHARACTER!
HUF...
...
AND DON'T FORGET TO SMILE!
HUF... GOT IT.
YO, MASTER!!
JUST "MASTER," PLEASE.
FINE. IF THAT'S WHAT IT TAKES, I'LL PUT ON A SHOW.
CRUD...
WHAT KIND OF CHARACTER DO YOU PLAY TO GET SO POPULAR, KOHAKOBE?
ME?
I DON'T NEED TO ACT.
I'M NATU-RALLY CUTE.
Mahstar... Marster...
MOST VAMPIRES ARE.
PSST

HERE'S YOUR TEA...
...WITH A DASH OF LOVE!
...
TNK
SIP
TNK
...
NICE.
SWEET... BUT NOT CLOYING.
AW... YOU'RE TOO KIND, SIR!
YOUR TEA SERVICE HAS REALLY IMPROVED.

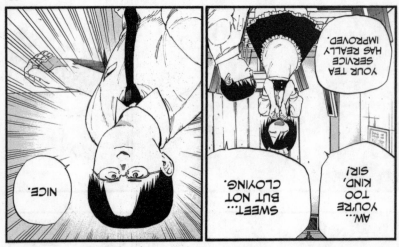

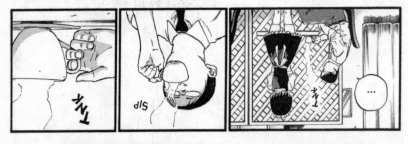

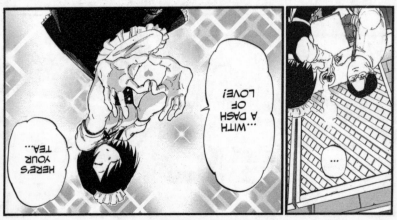

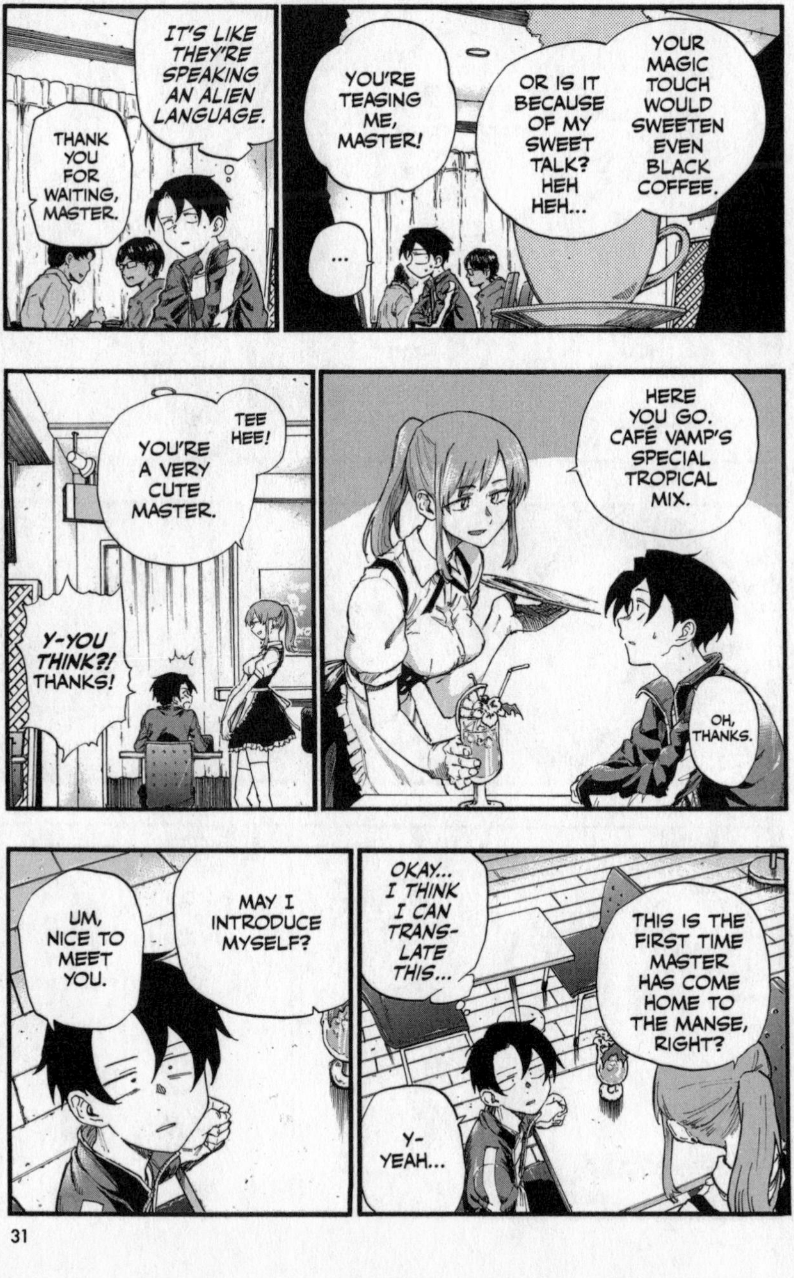
YOUR MAGIC TOUCH WOULD SWEETEN EVEN BLACK COFFEE.
OR IS IT BECAUSE OF MY SWEET TALK? HEH HEH...
YOU'RE TEASING ME, MASTER!
...
IT'S LIKE THEY'RE SPEAKING AN ALIEN LANGUAGE.
THANK YOU FOR WAITING, MASTER.
HERE YOU GO. CAFÉ VAMP'S SPECIAL TROPICAL MIX.
OH, THANKS.
TEE HEE!
YOU'RE A VERY CUTE MASTER.
Y-YOU THINK?! THANKS!
THIS IS THE FIRST TIME MASTER HAS COME HOME TO THE MANSE, RIGHT?
OKAY... I THINK I CAN TRANS-LATE THIS...
Y-YEAH...
MAY I INTRODUCE MYSELF?
UM, NICE TO MEET YOU.

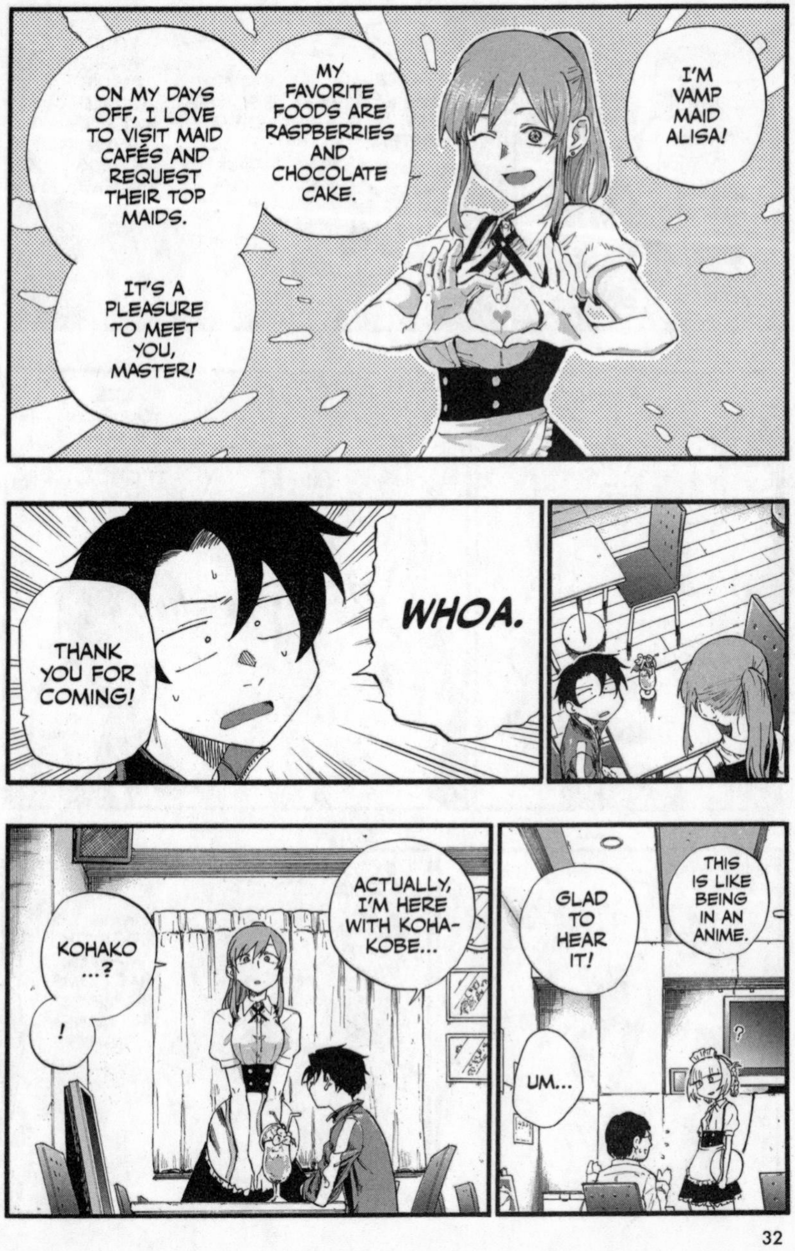
I'M VAMP MAID ALISA!
MY FAVORITE FOODS ARE RASPBERRIES AND CHOCOLATE CAKE.
ON MY DAYS OFF, I LOVE TO VISIT MAID CAFÉS AND REQUEST THEIR TOP MAIDS.
IT'S A PLEASURE TO MEET YOU, MASTER!
WHOA.
THANK YOU FOR COMING!
THIS IS LIKE BEING IN AN ANIME.
GLAD TO HEAR IT!
UM...
?
ACTUALLY, I'M HERE WITH KOHA-KOBE...
KOHAKO ...?
!

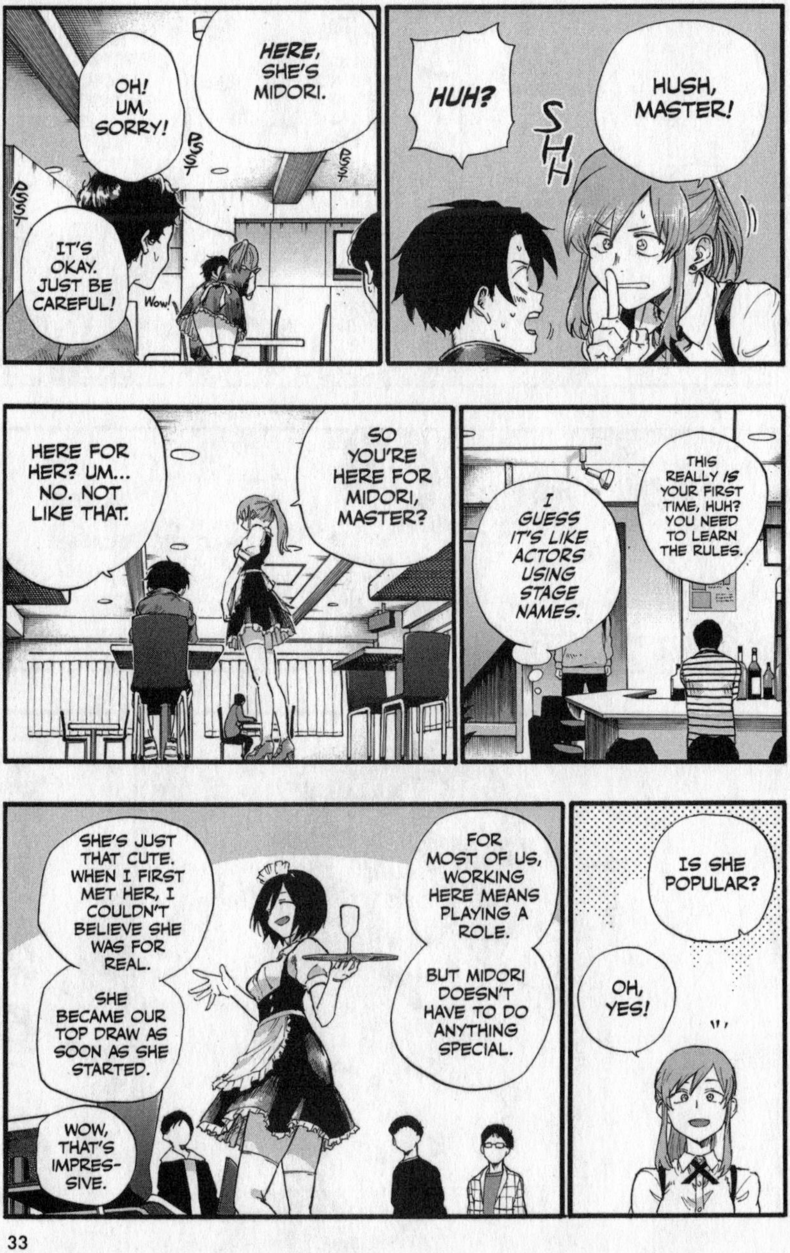
HUSH, MASTER!
SHH
HUH?
HERE, SHE'S MIDORI.
OH! UM, SORRY!
PSST
PSST
PSST
IT'S OKAY. JUST BE CAREFUL!
Wow!
THIS REALLY IS YOUR FIRST TIME, HUH? YOU NEED TO LEARN THE RULES.
I GUESS IT'S LIKE ACTORS USING STAGE NAMES.
SO YOU'RE HERE FOR MIDORI, MASTER?
HERE FOR HER? UM... NO. NOT LIKE THAT.
IS SHE POPULAR?
OH, YES!
FOR MOST OF US, WORKING HERE MEANS PLAYING A ROLE.
BUT MIDORI DOESN'T HAVE TO DO ANYTHING SPECIAL.
SHE'S JUST THAT CUTE. WHEN I FIRST MET HER, I COULDN'T BELIEVE SHE WAS FOR REAL.
SHE BECAME OUR TOP DRAW AS SOON AS SHE STARTED.
WOW, THAT'S IMPRES-SIVE.

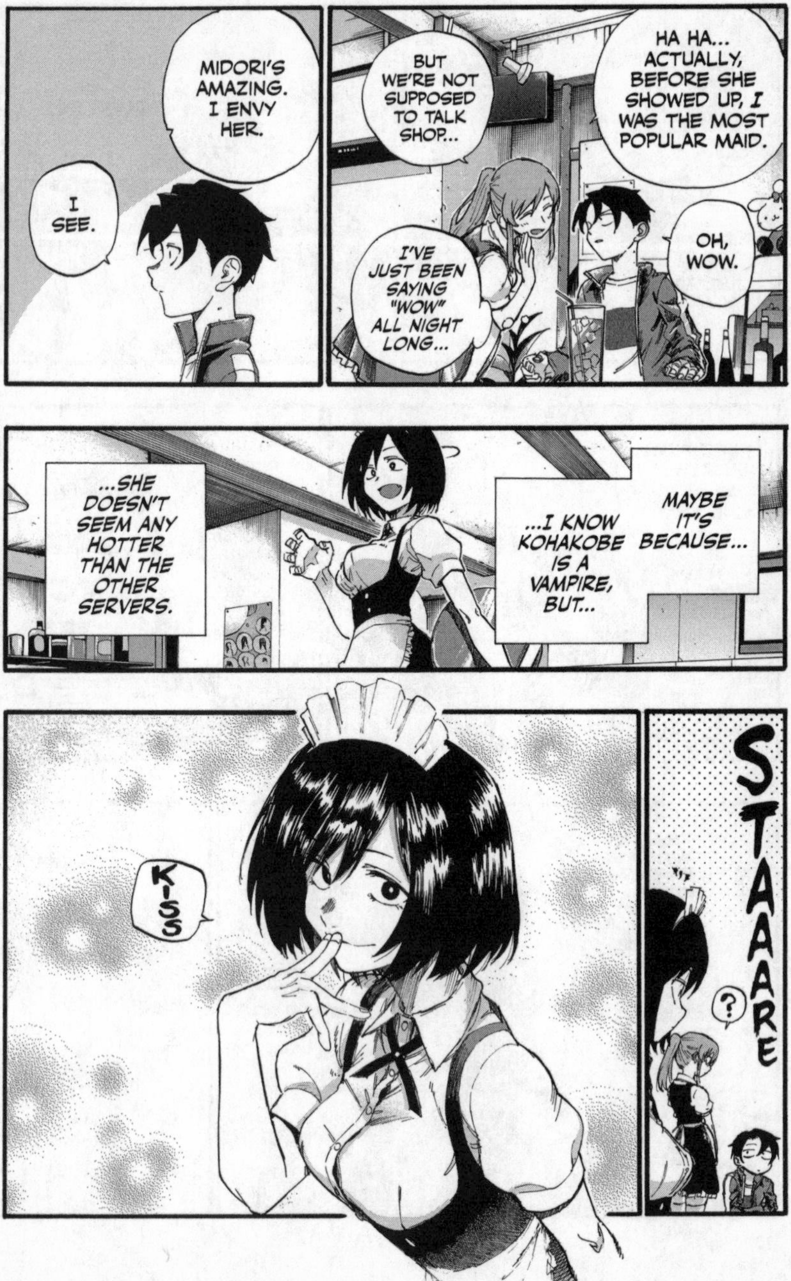
HA HA... ACTUALLY, BEFORE SHE SHOWED UP, I WAS THE MOST POPULAR MAID.
OH, WOW.
BUT WE'RE NOT SUPPOSED TO TALK SHOP...
I'VE JUST BEEN SAYING "WOW" ALL NIGHT LONG...
MIDORI'S AMAZING. I ENVY HER.
I SEE.
MAYBE IT'S BECAUSE...
...I KNOW KOHAKOBE IS A VAMPIRE, BUT...
...SHE DOESN'T SEEM ANY HOTTER THAN THE OTHER SERVERS.
STAAARE
?
KISS

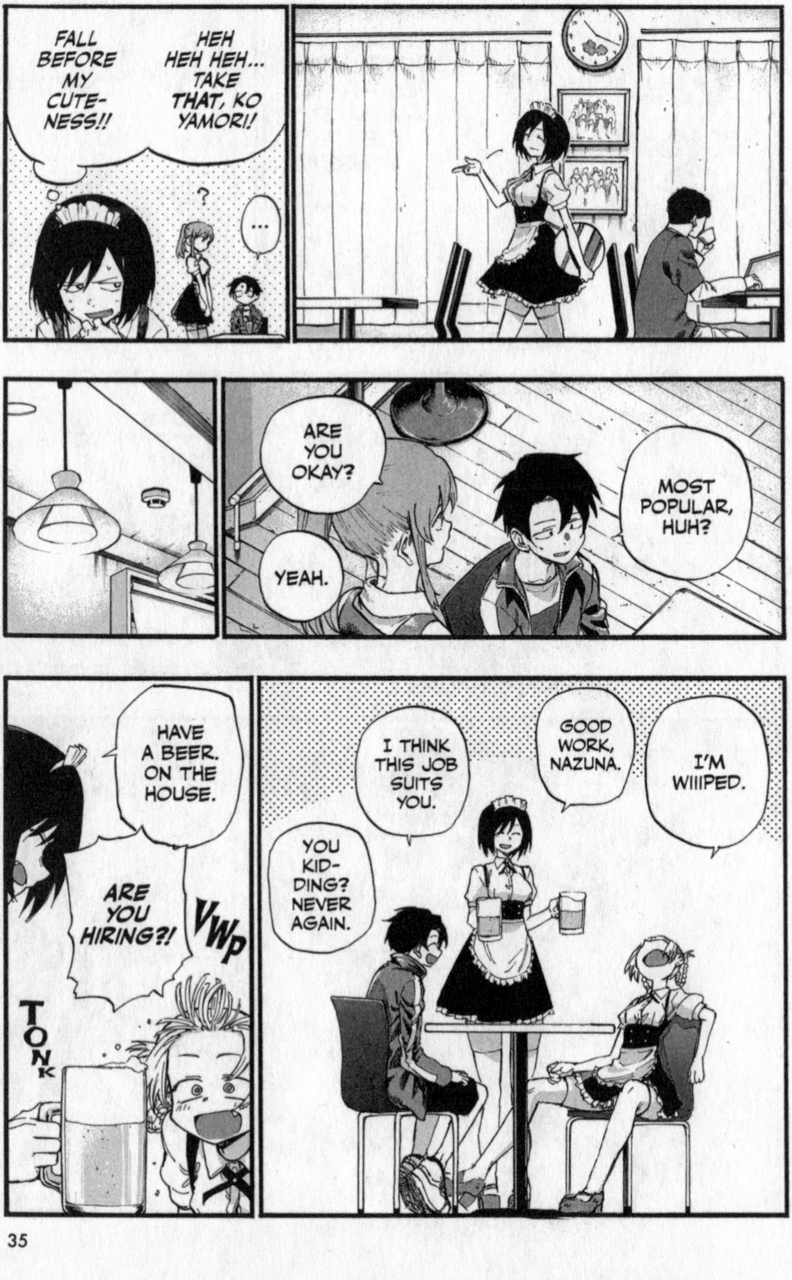
HEH HEH HEH... TAKE THAT, KO YAMORI!
FALL BEFORE MY CUTE-NESS!!
?
...
MOST POPULAR, HUH?
ARE YOU OKAY?
YEAH.
I'M WIIIPED.
GOOD WORK, NAZUNA.
I THINK THIS JOB SUITS YOU.
YOU KID-DING? NEVER AGAIN.
HAVE A BEER. ON THE HOUSE.
VWP
ARE YOU HIRING?!
TONK

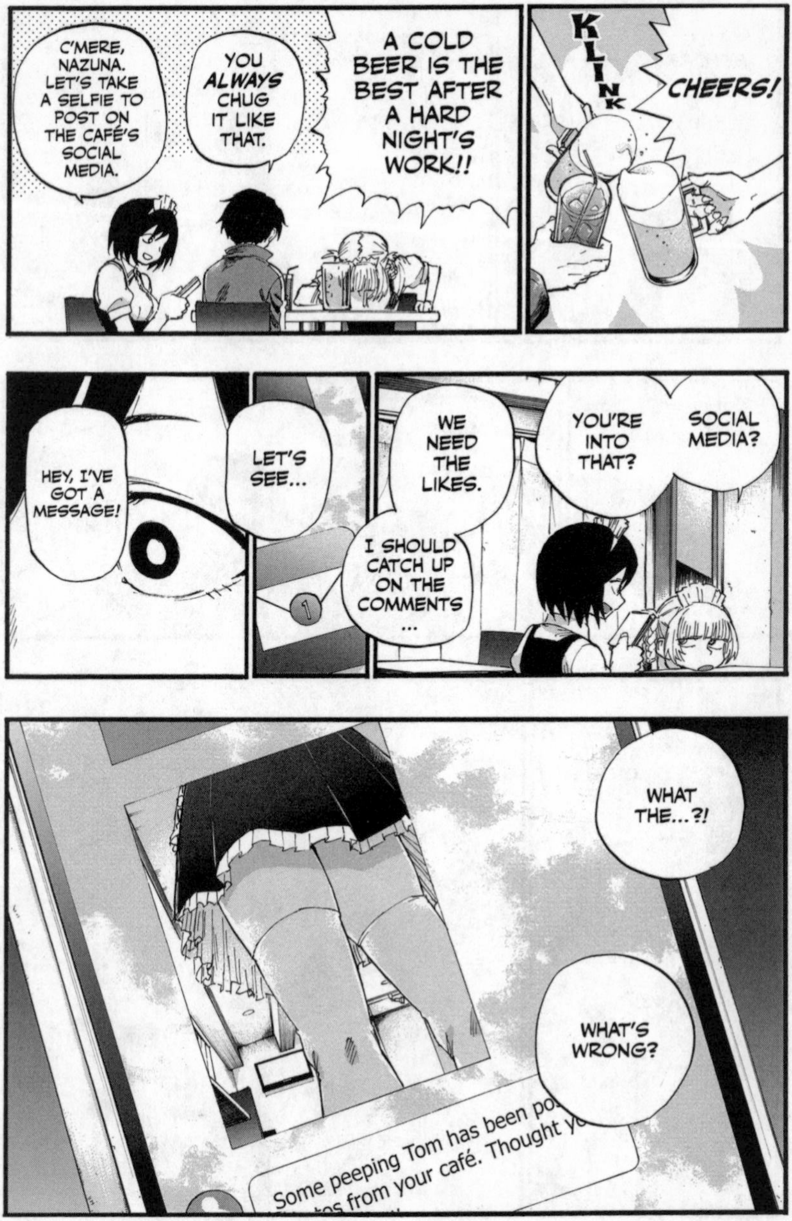
KLINK
CHEERS!
A COLD BEER IS THE BEST AFTER A HARD NIGHT'S WORK!!
YOU ALWAYS CHUG IT LIKE THAT.
C'MERE, NAZUNA. LET'S TAKE A SELFIE TO POST ON THE CAFÉ'S SOCIAL MEDIA.
SOCIAL MEDIA?
YOU'RE INTO THAT?
WE NEED THE LIKES.
I SHOULD CATCH UP ON THE COMMENTS ...
LET'S SEE...
HEY, I'VE GOT A MESSAGE!
WHAT THE...?!
WHAT'S WRONG?
Some peeping Tom has been po
from your café. Thought y

NIGHT 32: ENLARGE THE PEEPING-TOM PHOTOS

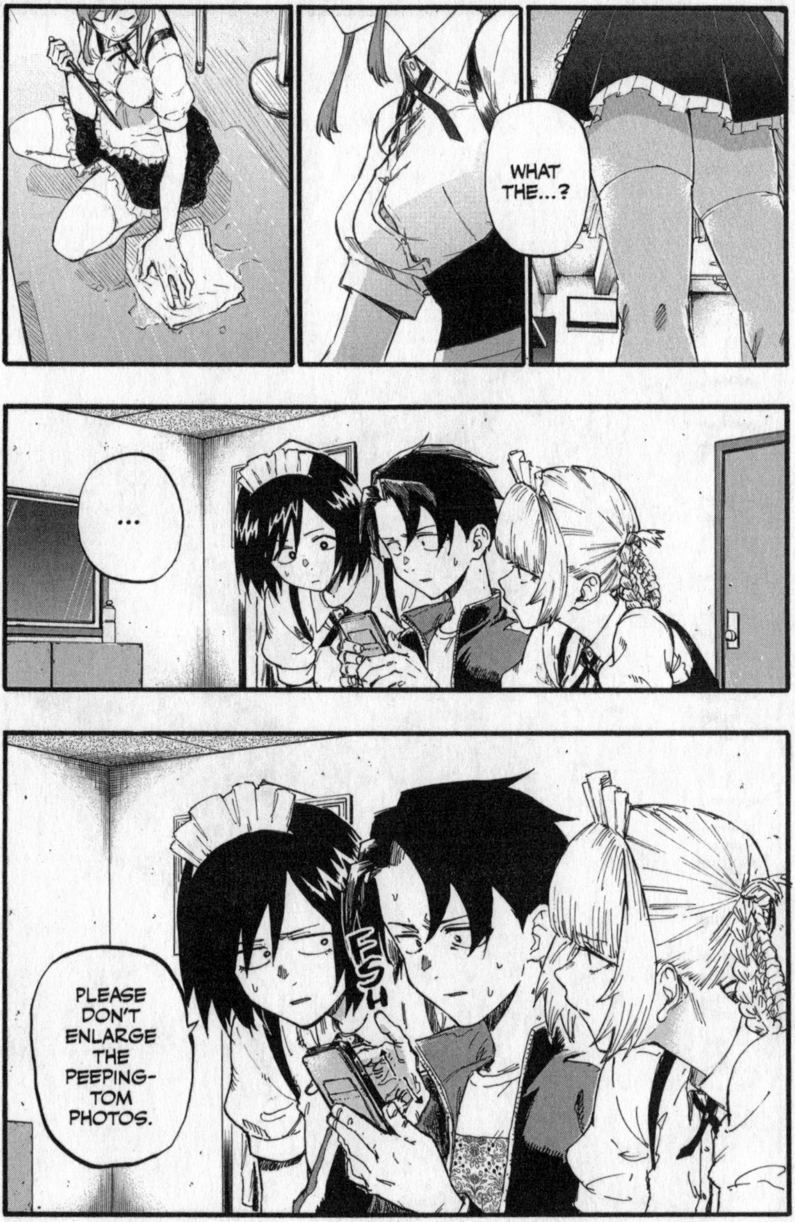

WHAT THE...?
...
PLEASE DON'T ENLARGE THE PEEPING-TOM PHOTOS.
FSH

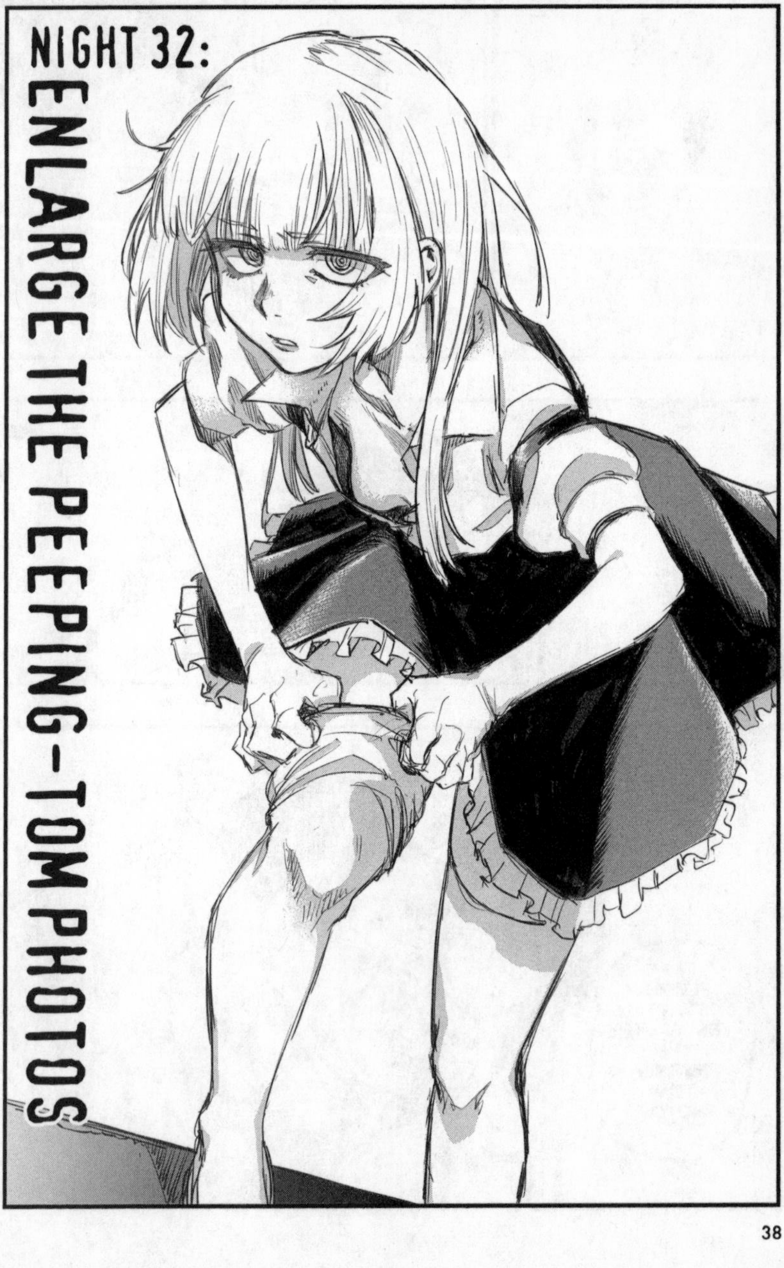
NIGHT 32:
ENLARGE THE PEEPING-TOM PHOTOS

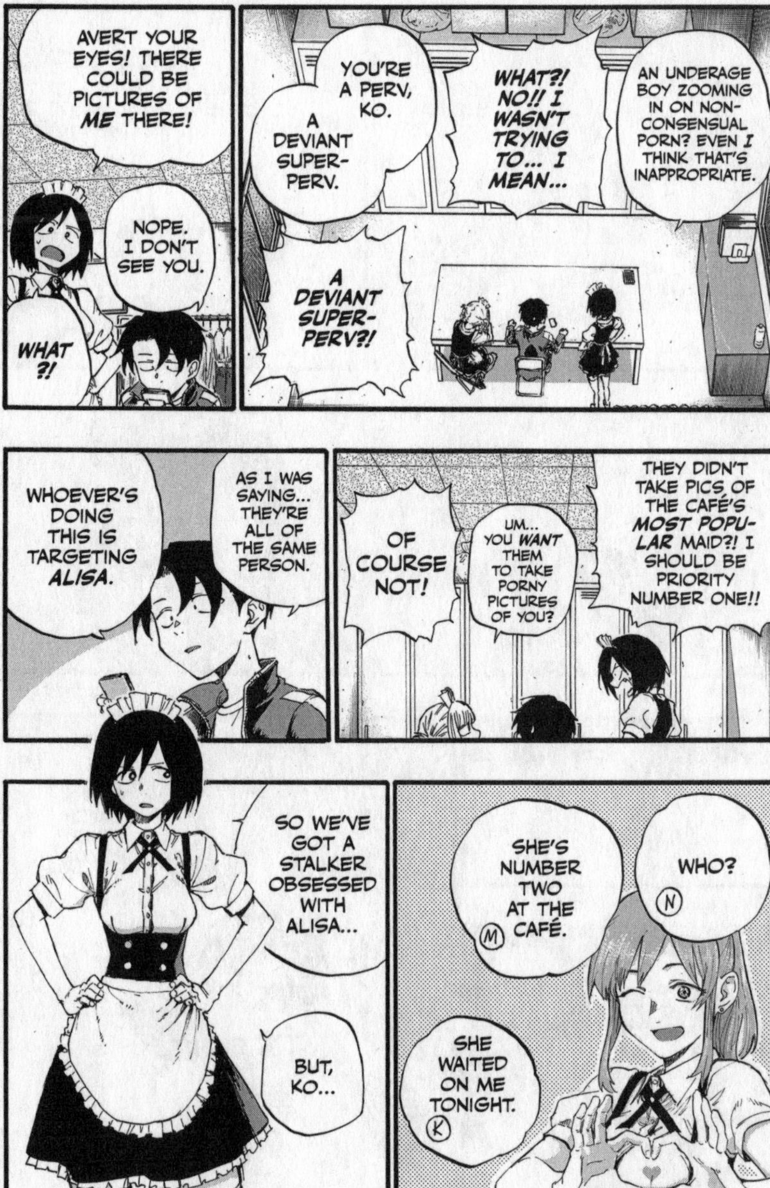
AN UNDERAGE BOY ZOOMING IN ON NON-CONSENSUAL PORN? EVEN *I* THINK THAT'S INAPPROPRIATE.
WHAT?! NO!! I WASN'T TRYING TO... I MEAN...
YOU'RE A PERV, KO.
A DEVIANT SUPER-PERV.
A DEVIANT SUPER-PERV?!
AVERT YOUR EYES! THERE COULD BE PICTURES OF *ME* THERE!
NOPE. I DON'T SEE YOU.
WHAT ?!
THEY DIDN'T TAKE PICS OF THE CAFÉ'S *MOST POPULAR* MAID?! I SHOULD BE PRIORITY NUMBER ONE!!
UM... YOU *WANT* THEM TO TAKE PORNY PICTURES OF YOU?
OF COURSE NOT!
AS I WAS SAYING... THEY'RE ALL OF THE SAME PERSON.
WHOEVER'S DOING THIS IS TARGETING *ALISA*.
WHO?
N
SHE'S NUMBER TWO AT THE CAFÉ.
M
SHE WAITED ON ME TONIGHT.
K
SO WE'VE GOT A STALKER OBSESSED WITH ALISA...
BUT, KO...

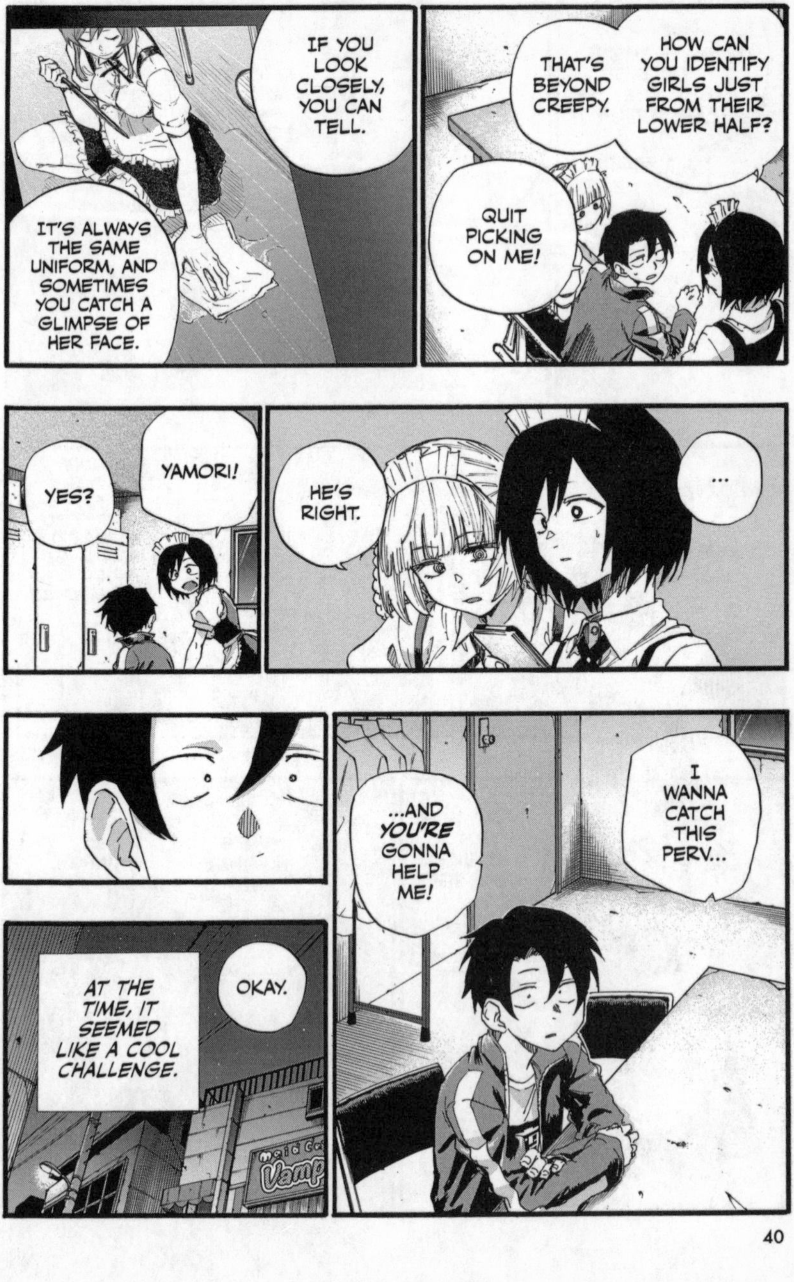

HOW CAN YOU IDENTIFY GIRLS JUST FROM THEIR LOWER HALF?
THAT'S BEYOND CREEPY.
QUIT PICKING ON ME!
IF YOU LOOK CLOSELY, YOU CAN TELL.
IT'S ALWAYS THE SAME UNIFORM, AND SOMETIMES YOU CATCH A GLIMPSE OF HER FACE.
...
HE'S RIGHT.
YAMORI!
YES?
I WANNA CATCH THIS PERV...
...AND YOU'RE GONNA HELP ME!
OKAY.
AT THE TIME, IT SEEMED LIKE A COOL CHALLENGE.

THE NEXT DAY...
BUT REALISTICALLY...
...I HAVE NO IDEA HOW TO DO DETECTIVE WORK!
OK
AND THAT'S HOW I'VE ENDED UP IN THE BREAK ROOM OF CAFÉ VAMP...
...SCROLLING THROUGH SKEEVY PHOTOS AND TRYING TO COME UP WITH A PLAN.
...
THERE SHE IS CHANGING HER OUTFIT...
...
THAT'S ALISA, ALL RIGHT...

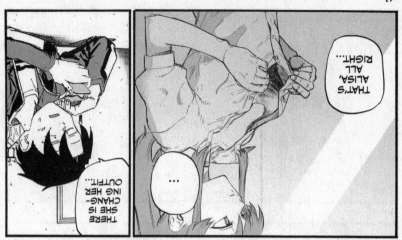

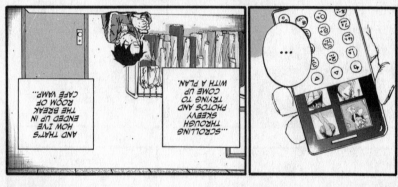

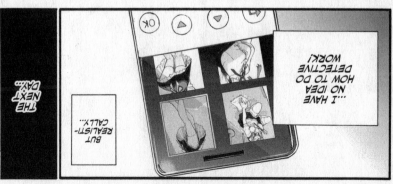

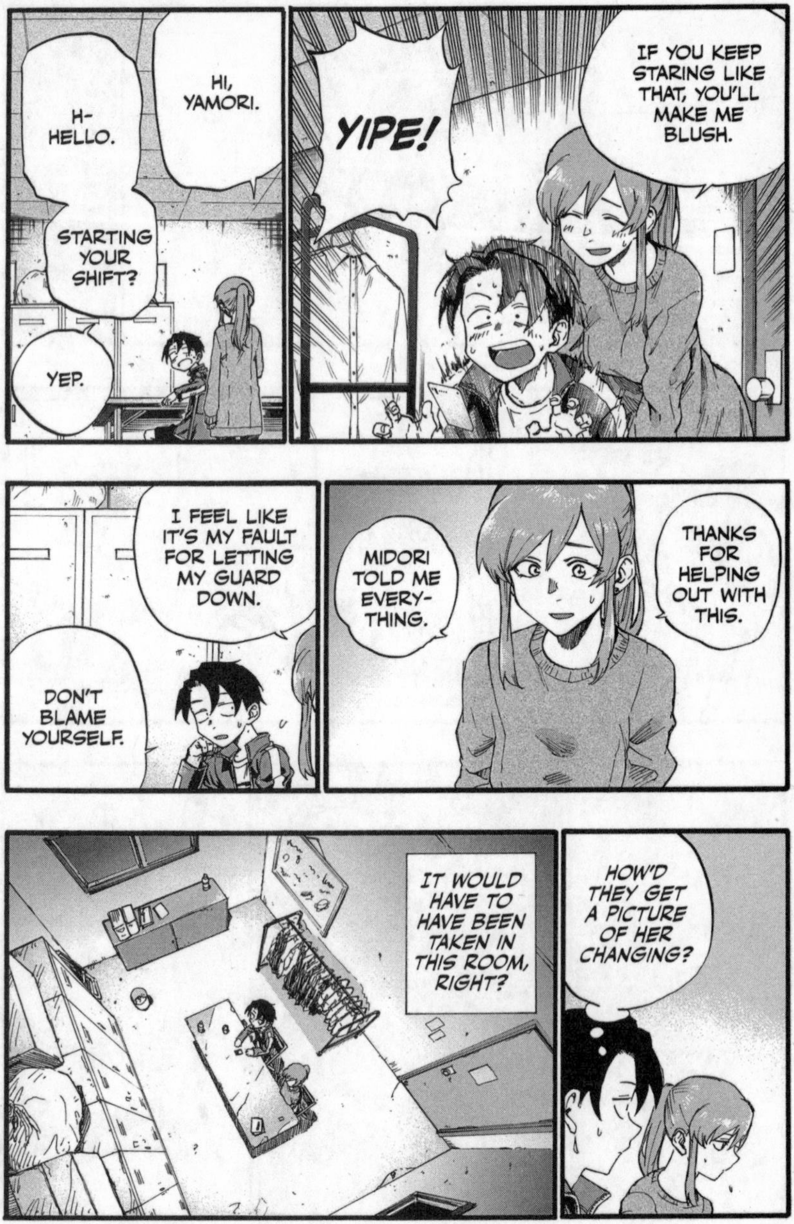
IF YOU KEEP STARING LIKE THAT, YOU'LL MAKE ME BLUSH.
YIPE!
HI, YAMORI.
H-HELLO.
STARTING YOUR SHIFT?
YEP.
THANKS FOR HELPING OUT WITH THIS.
MIDORI TOLD ME EVERYTHING.
I FEEL LIKE IT'S MY FAULT FOR LETTING MY GUARD DOWN.
DON'T BLAME YOURSELF.
HOW'D THEY GET A PICTURE OF HER CHANGING?
IT WOULD HAVE TO HAVE BEEN TAKEN IN THIS ROOM, RIGHT?

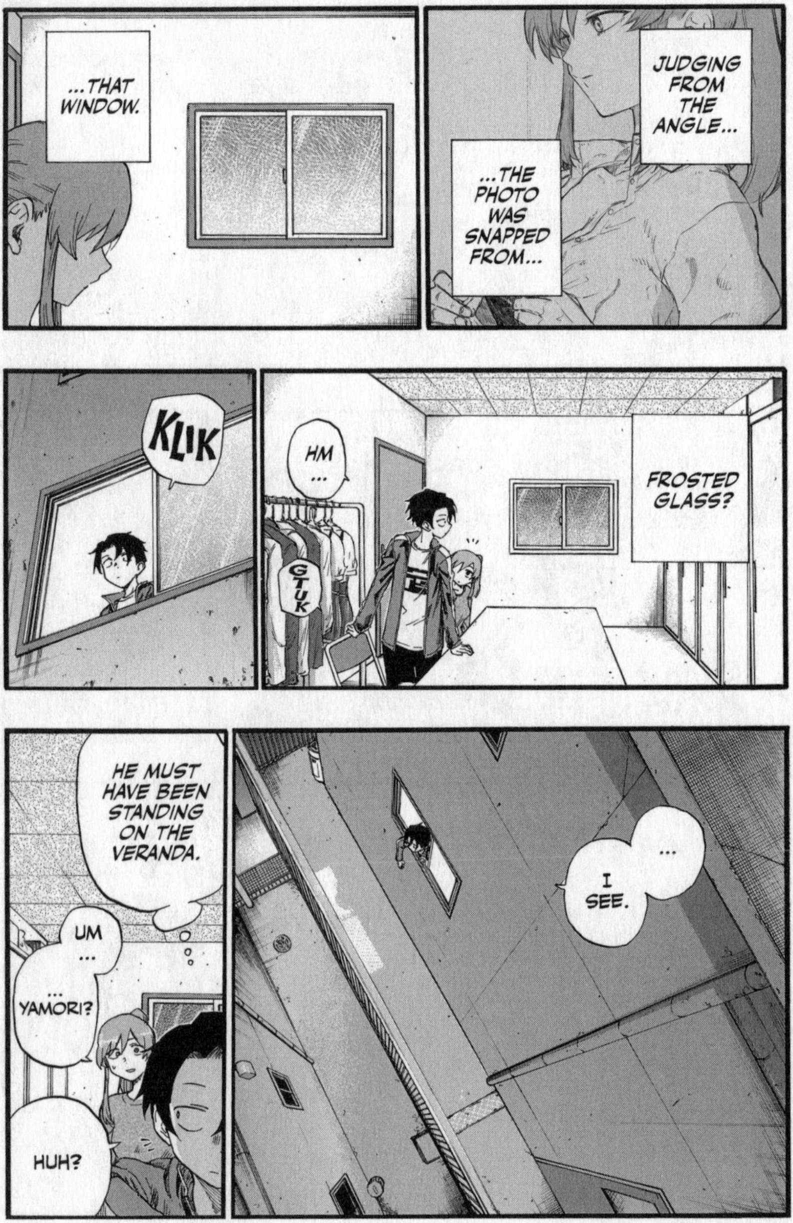
JUDGING FROM THE ANGLE...
...THE PHOTO WAS SNAPPED FROM...
...THAT WINDOW.
FROSTED GLASS?
HM ...
GTUK
KLIK
...
I SEE.
HE MUST HAVE BEEN STANDING ON THE VERANDA.
UM ...
... YAMORI?
HUH?

UM...
...I NEED TO GET CHANGED AND START MY SHIFT.
OOPS!
SORRY, I WASN'T THINKING!
TEE HEE! NO, WORRIES. SORRY TO KICK YOU OUT.
KRMBL
I'M LEAVING NOW!!
SLAM
WHEW.
...
HEY!
HM...

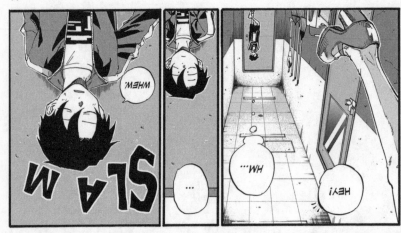

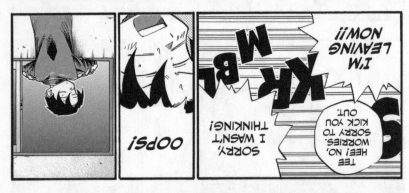

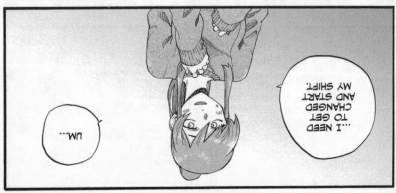

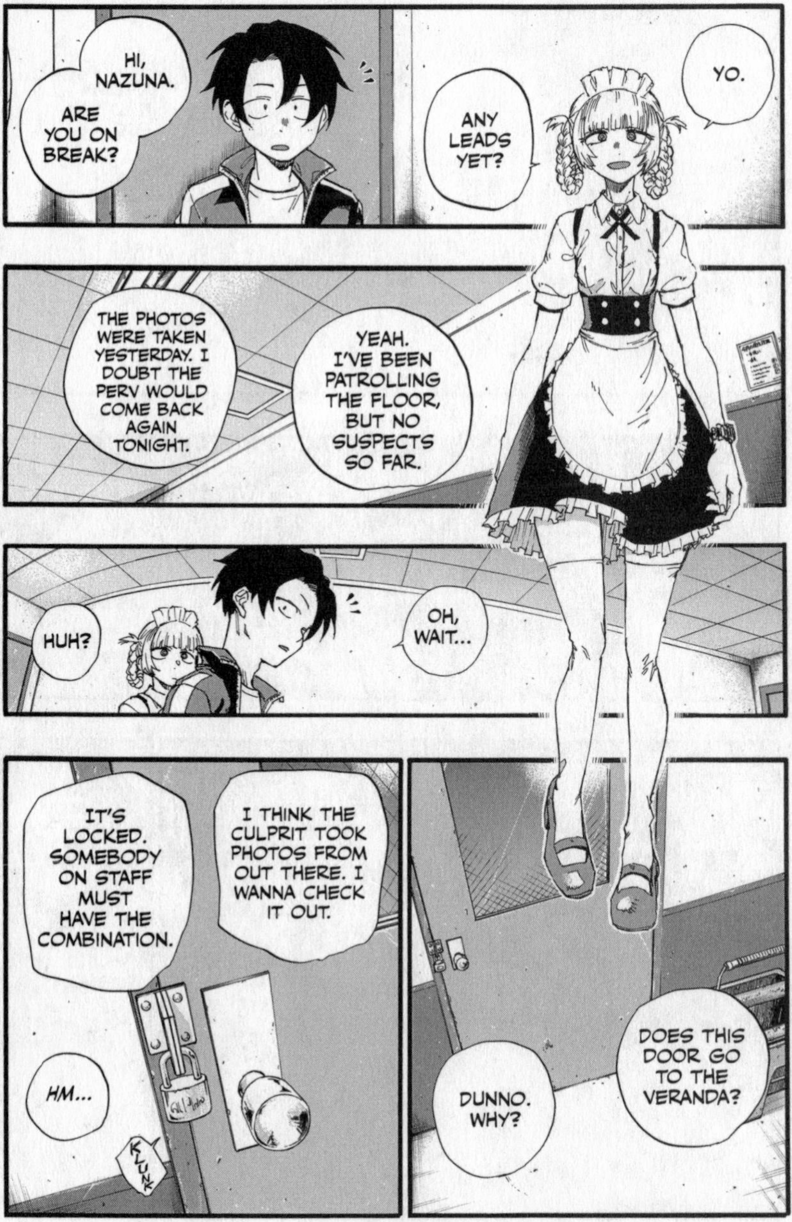
YO.
ANY LEADS YET?
HI, NAZUNA.
ARE YOU ON BREAK?
YEAH. I'VE BEEN PATROLLING THE FLOOR, BUT NO SUSPECTS SO FAR.
THE PHOTOS WERE TAKEN YESTERDAY. I DOUBT THE PERV WOULD COME BACK AGAIN TONIGHT.
OH, WAIT...
HUH?
DOES THIS DOOR GO TO THE VERANDA?
DUNNO. WHY?
I THINK THE CULPRIT TOOK PHOTOS FROM OUT THERE. I WANNA CHECK IT OUT.
IT'S LOCKED. SOMEBODY ON STAFF MUST HAVE THE COMBINATION.
HM...
KLUNK

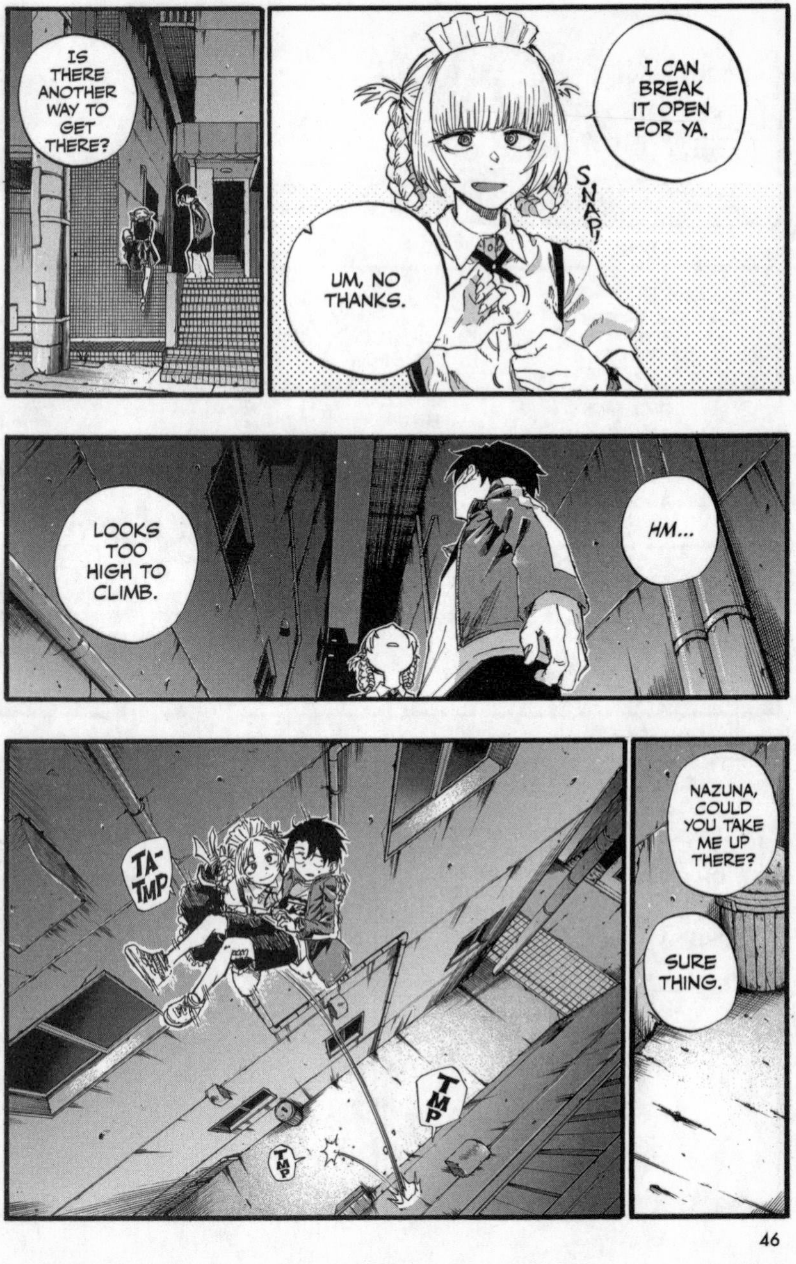
I CAN BREAK IT OPEN FOR YA.
SNAP!
UM, NO THANKS.
IS THERE ANOTHER WAY TO GET THERE?
HM...
LOOKS TOO HIGH TO CLIMB.
NAZUNA, COULD YOU TAKE ME UP THERE?
SURE THING.
TA-TMP
TMP
TMP

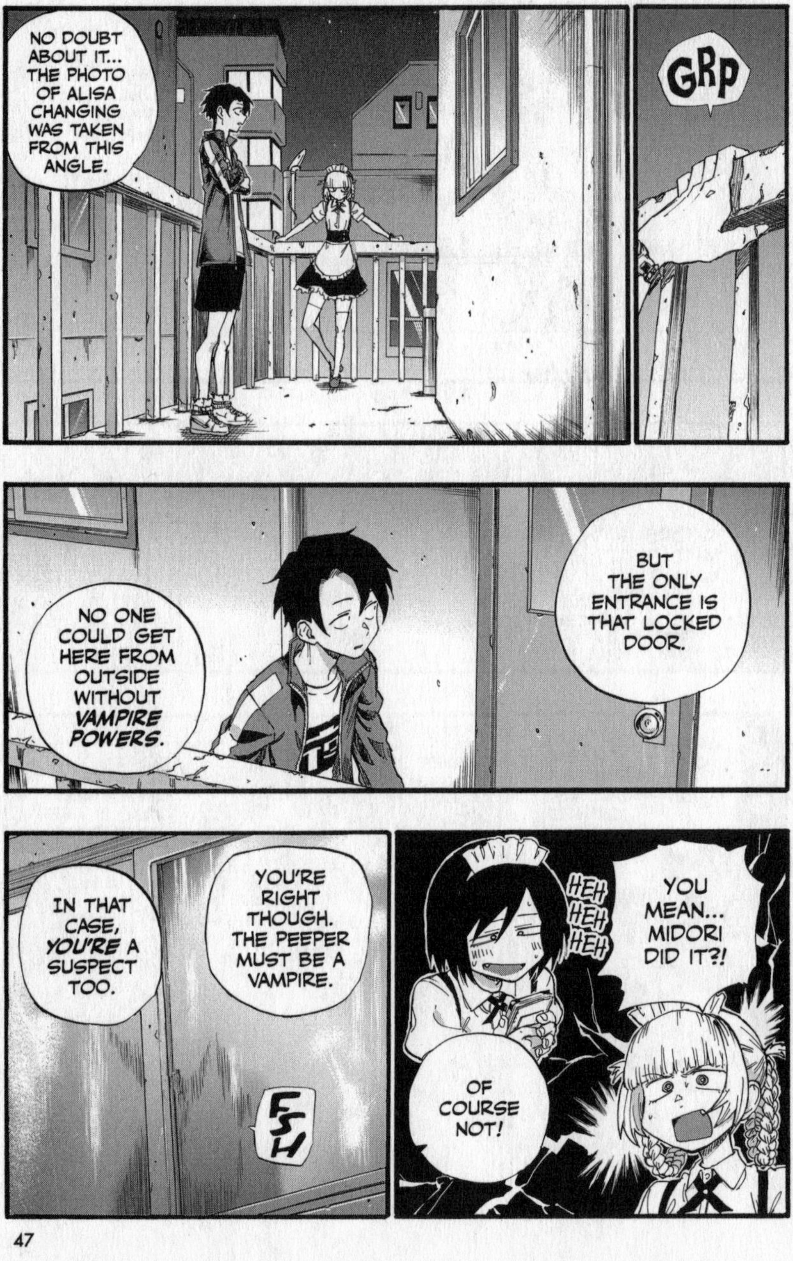
GRP
NO DOUBT ABOUT IT... THE PHOTO OF ALISA CHANGING WAS TAKEN FROM THIS ANGLE.
BUT THE ONLY ENTRANCE IS THAT LOCKED DOOR.
NO ONE COULD GET HERE FROM OUTSIDE WITHOUT *VAMPIRE POWERS*.
YOU MEAN... MIDORI DID IT?!
HEH HEH HEH
OF COURSE NOT!
YOU'RE RIGHT THOUGH. THE PEEPER MUST BE A VAMPIRE.
IN THAT CASE, *YOU'RE* A SUSPECT TOO.
FSH

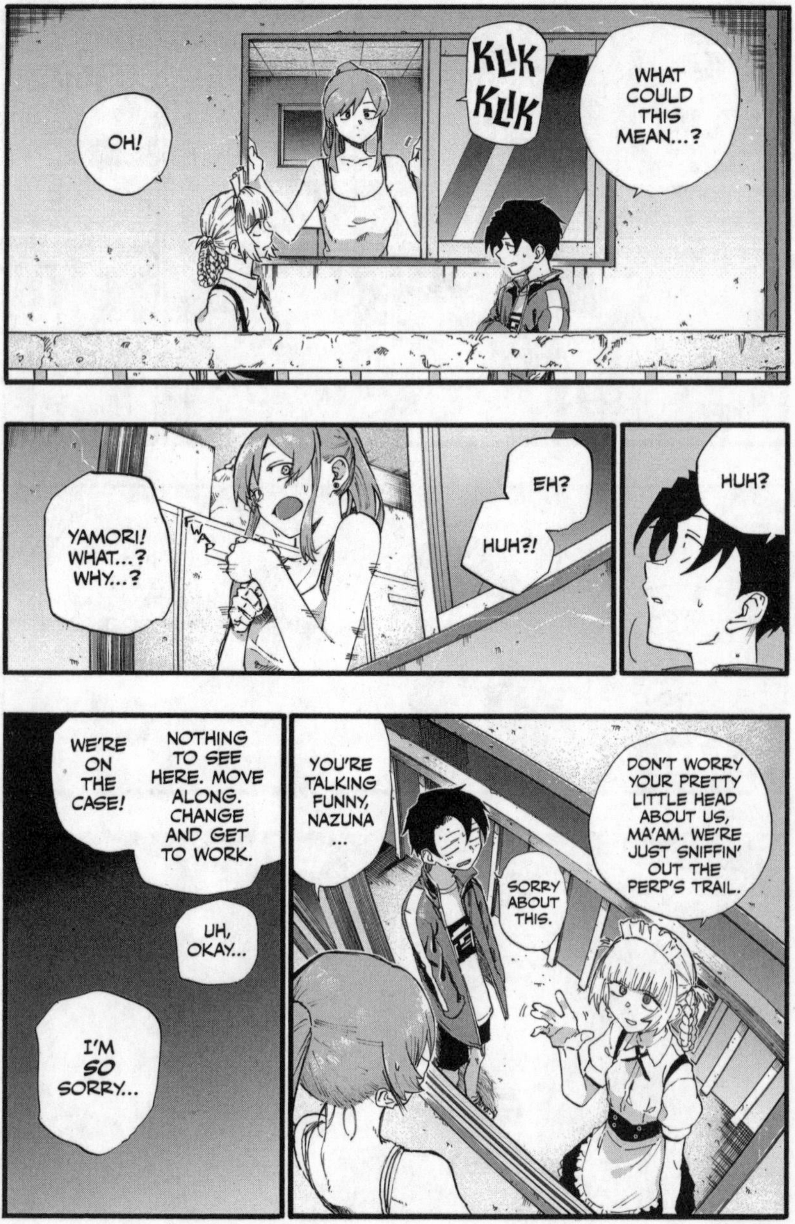
WHAT COULD THIS MEAN...?
KLIK KLIK
OH!
HUH?
EH?
HUH?!
YAMORI! WHAT...? WHY...?
DON'T WORRY YOUR PRETTY LITTLE HEAD ABOUT US, MA'AM. WE'RE JUST SNIFFIN' OUT THE PERP'S TRAIL.
SORRY ABOUT THIS.
YOU'RE TALKING FUNNY, NAZUNA ...
NOTHING TO SEE HERE. MOVE ALONG. CHANGE AND GET TO WORK.
WE'RE ON THE CASE!
UH, OKAY...
I'M SO SORRY...

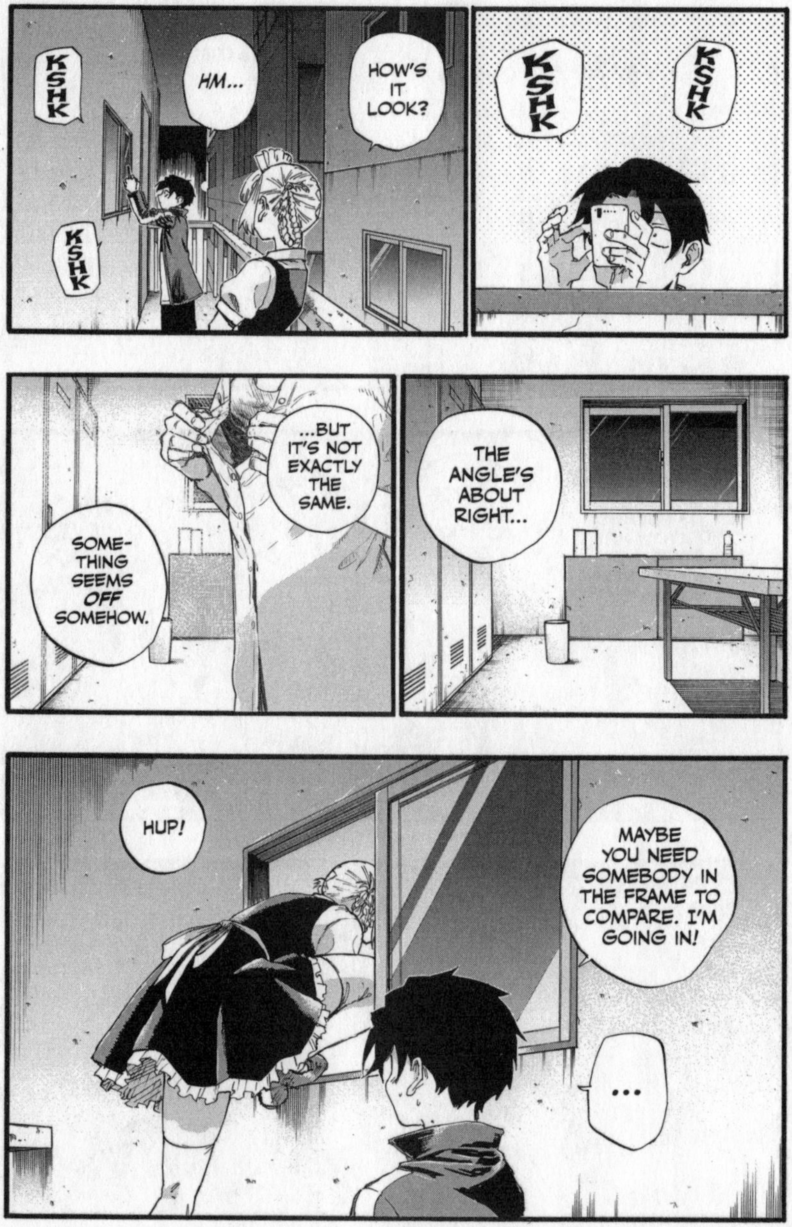
KSHK
KSHK
HOW'S IT LOOK?
HM...
KSHK
KSHK
THE ANGLE'S ABOUT RIGHT...
...BUT IT'S NOT EXACTLY THE SAME.
SOME-THING SEEMS *OFF* SOMEHOW.
MAYBE YOU NEED SOMEBODY IN THE FRAME TO COMPARE. I'M GOING IN!
HUP!
...

KSHK
NAZUNA? YOU LOOK AWFUL!!
I'M GONNA PULVER-IZE YOU...
WHOA, I DO LOOK AWFUL!
RIGHT?
THERE ARE HACKS TO TAKING GOOD PHOTOS.
I GUESS IF YOU TOOK A LOT OF SELFIES, YOU'D KNOW HOW TO POSE AND MAKE THE RIGHT FACES.
=
same person
GOOD PHOTOS...
...
HUH?
...
WHAT'S UP, KO?

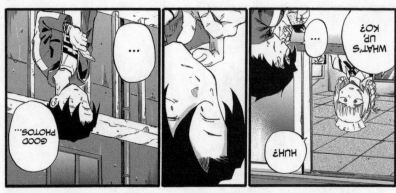

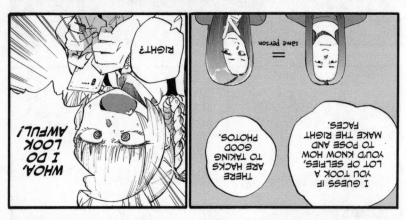

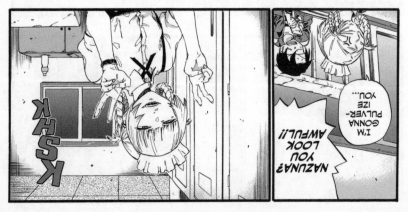

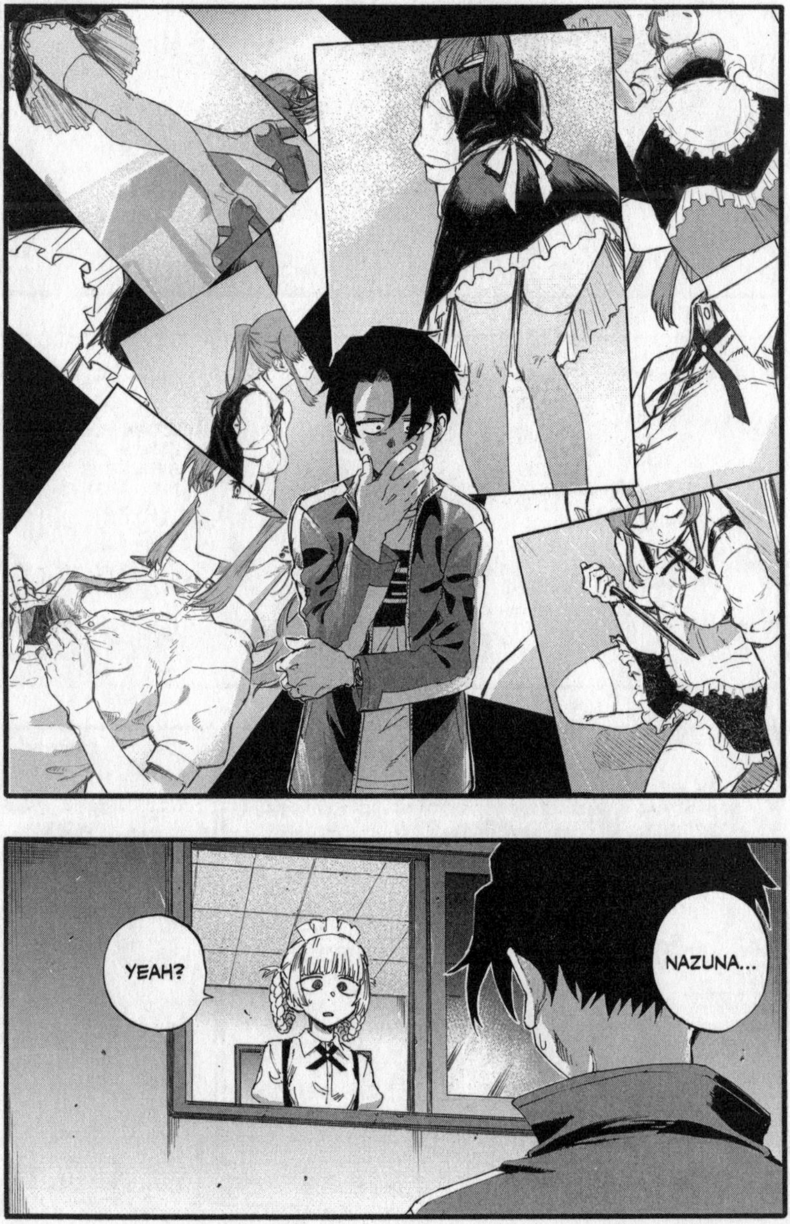
NAZUNA...
YEAH?

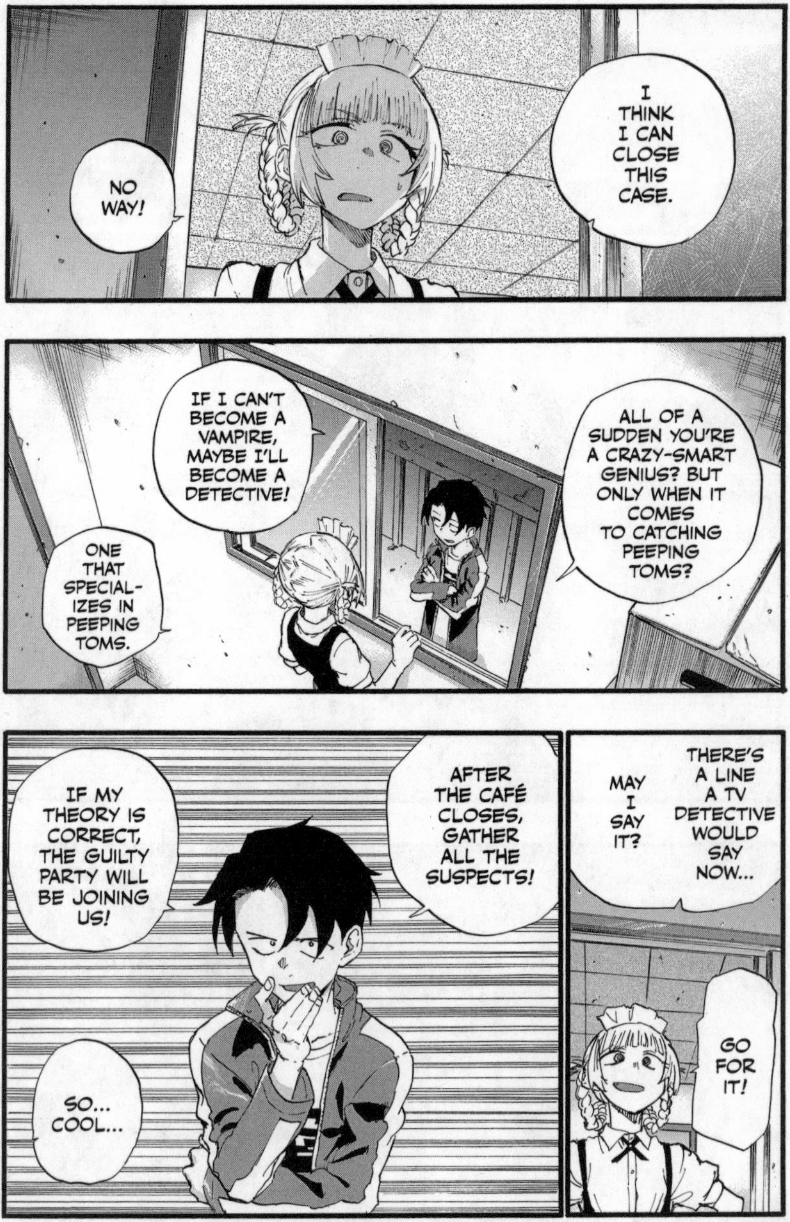
I THINK I CAN CLOSE THIS CASE.
NO WAY!
ALL OF A SUDDEN YOU'RE A CRAZY-SMART GENIUS? BUT ONLY WHEN IT COMES TO CATCHING PEEPING TOMS?
IF I CAN'T BECOME A VAMPIRE, MAYBE I'LL BECOME A DETECTIVE!
ONE THAT SPECIAL-IZES IN PEEPING TOMS.
THERE'S A LINE A TV DETECTIVE WOULD SAY NOW...
MAY I SAY IT?
GO FOR IT!
AFTER THE CAFÉ CLOSES, GATHER ALL THE SUSPECTS!
IF MY THEORY IS CORRECT, THE GUILTY PARTY WILL BE JOINING US!
SO... COOL...

Call of the Night

Call of the Night

NIGHT 33: WE MIGHT FIND OUT IF WE'RE LUCKY

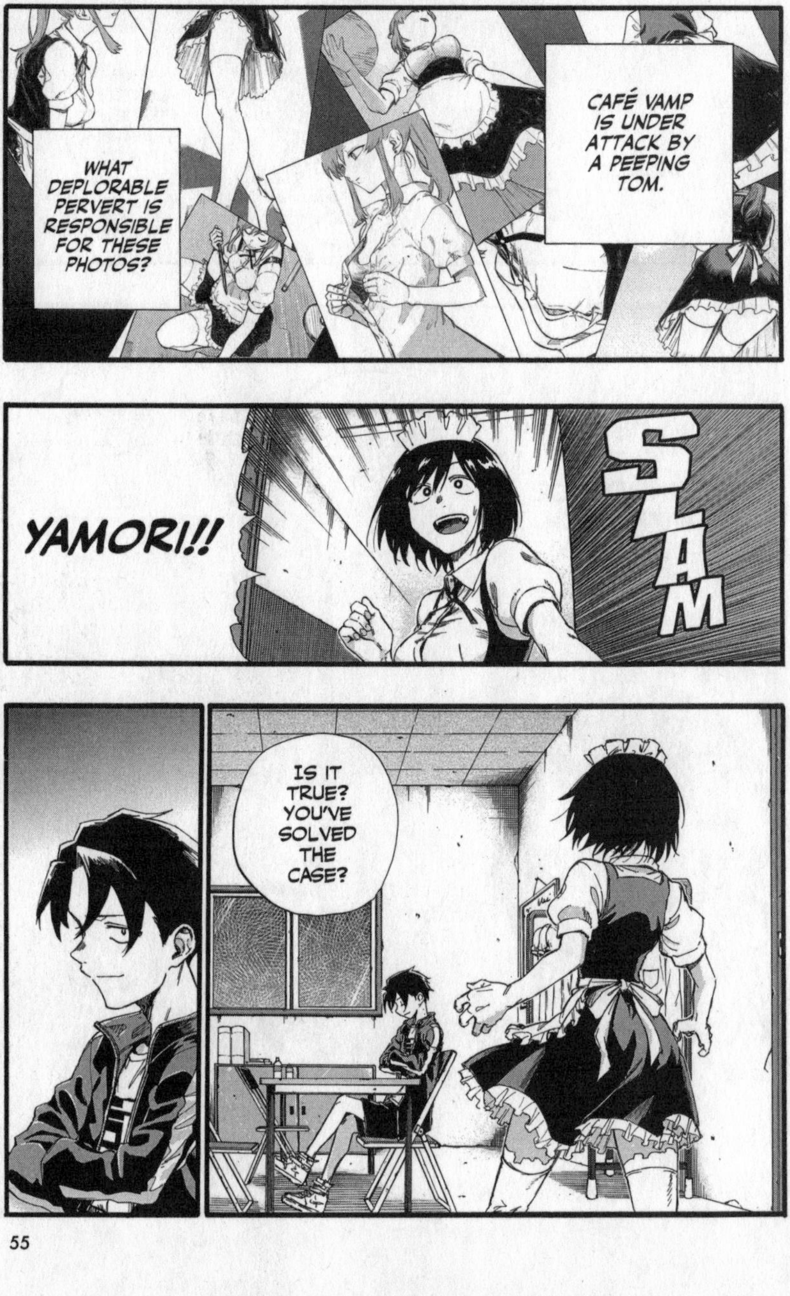
CAFÉ VAMP IS UNDER ATTACK BY A PEEPING TOM.
WHAT DEPLORABLE PERVERT IS RESPONSIBLE FOR THESE PHOTOS?
SLAM
YAMORI!!
IS IT TRUE? YOU'VE SOLVED THE CASE?

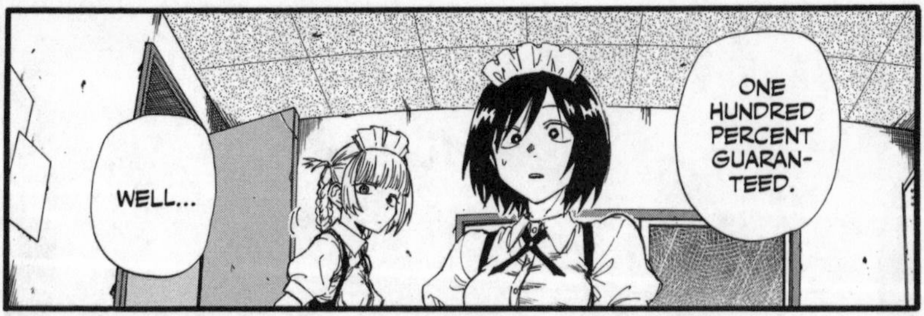
ONE HUNDRED PERCENT GUARAN-TEED.
WELL...

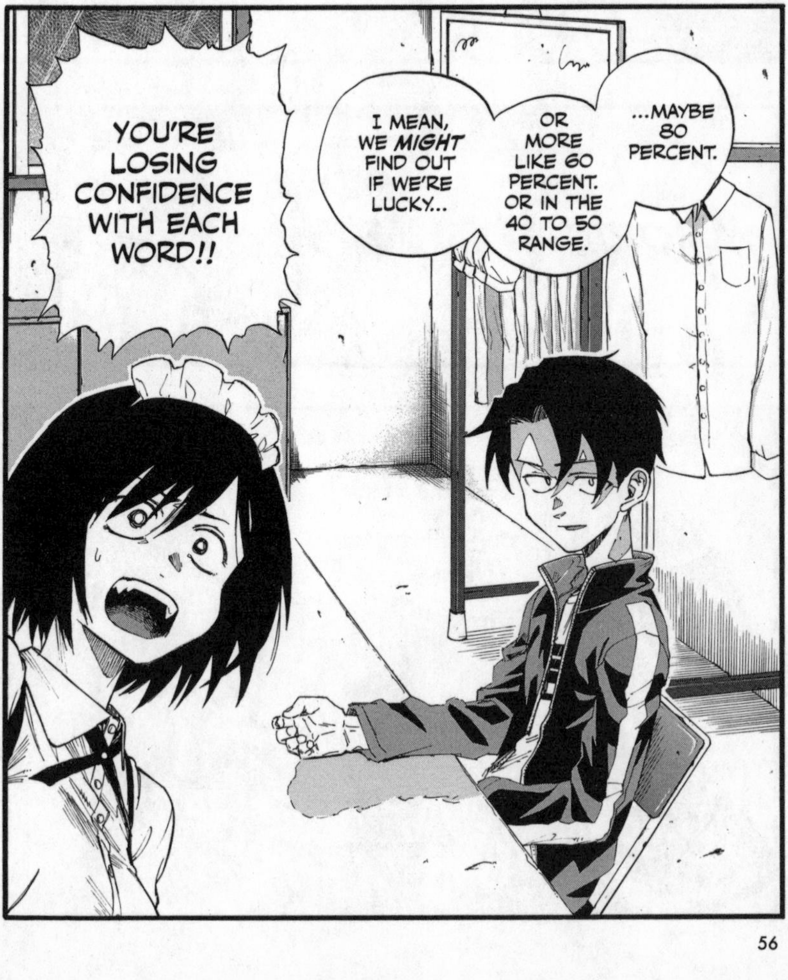
...MAYBE 80 PERCENT.
OR MORE LIKE 60 PERCENT. OR IN THE 40 TO 50 RANGE.
I MEAN, WE *MIGHT* FIND OUT IF WE'RE LUCKY...
YOU'RE LOSING CONFIDENCE WITH EACH WORD!!

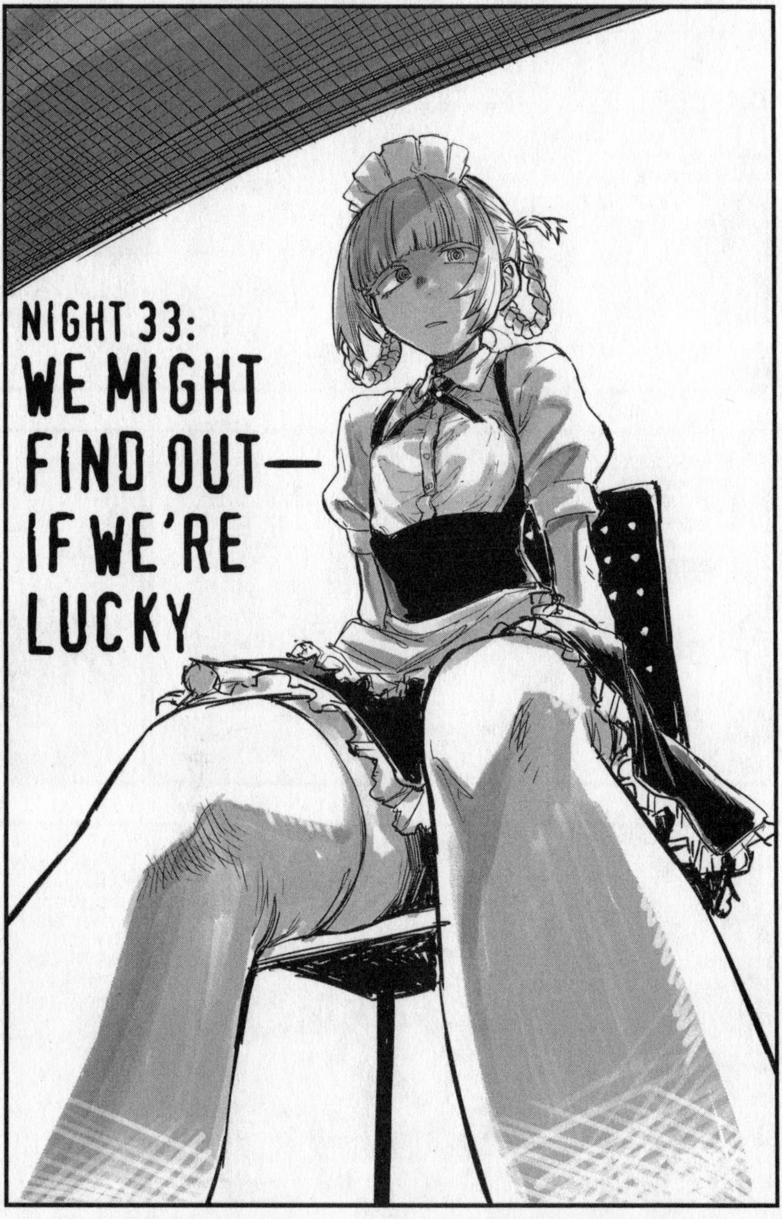
NIGHT 33:
WE MIGHT FIND OUT— IF WE'RE LUCKY

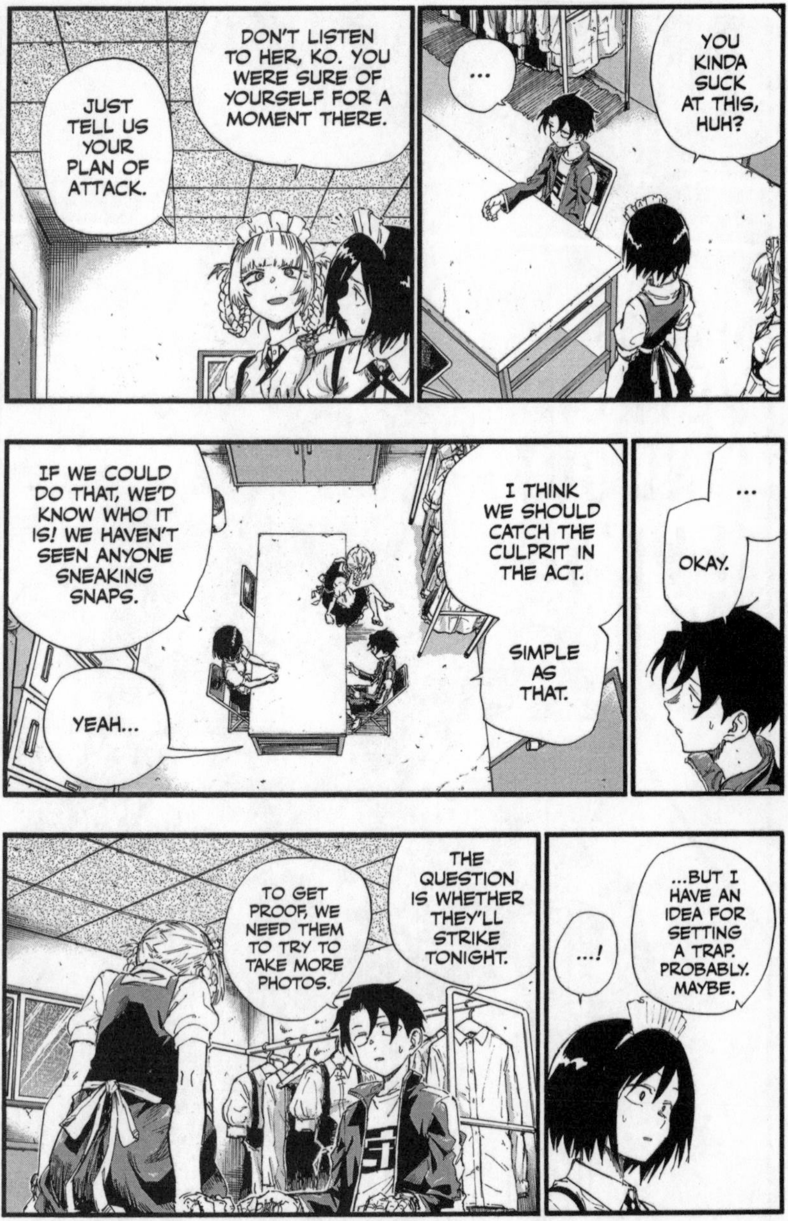
YOU KINDA SUCK AT THIS, HUH?
...
DON'T LISTEN TO HER, KO. YOU WERE SURE OF YOURSELF FOR A MOMENT THERE.
JUST TELL US YOUR PLAN OF ATTACK.
...
OKAY.
I THINK WE SHOULD CATCH THE CULPRIT IN THE ACT.
SIMPLE AS THAT.
IF WE COULD DO THAT, WE'D KNOW WHO IT IS! WE HAVEN'T SEEN ANYONE SNEAKING SNAPS.
YEAH...
...BUT I HAVE AN IDEA FOR SETTING A TRAP. PROBABLY. MAYBE.
...!
THE QUESTION IS WHETHER THEY'LL STRIKE TONIGHT.
TO GET PROOF, WE NEED THEM TO TRY TO TAKE MORE PHOTOS.

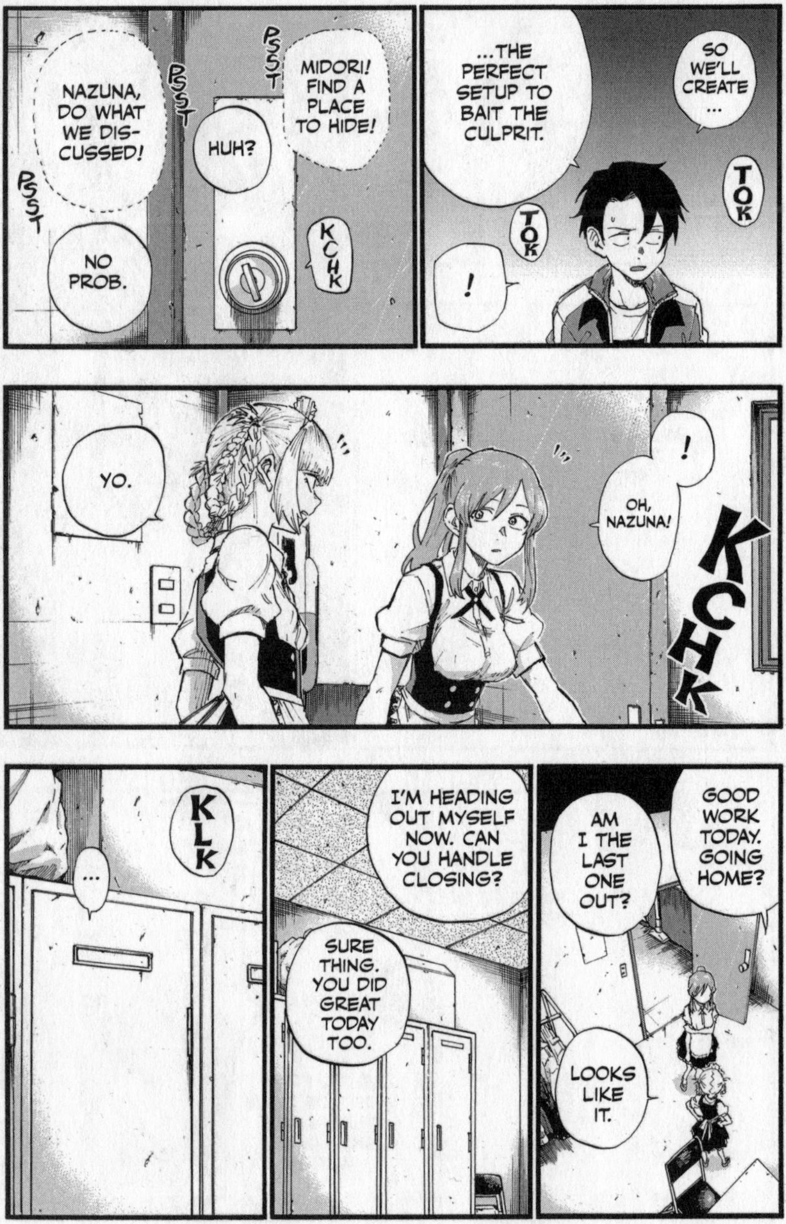
SO WE'LL CREATE ...
TOK
...THE PERFECT SETUP TO BAIT THE CULPRIT.
TOK
!
MIDORI! FIND A PLACE TO HIDE!
PSST
HUH?
KCHK
NAZUNA, DO WHAT WE DISCUSSED!
PSST
NO PROB.
!
OH, NAZUNA!
KCHK
YO.
GOOD WORK TODAY. GOING HOME?
AM I THE LAST ONE OUT?
LOOKS LIKE IT.
I'M HEADING OUT MYSELF NOW. CAN YOU HANDLE CLOSING?
SURE THING. YOU DID GREAT TODAY TOO.
KLK
...

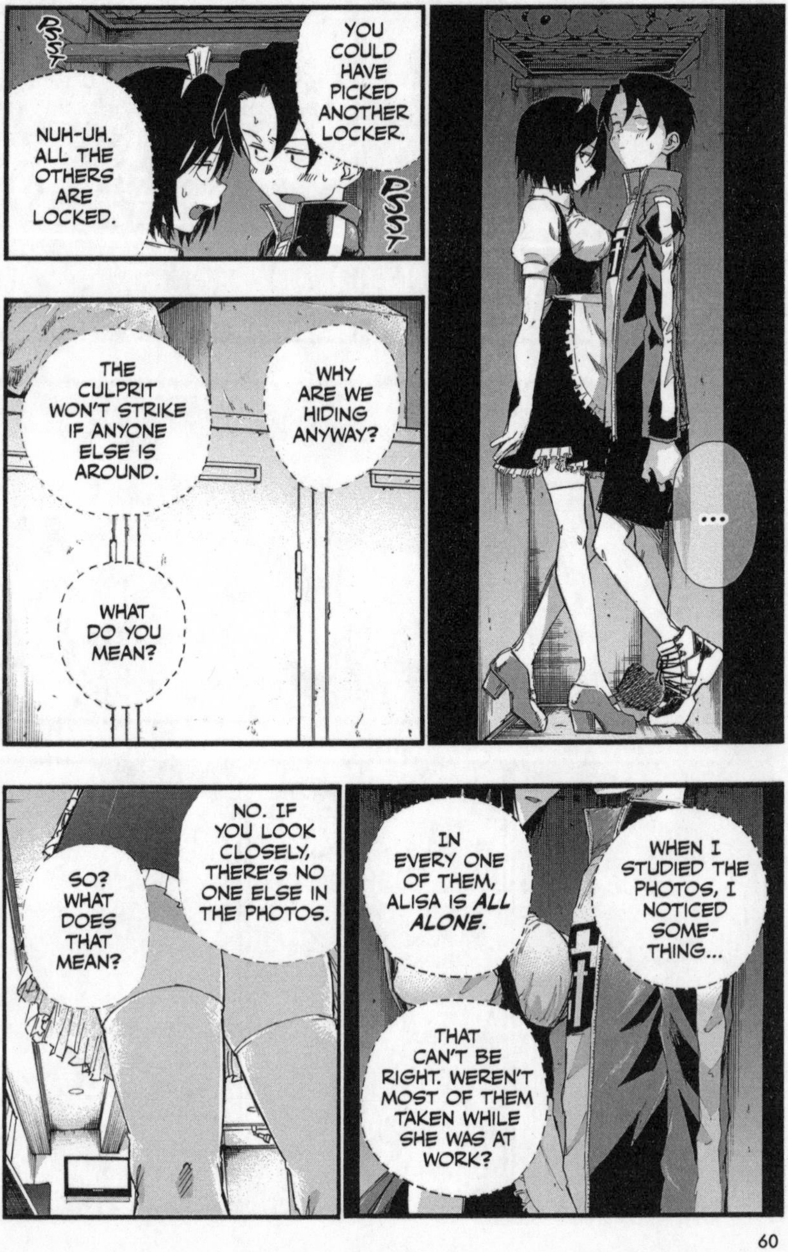
...
YOU COULD HAVE PICKED ANOTHER LOCKER.
PSST
PSST
NUH-UH. ALL THE OTHERS ARE LOCKED.
WHY ARE WE HIDING ANYWAY?
THE CULPRIT WON'T STRIKE IF ANYONE ELSE IS AROUND.
WHAT DO YOU MEAN?
WHEN I STUDIED THE PHOTOS, I NOTICED SOME-THING...
IN EVERY ONE OF THEM, ALISA IS *ALL ALONE*.
THAT CAN'T BE RIGHT. WEREN'T MOST OF THEM TAKEN WHILE SHE WAS AT WORK?
NO. IF YOU LOOK CLOSELY, THERE'S NO ONE ELSE IN THE PHOTOS.
SO? WHAT DOES THAT MEAN?

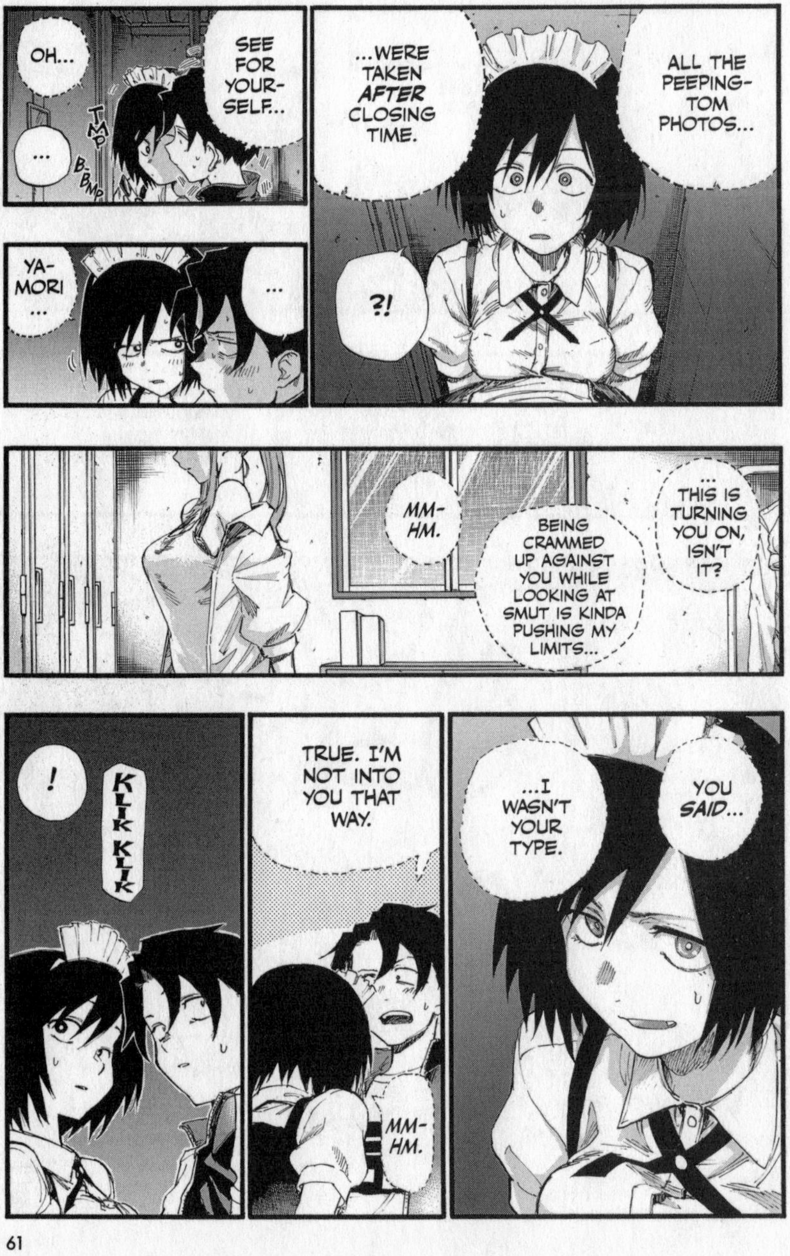
ALL THE PEEPING-TOM PHOTOS...
...WERE TAKEN *AFTER* CLOSING TIME.
?!
SEE FOR YOUR-SELF...
OH...
TMP
...
B-BMP
...
YA-MORI ...
... THIS IS TURNING YOU ON, ISN'T IT?
BEING CRAMMED UP AGAINST YOU WHILE LOOKING AT SMUT IS KINDA PUSHING MY LIMITS...
MM-HM.
YOU *SAID*...
...I WASN'T YOUR TYPE.
TRUE. I'M NOT INTO YOU THAT WAY.
MM-HM.
!
KLIK KLIK

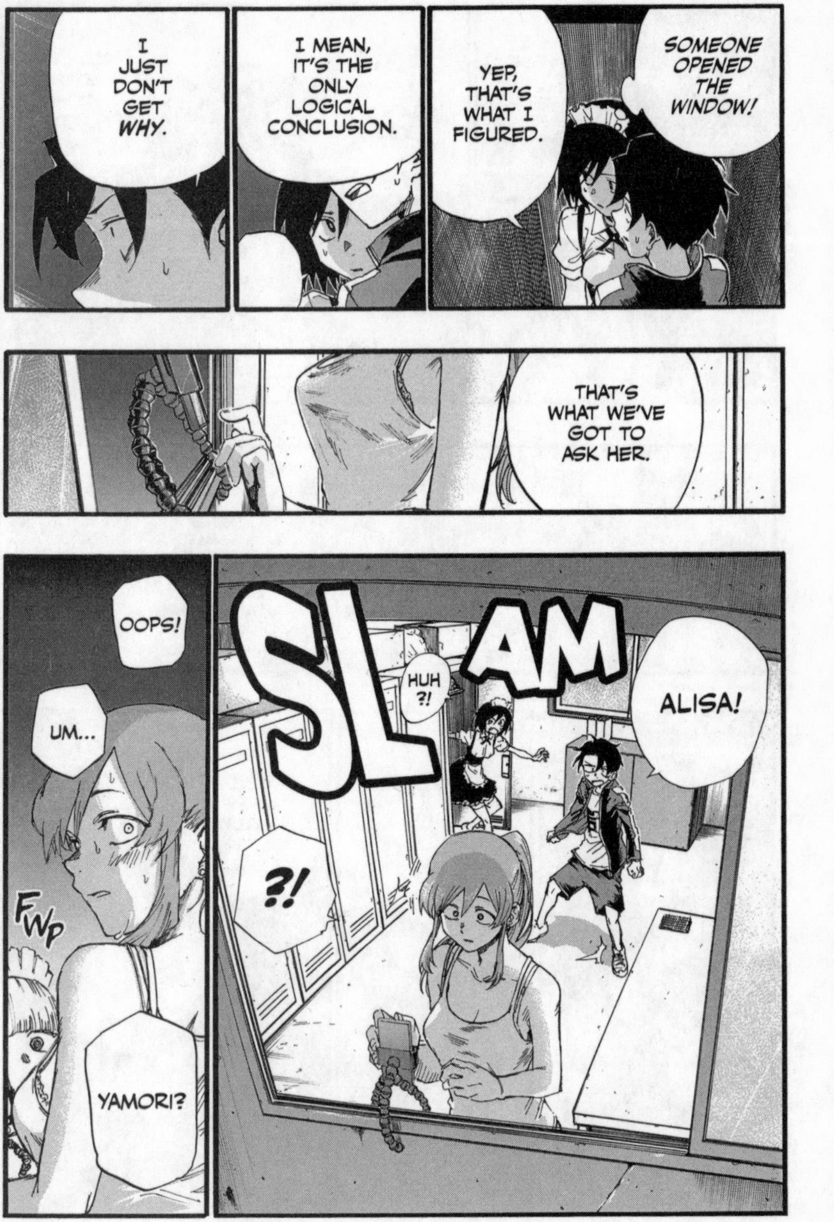
SOMEONE OPENED THE WINDOW!
YEP, THAT'S WHAT I FIGURED.
I MEAN, IT'S THE ONLY LOGICAL CONCLUSION.
I JUST DON'T GET WHY.
THAT'S WHAT WE'VE GOT TO ASK HER.
ALISA!
SLAM
HUH ?!
?!
OOPS!
UM...
FWP
YAMORI?

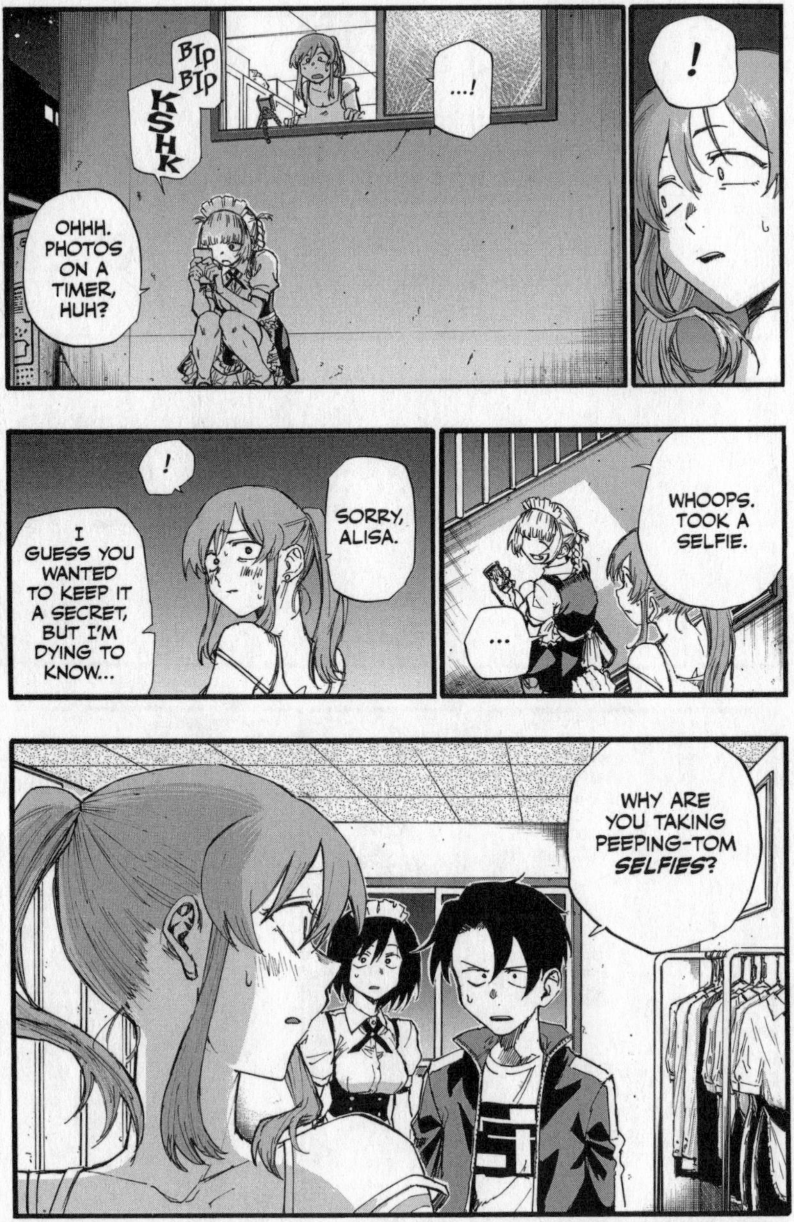
!
...!
BIP BIP
KSHK
OHHH. PHOTOS ON A TIMER, HUH?
WHOOPS. TOOK A SELFIE.
...
SORRY, ALISA.
!
I GUESS YOU WANTED TO KEEP IT A SECRET, BUT I'M DYING TO KNOW...
WHY ARE YOU TAKING PEEPING-TOM *SELFIES*?

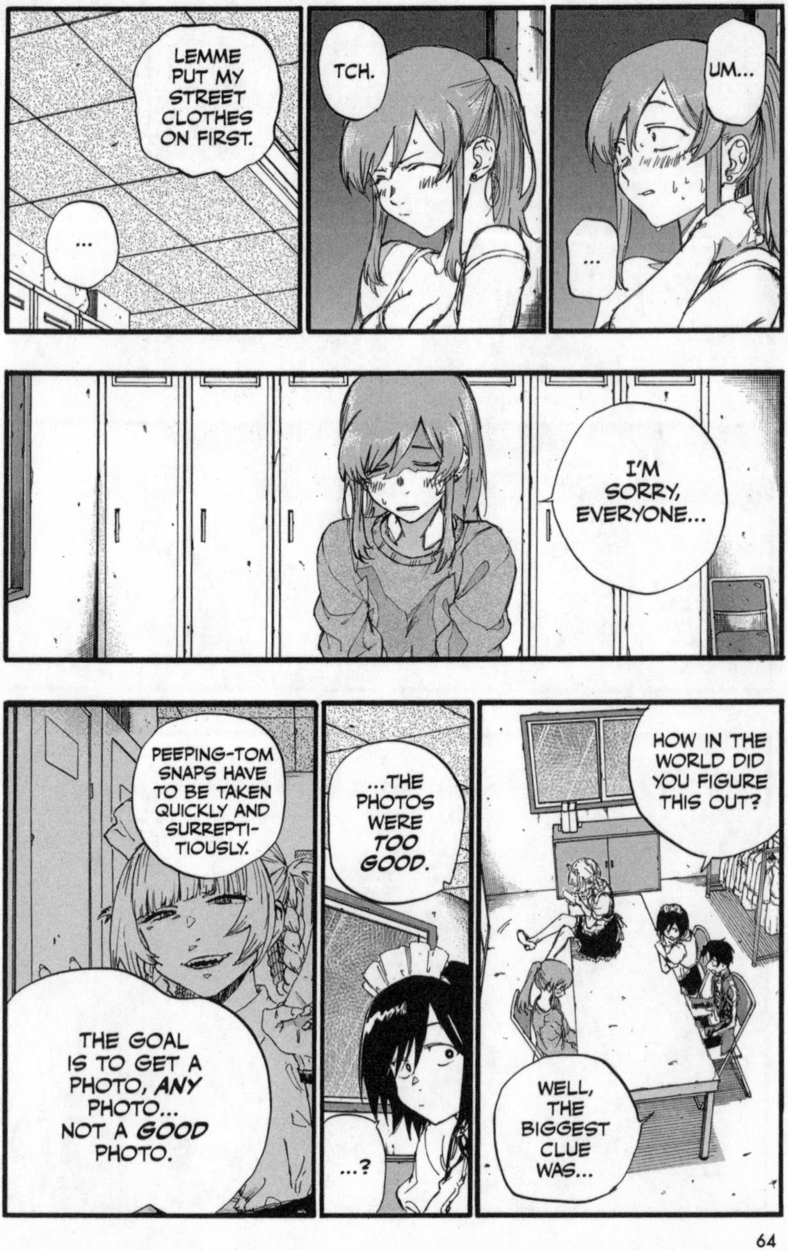
UM...
...
TCH.
LEMME PUT MY STREET CLOTHES ON FIRST.
...
I'M SORRY, EVERYONE...
HOW IN THE WORLD DID YOU FIGURE THIS OUT?
WELL, THE BIGGEST CLUE WAS...
...THE PHOTOS WERE *TOO GOOD*.
...?
PEEPING-TOM SNAPS HAVE TO BE TAKEN QUICKLY AND SURREPTI-TIOUSLY.
THE GOAL IS TO GET A PHOTO, *ANY* PHOTO... NOT A *GOOD* PHOTO.

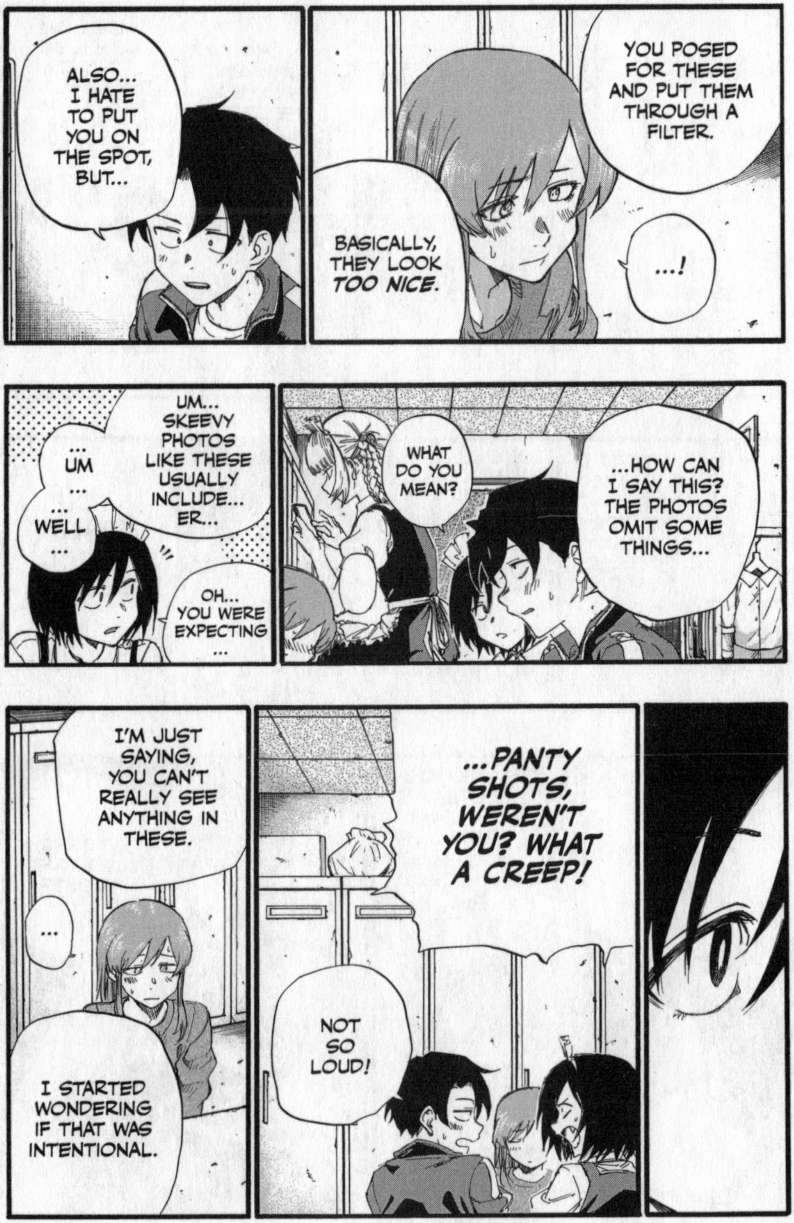
YOU POSED FOR THESE AND PUT THEM THROUGH A FILTER.
...!
BASICALLY, THEY LOOK *TOO NICE*.
ALSO... I HATE TO PUT YOU ON THE SPOT, BUT...
...HOW CAN I SAY THIS? THE PHOTOS OMIT SOME THINGS...
WHAT DO YOU MEAN?
UM... SKEEVY PHOTOS LIKE THESE USUALLY INCLUDE... ER...
... UM ...
... WELL ...
OH... YOU WERE EXPECTING ...
...PANTY SHOTS, WEREN'T YOU? WHAT A CREEP!
NOT SO LOUD!
I'M JUST SAYING, YOU CAN'T REALLY SEE ANYTHING IN THESE.
...
I STARTED WONDERING IF THAT WAS INTENTIONAL.

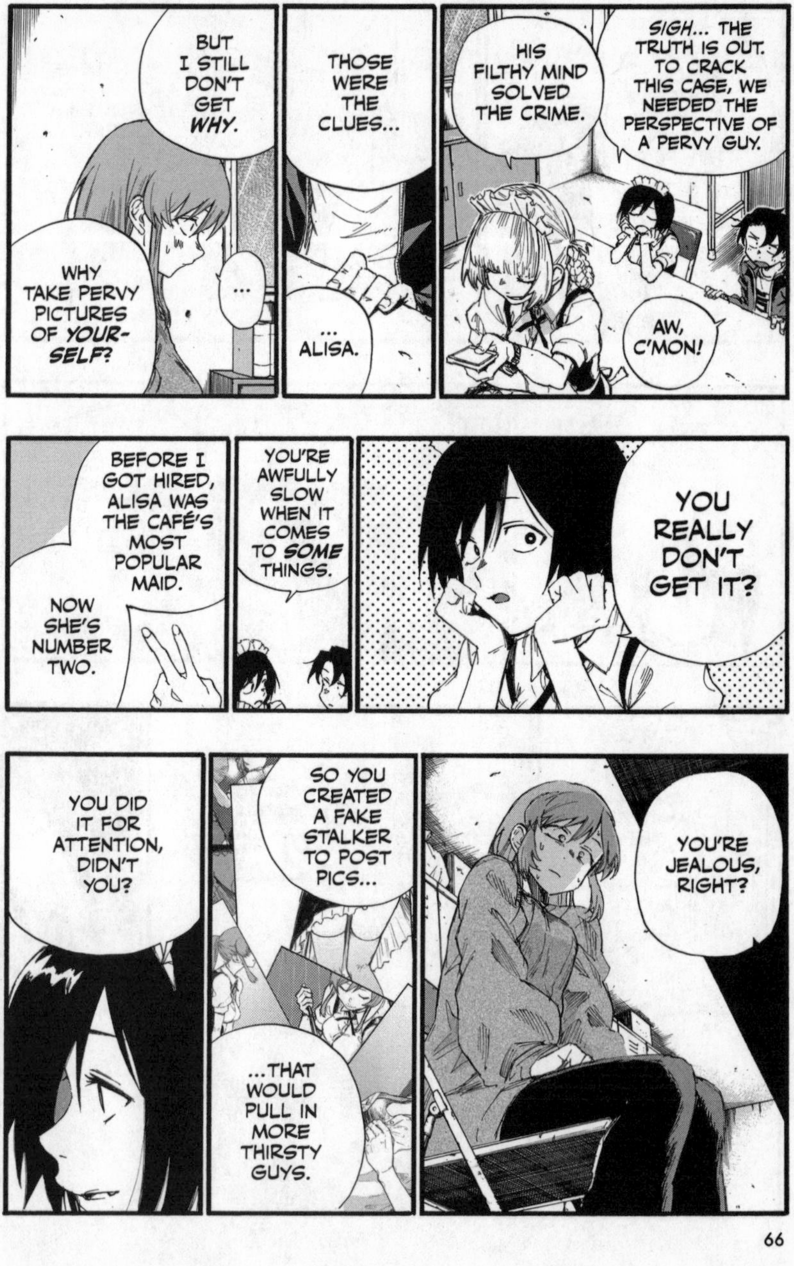
SIGH... THE TRUTH IS OUT. TO CRACK THIS CASE, WE NEEDED THE PERSPECTIVE OF A PERVY GUY.
HIS FILTHY MIND SOLVED THE CRIME.
AW, C'MON!
THOSE WERE THE CLUES...
... ALISA.
BUT I STILL DON'T GET WHY.
...
WHY TAKE PERVY PICTURES OF YOURSELF?
YOU REALLY DON'T GET IT?
YOU'RE AWFULLY SLOW WHEN IT COMES TO SOME THINGS.
BEFORE I GOT HIRED, ALISA WAS THE CAFÉ'S MOST POPULAR MAID.
NOW SHE'S NUMBER TWO.
YOU'RE JEALOUS, RIGHT?
SO YOU CREATED A FAKE STALKER TO POST PICS...
...THAT WOULD PULL IN MORE THIRSTY GUYS.
YOU DID IT FOR ATTENTION, DIDN'T YOU?

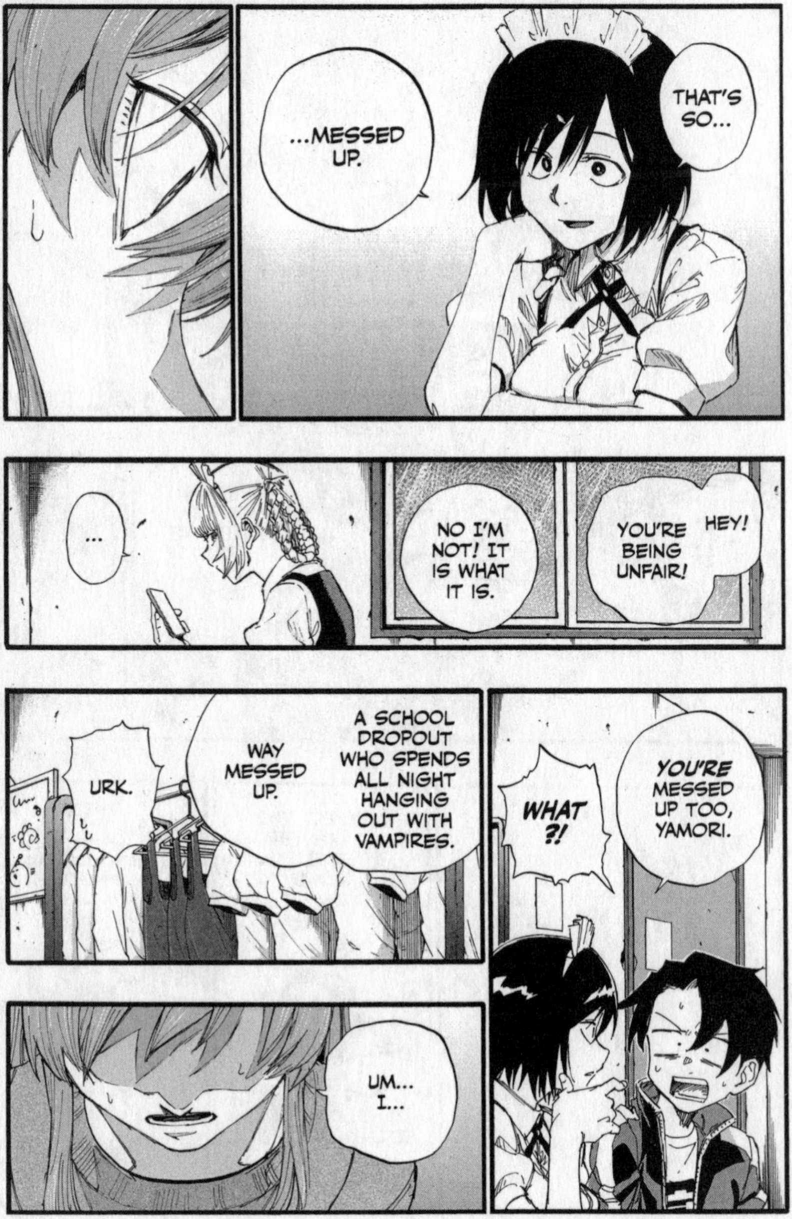
THAT'S SO...
...MESSED UP.
HEY!
YOU'RE BEING UNFAIR!
NO I'M NOT! IT IS WHAT IT IS.
...
YOU'RE MESSED UP TOO, YAMORI.
WHAT ?!
A SCHOOL DROPOUT WHO SPENDS ALL NIGHT HANGING OUT WITH VAMPIRES.
WAY MESSED UP.
URK.
UM... I...

I QUIT!
HOLD UP, ALISA...
IT'S OKAY TO BE MESSED UP.
IN FACT, YOU'RE MESSED UP IN A PRETTY NORMAL WAY.
LOTS OF PEOPLE ACT OUT TO GET NOTICED.
DON'T YOU THINK?
MYSELF INCLUD-ED.
IN FACT, ALL THE GIRLS WHO WORK HERE ARE KINDA MESSED UP. THEY ALL CRAVE ATTENTION.
AND THE "MASTERS" SHELL OUT MONEY TO GIVE IT TO THEM.
THIS WHOLE SITUATION IS WEIRD.
ALISA, YOUR WEIRDNESS IS TOTALLY NORMAL!
SO YOU WENT A LITTLE TOO FAR...
ANYWAY, THOSE WERE REALLY GOOD PHOTOS...

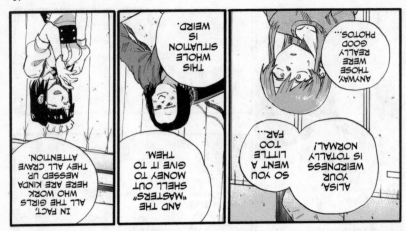

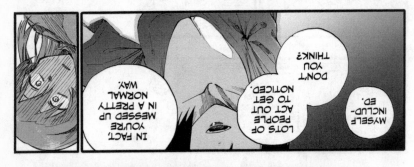

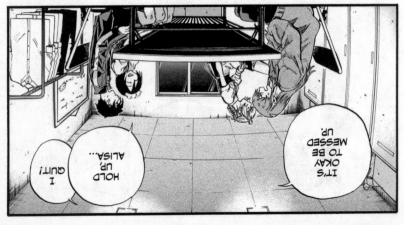

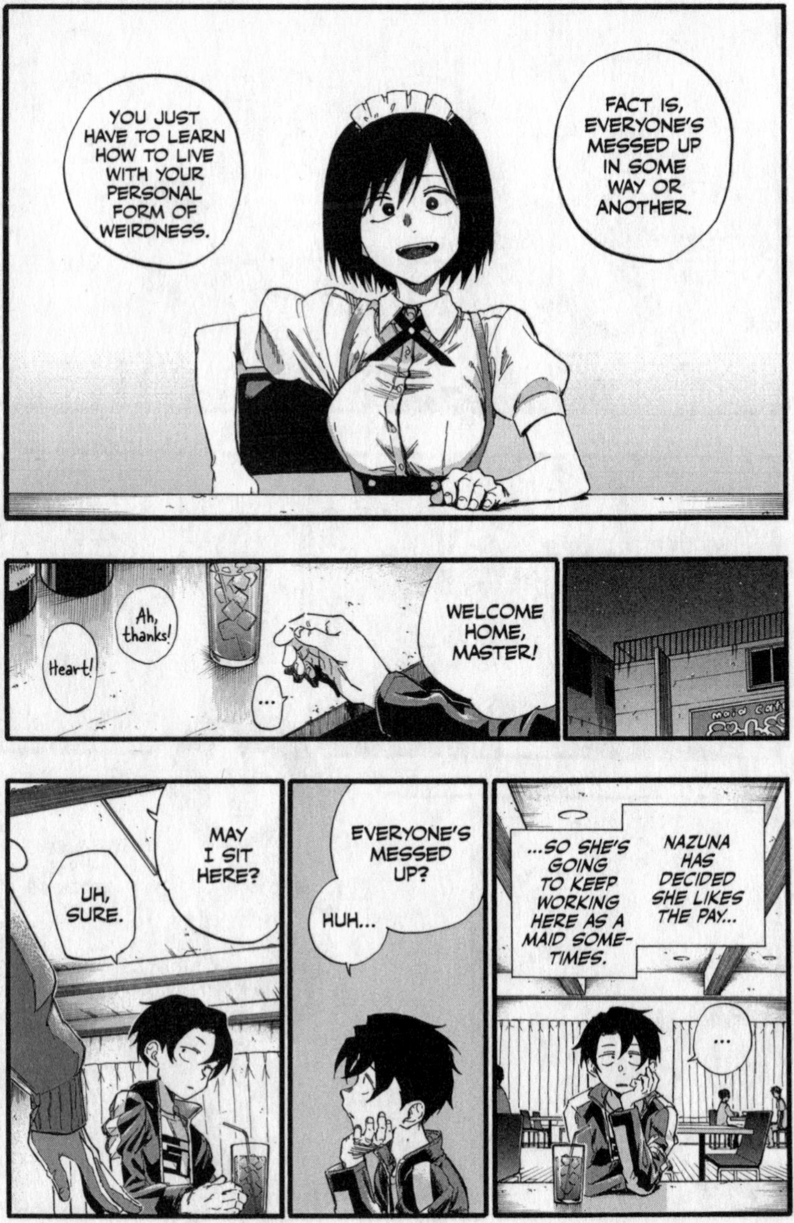
FACT IS, EVERYONE'S MESSED UP IN SOME WAY OR ANOTHER.
YOU JUST HAVE TO LEARN HOW TO LIVE WITH YOUR PERSONAL FORM OF WEIRDNESS.
WELCOME HOME, MASTER!
...
Ah, thanks!
Heart!
NAZUNA HAS DECIDED SHE LIKES THE PAY...
...SO SHE'S GOING TO KEEP WORKING HERE AS A MAID SOME-TIMES.
...
EVERYONE'S MESSED UP?
HUH...
MAY I SIT HERE?
UH, SURE.

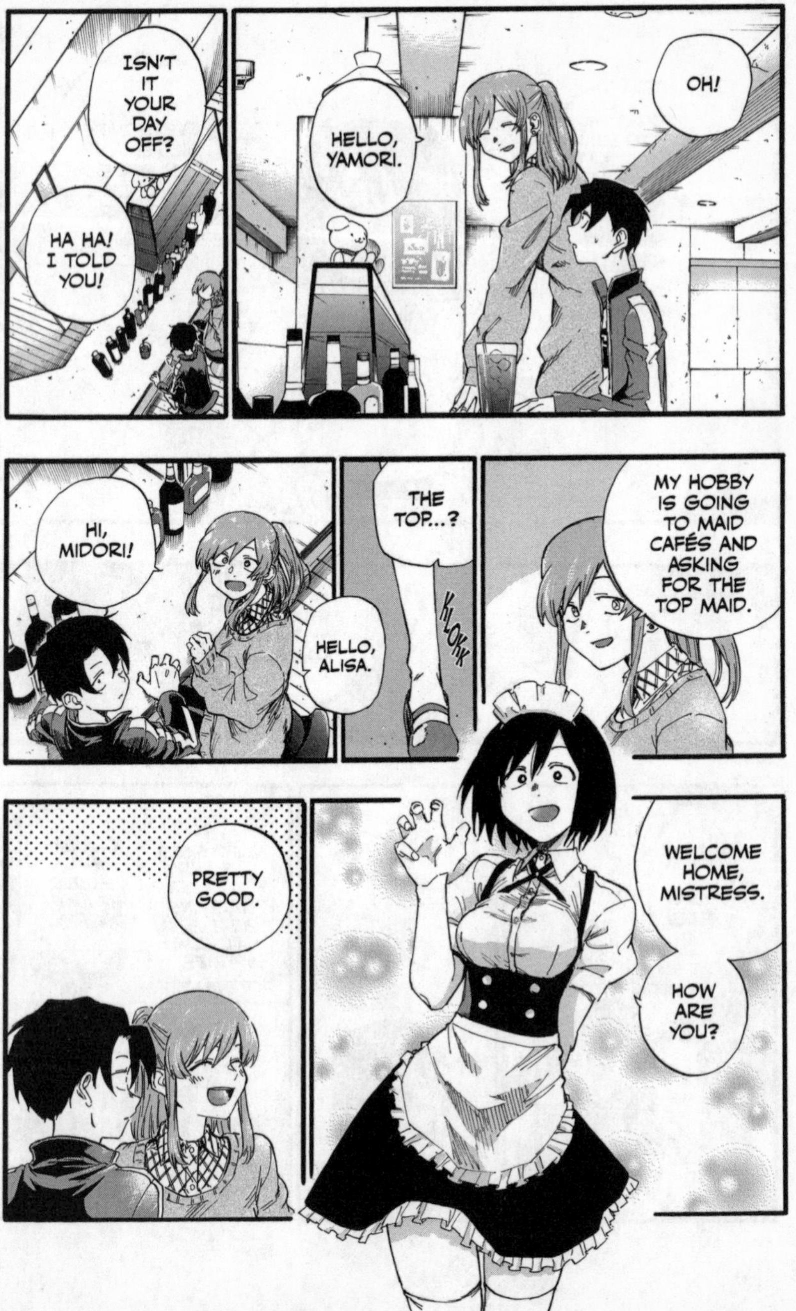
OH!
HELLO, YAMORI.
ISN'T IT YOUR DAY OFF?
HA HA! I TOLD YOU!
MY HOBBY IS GOING TO MAID CAFÉS AND ASKING FOR THE TOP MAID.
THE TOP...?
KLOKK
HI, MIDORI!
HELLO, ALISA.
WELCOME HOME, MISTRESS.
HOW ARE YOU?
PRETTY GOOD.

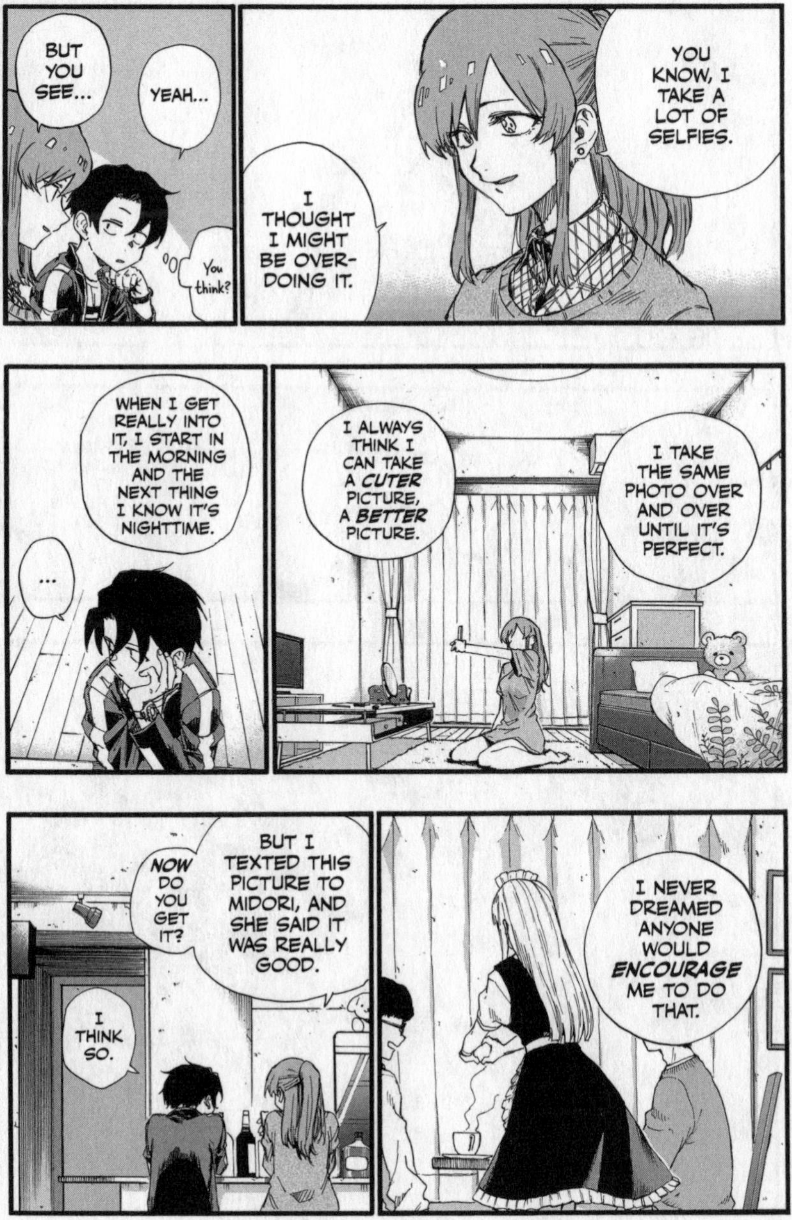
YOU KNOW, I TAKE A LOT OF SELFIES.
I THOUGHT I MIGHT BE OVER-DOING IT.
BUT YOU SEE...
YEAH...
You think?
I TAKE THE SAME PHOTO OVER AND OVER UNTIL IT'S PERFECT.
I ALWAYS THINK I CAN TAKE A *CUTER* PICTURE, A *BETTER* PICTURE.
WHEN I GET REALLY INTO IT, I START IN THE MORNING AND THE NEXT THING I KNOW IT'S NIGHTTIME.
...
I NEVER DREAMED ANYONE WOULD *ENCOURAGE* ME TO DO THAT.
BUT I TEXTED THIS PICTURE TO MIDORI, AND SHE SAID IT WAS REALLY GOOD.
NOW DO YOU GET IT?
I THINK SO.

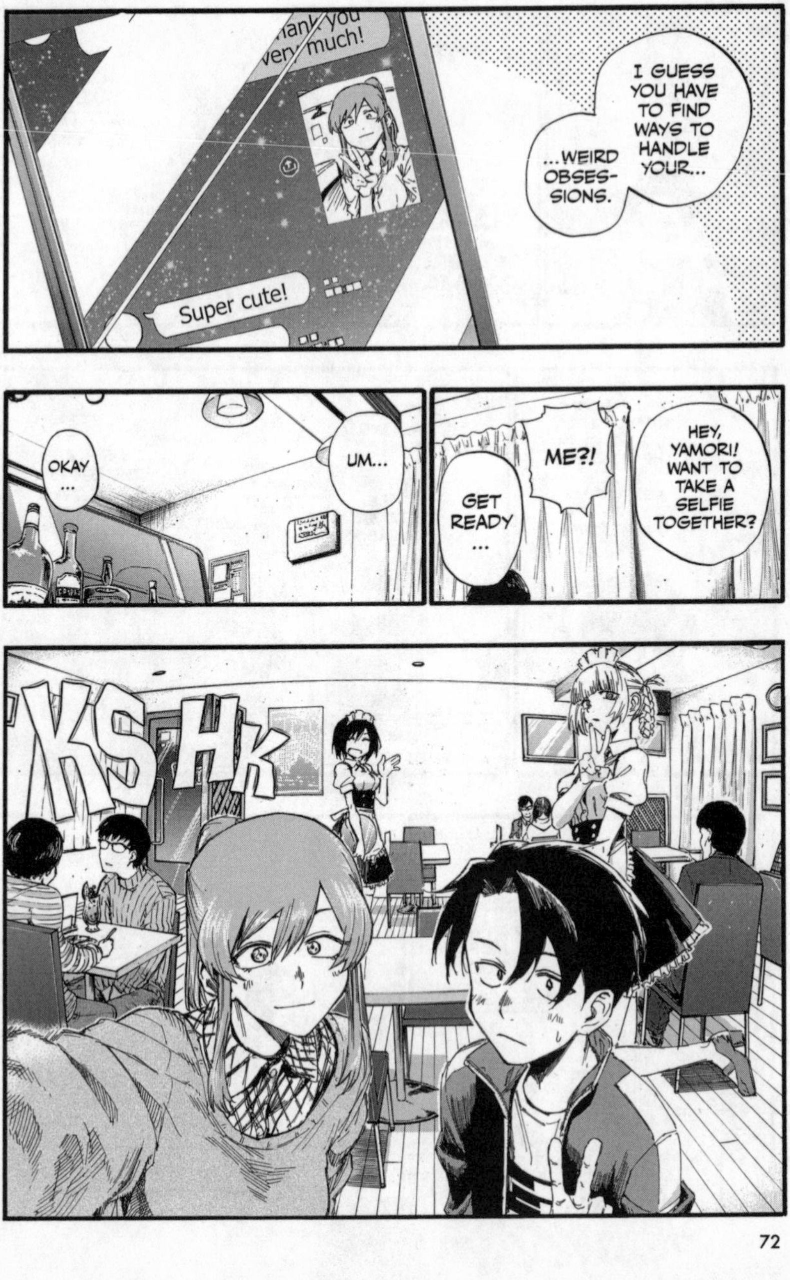
I GUESS YOU HAVE TO FIND WAYS TO HANDLE YOUR...
...WEIRD OBSES-SIONS.
Thank you very much!
Super cute!
HEY, YAMORI! WANT TO TAKE A SELFIE TOGETHER?
ME?!
GET READY ...
UM...
OKAY ...
KSHK

Call of the Night

Call of the Night

NIGHT 34: AM I THE WORST?

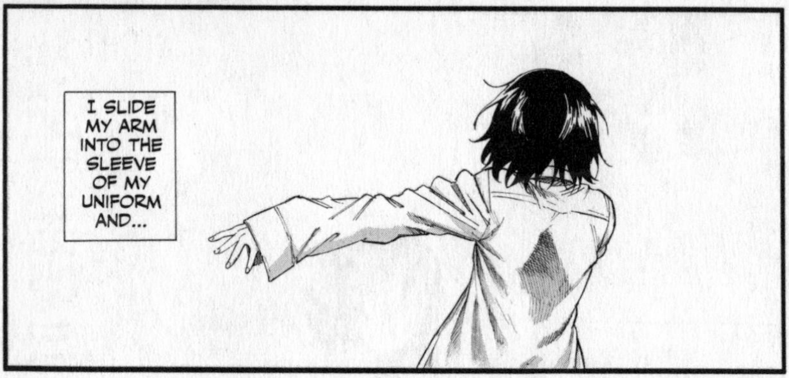
I SLIDE MY ARM INTO THE SLEEVE OF MY UNIFORM AND...

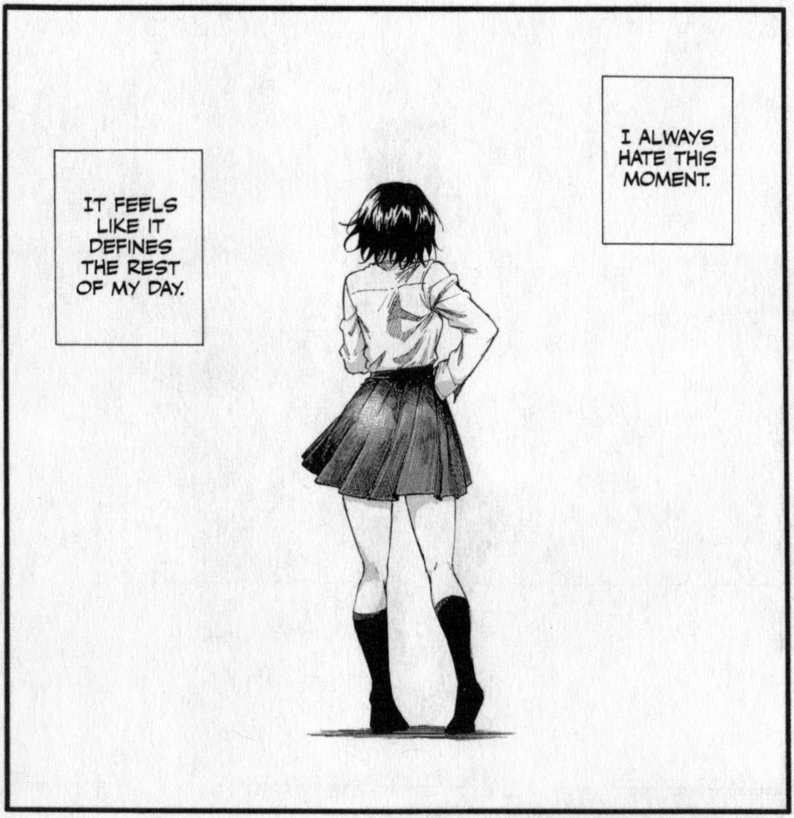
I ALWAYS HATE THIS MOMENT.
IT FEELS LIKE IT DEFINES THE REST OF MY DAY.

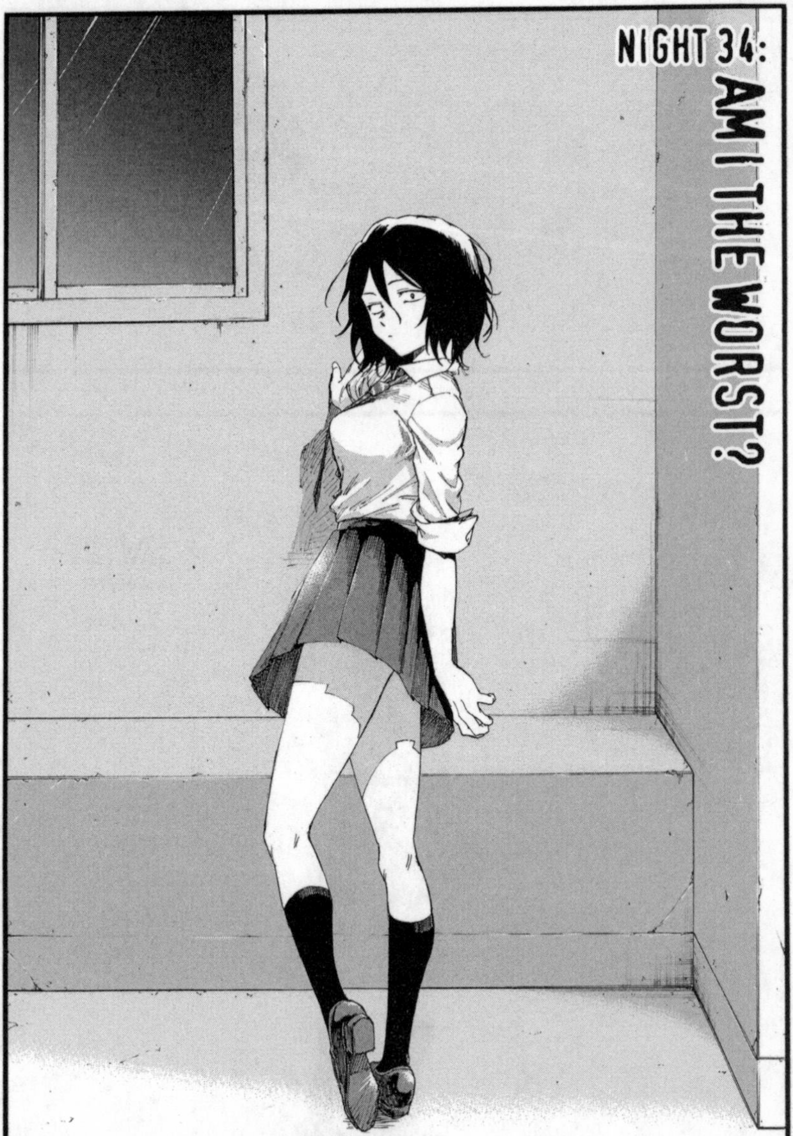
NIGHT 34:
AM I THE WORST?

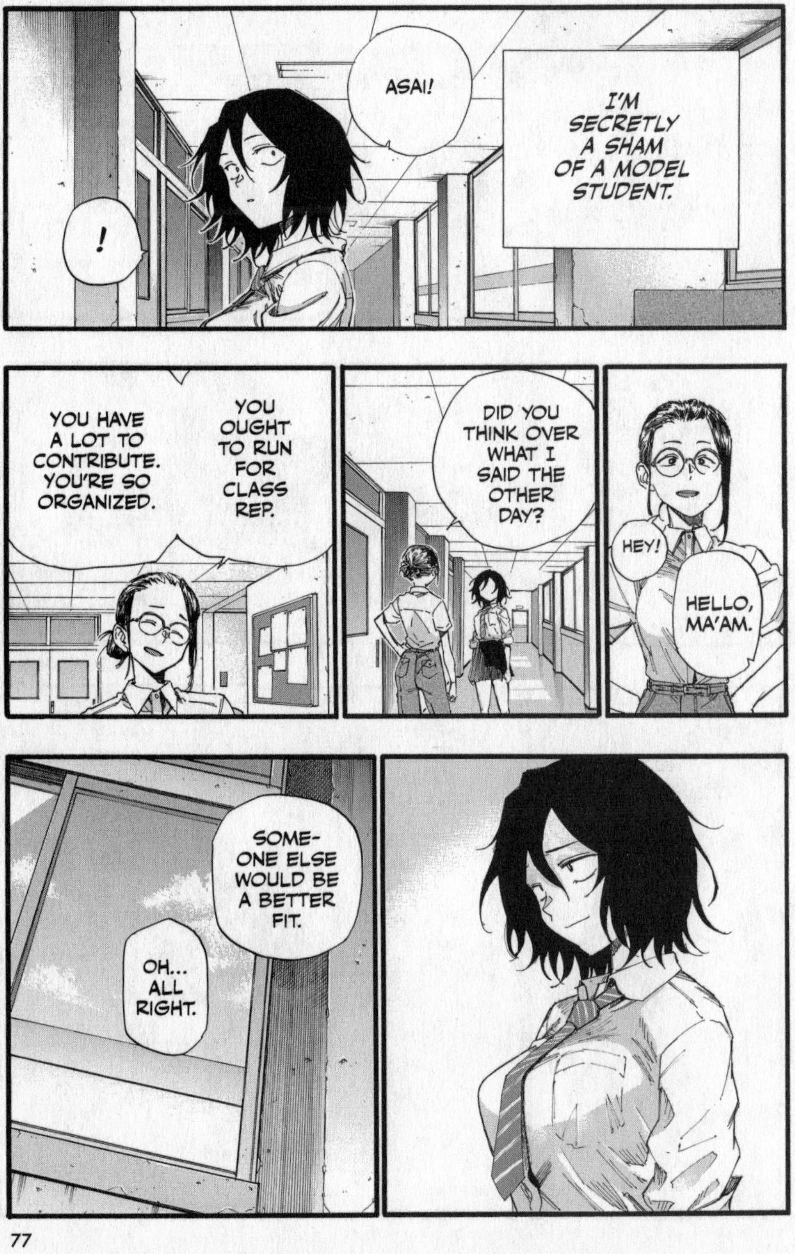

I'M SECRETLY A SHAM OF A MODEL STUDENT.
ASAI!
!
HEY!
HELLO, MA'AM.
DID YOU THINK OVER WHAT I SAID THE OTHER DAY?
YOU OUGHT TO RUN FOR CLASS REP.
YOU HAVE A LOT TO CONTRIBUTE. YOU'RE SO ORGANIZED.
SOME-ONE ELSE WOULD BE A BETTER FIT.
OH... ALL RIGHT.

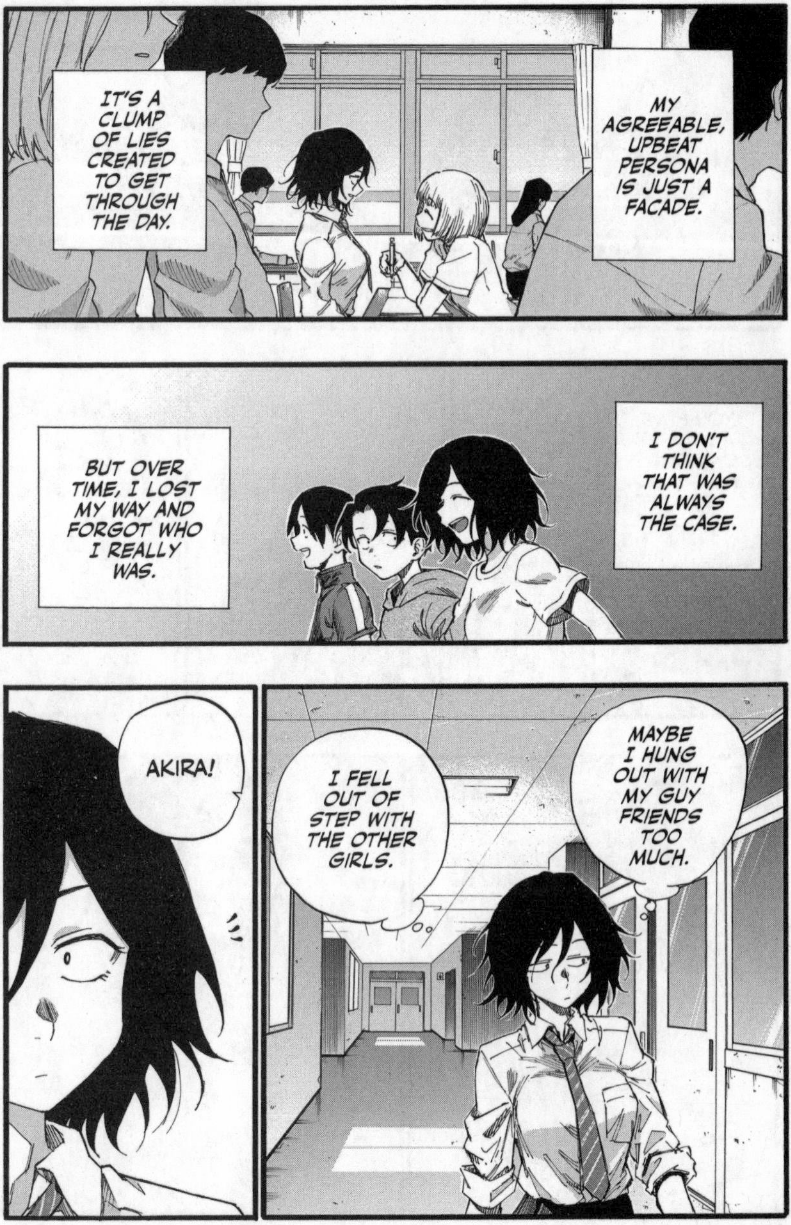
MY AGREEABLE, UPBEAT PERSONA IS JUST A FACADE.
IT'S A CLUMP OF LIES CREATED TO GET THROUGH THE DAY.
I DON'T THINK THAT WAS ALWAYS THE CASE.
BUT OVER TIME, I LOST MY WAY AND FORGOT WHO I REALLY WAS.
MAYBE I HUNG OUT WITH MY GUY FRIENDS TOO MUCH.
I FELL OUT OF STEP WITH THE OTHER GIRLS.
AKIRA!

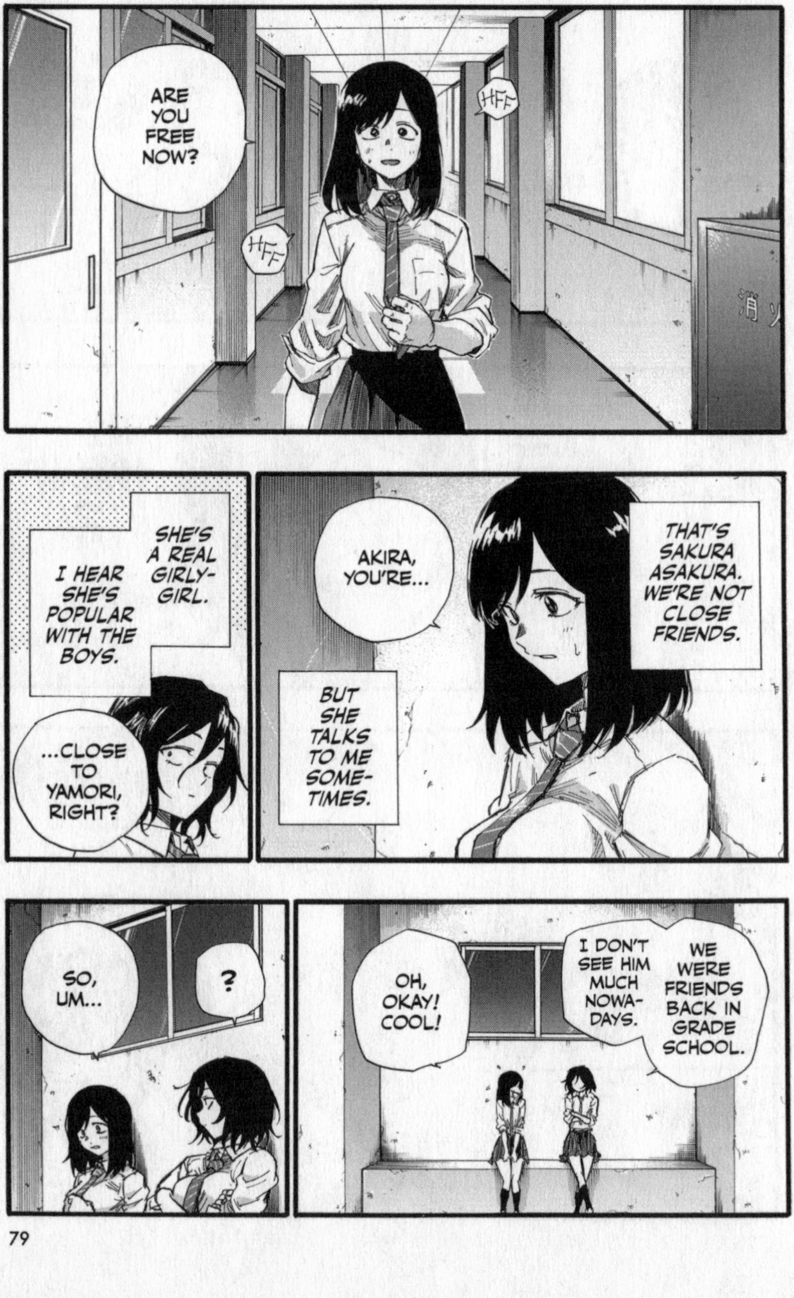
HFF
ARE YOU FREE NOW?
HFF
THAT'S SAKURA ASAKURA. WE'RE NOT CLOSE FRIENDS.
AKIRA, YOU'RE...
BUT SHE TALKS TO ME SOME-TIMES.
SHE'S A REAL GIRLY-GIRL.
I HEAR SHE'S POPULAR WITH THE BOYS.
...CLOSE TO YAMORI, RIGHT?
WE WERE FRIENDS BACK IN GRADE SCHOOL.
I DON'T SEE HIM MUCH NOWA-DAYS.
OH, OKAY! COOL!
?
SO, UM...

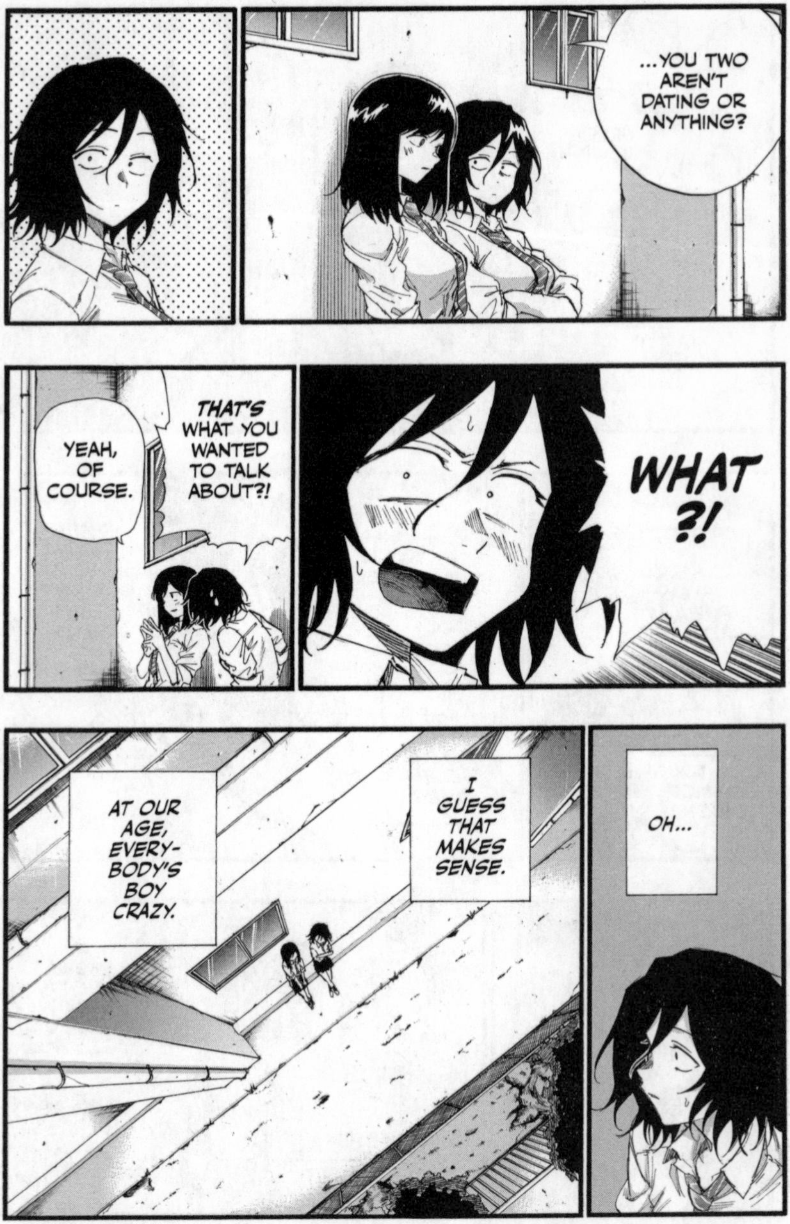
...YOU TWO AREN'T DATING OR ANYTHING?
WHAT ?!
THAT'S WHAT YOU WANTED TO TALK ABOUT?!
YEAH, OF COURSE.
OH...
I GUESS THAT MAKES SENSE.
AT OUR AGE, EVERY-BODY'S BOY CRAZY.

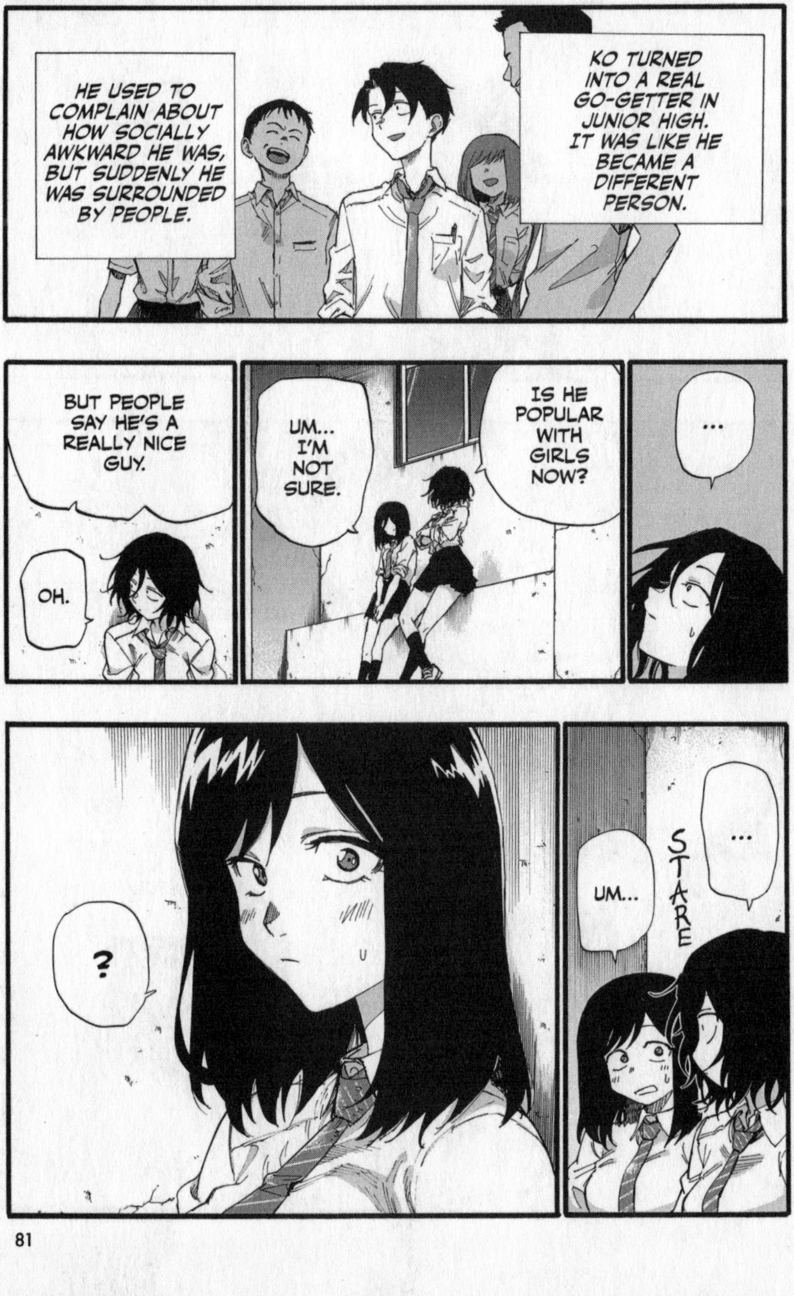
KO TURNED INTO A REAL GO-GETTER IN JUNIOR HIGH. IT WAS LIKE HE BECAME A DIFFERENT PERSON.
HE USED TO COMPLAIN ABOUT HOW SOCIALLY AWKWARD HE WAS, BUT SUDDENLY HE WAS SURROUNDED BY PEOPLE.
...
IS HE POPULAR WITH GIRLS NOW?
UM... I'M NOT SURE.
BUT PEOPLE SAY HE'S A REALLY NICE GUY.
OH.
...
STARE
UM...
?

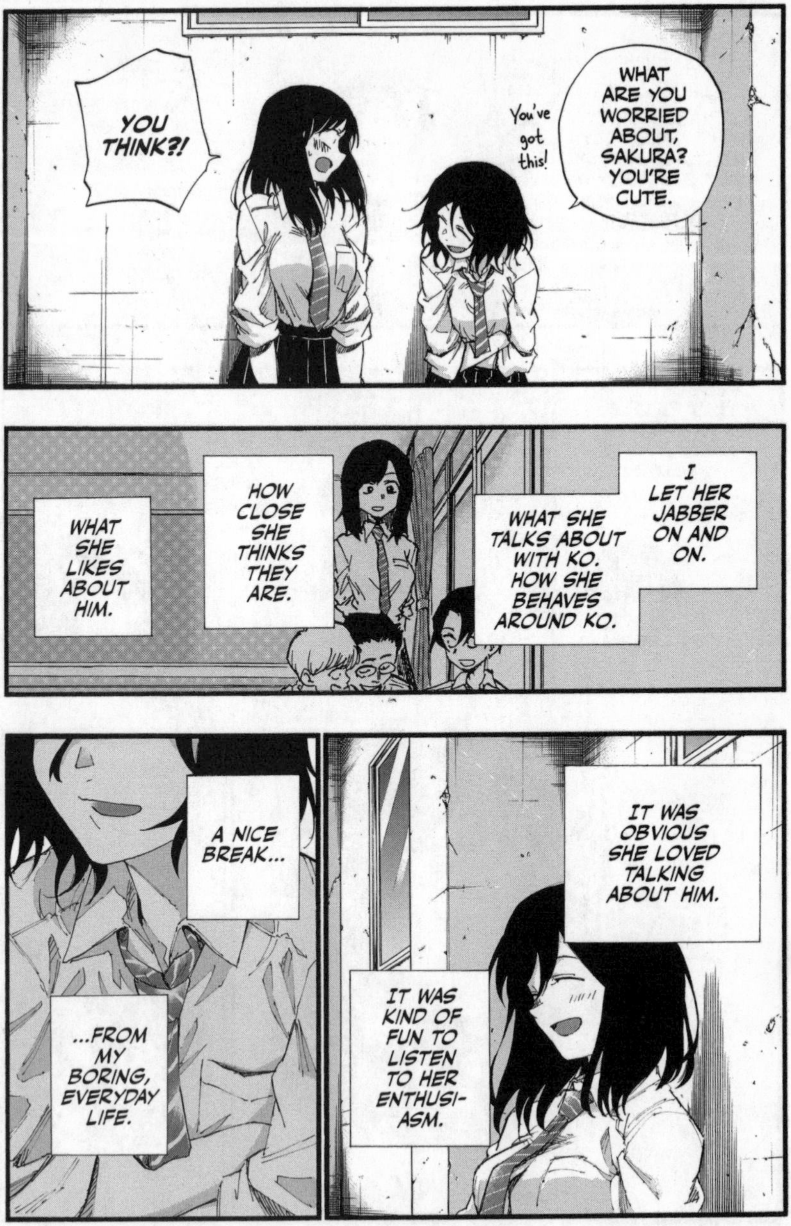
WHAT ARE YOU WORRIED ABOUT, SAKURA? YOU'RE CUTE.
You've got this!
YOU THINK?!
I LET HER JABBER ON AND ON.
WHAT SHE TALKS ABOUT WITH KO. HOW SHE BEHAVES AROUND KO.
HOW CLOSE SHE THINKS THEY ARE.
WHAT SHE LIKES ABOUT HIM.
IT WAS OBVIOUS SHE LOVED TALKING ABOUT HIM.
IT WAS KIND OF FUN TO LISTEN TO HER ENTHUSI-ASM.
A NICE BREAK...
...FROM MY BORING, EVERYDAY LIFE.

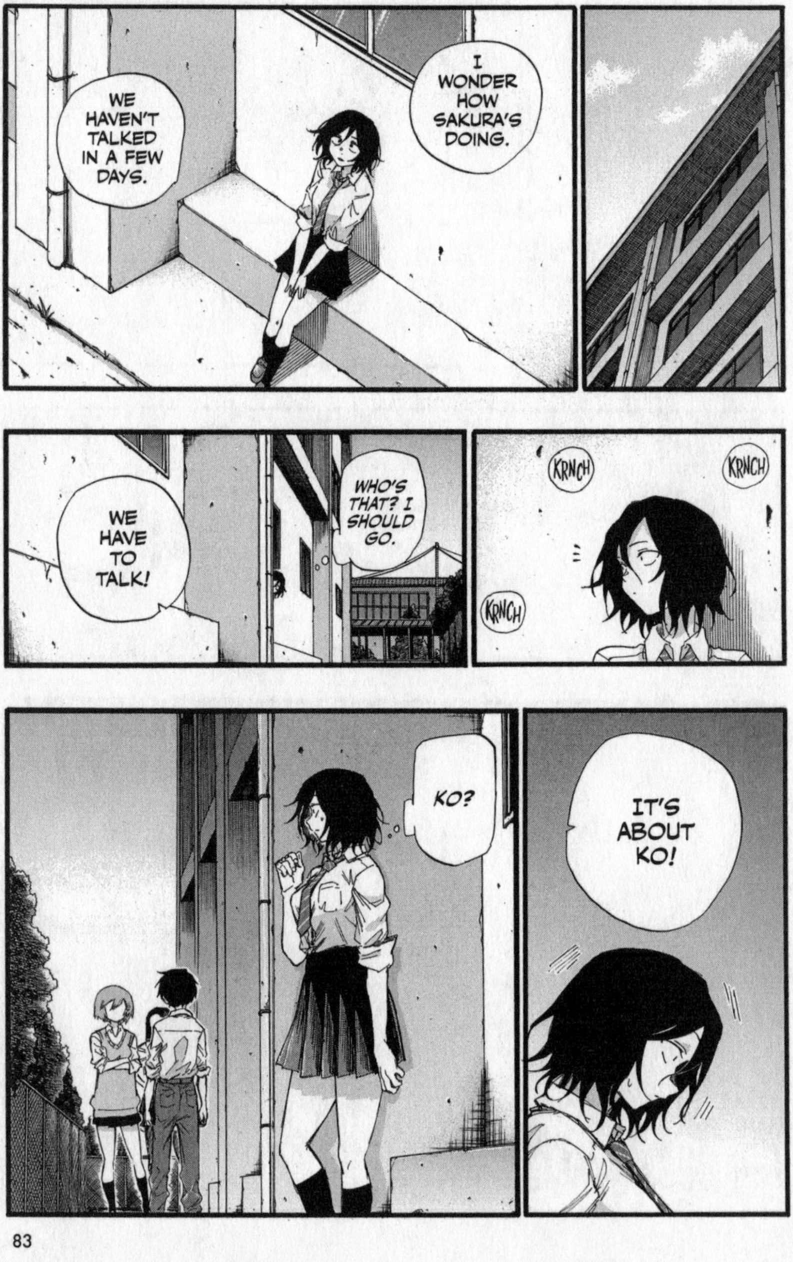
I WONDER HOW SAKURA'S DOING.
WE HAVEN'T TALKED IN A FEW DAYS.
KRNCH
KRNCH
KRNCH
WHO'S THAT? I SHOULD GO.
WE HAVE TO TALK!
IT'S ABOUT KO!
KO?

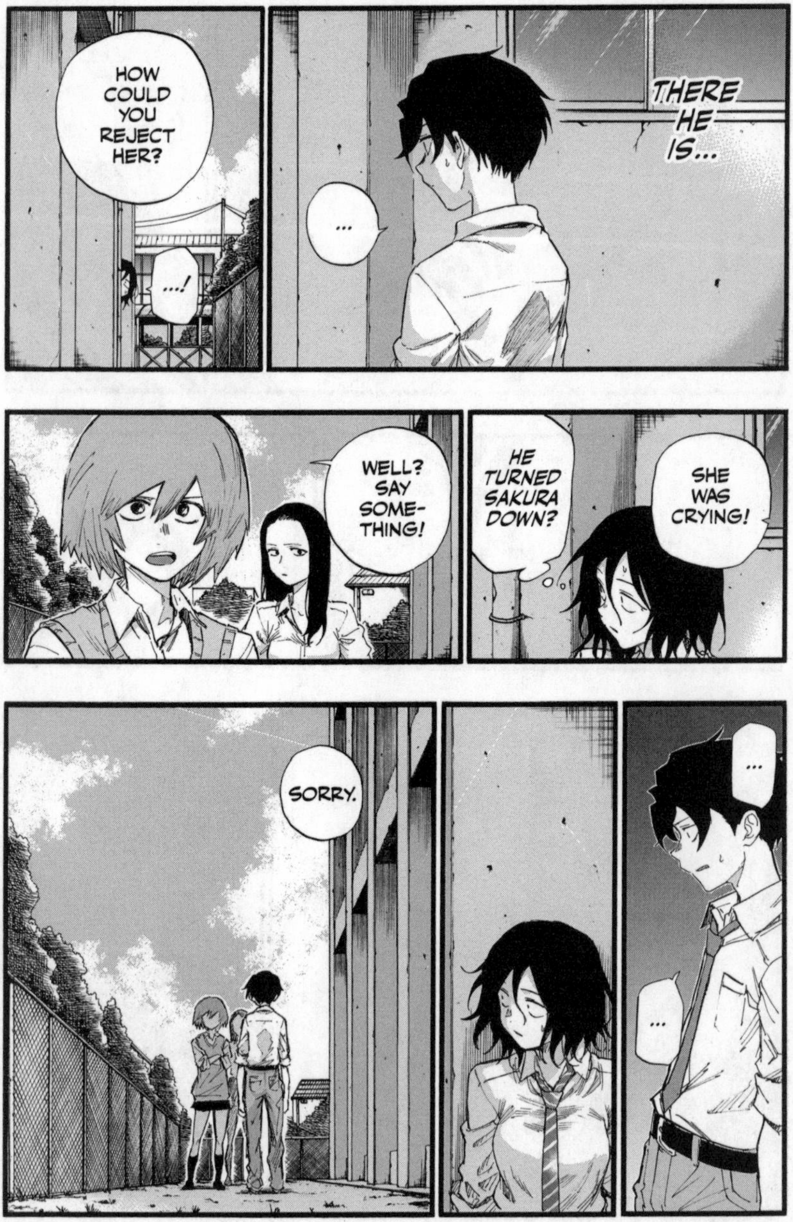
THERE HE IS...
...
HOW COULD YOU REJECT HER?
...!
SHE WAS CRYING!
HE TURNED SAKURA DOWN?
WELL? SAY SOME-THING!
...
...
SORRY.

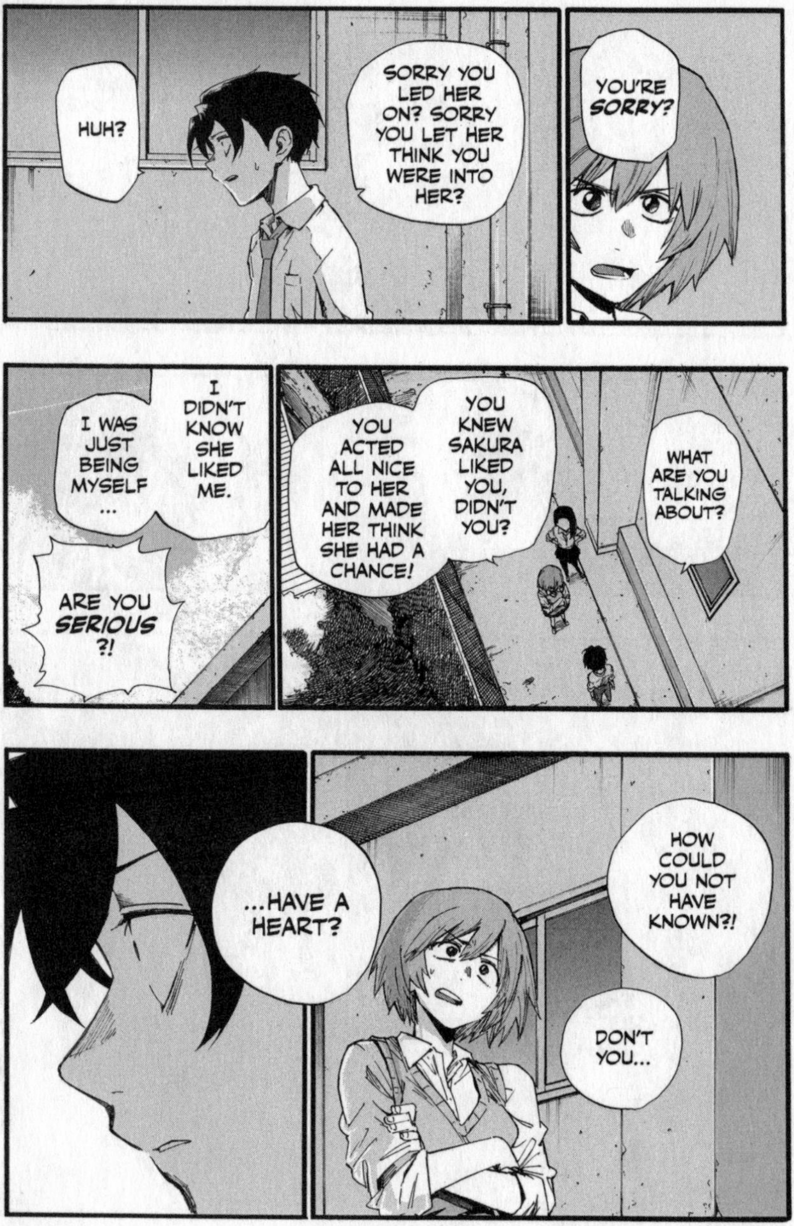
YOU'RE *SORRY?*
SORRY YOU LED HER ON? SORRY YOU LET HER THINK YOU WERE INTO HER?
HUH?
WHAT ARE YOU TALKING ABOUT?
YOU KNEW SAKURA LIKED YOU, DIDN'T YOU?
YOU ACTED ALL NICE TO HER AND MADE HER THINK SHE HAD A CHANCE!
I DIDN'T KNOW SHE LIKED ME.
I WAS JUST BEING MYSELF ...
ARE YOU *SERIOUS* ?!
HOW COULD YOU NOT HAVE KNOWN?!
DON'T YOU...
...HAVE A HEART?

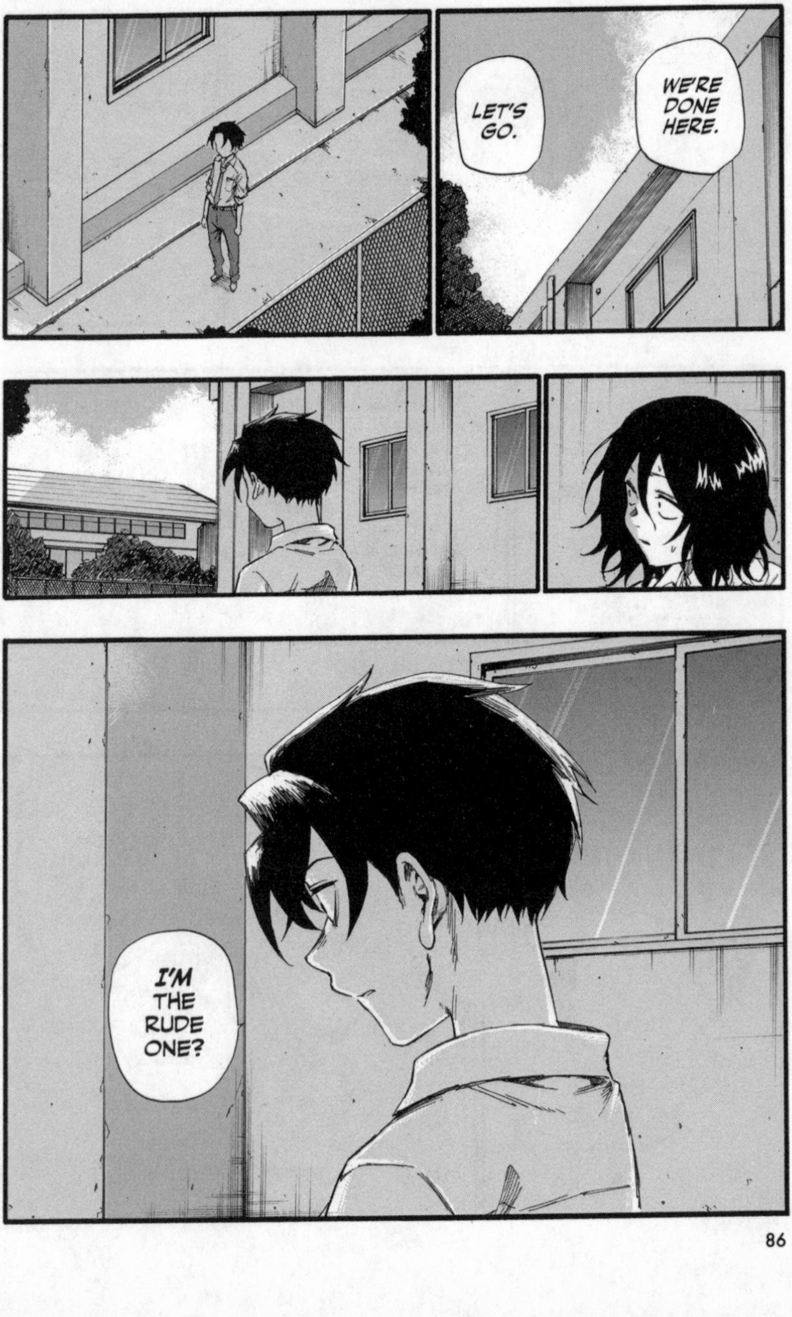
WE'RE DONE HERE.
LET'S GO.
I'M THE RUDE ONE?

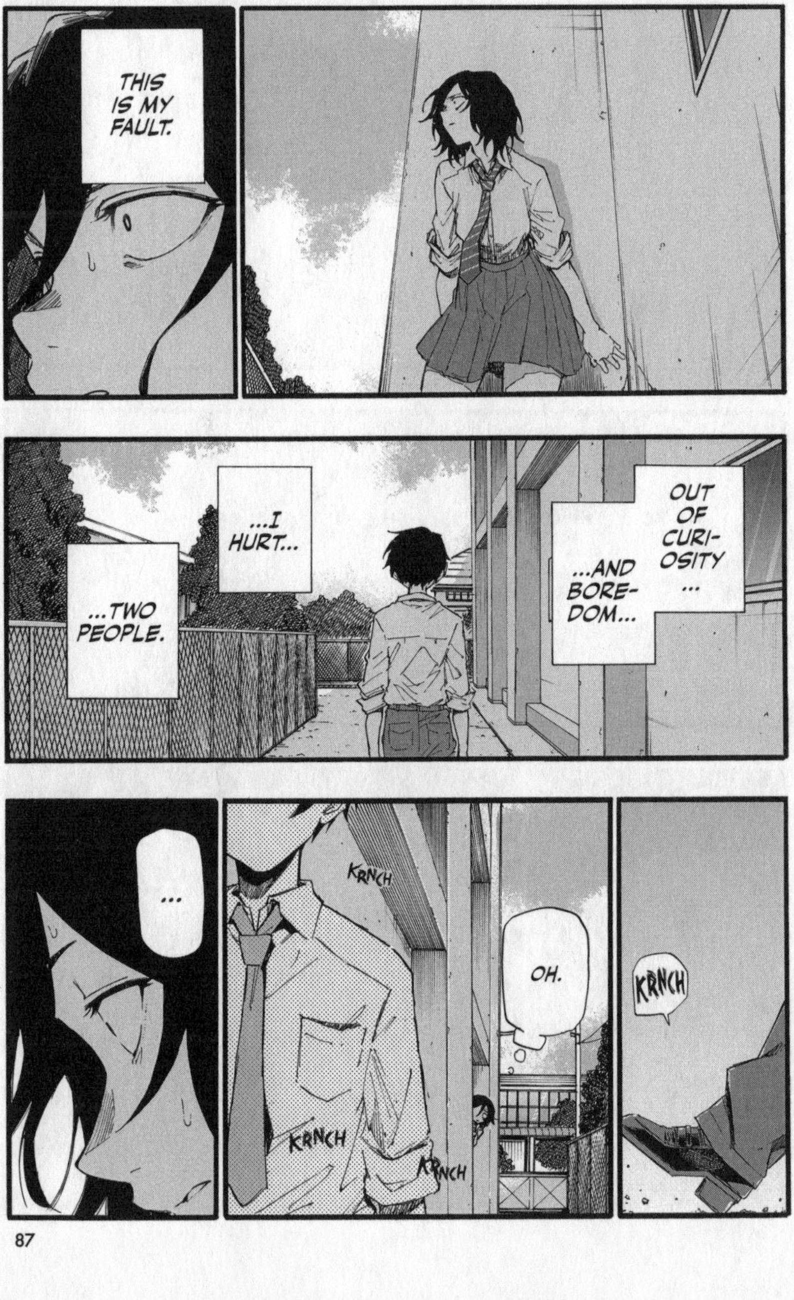
THIS IS MY FAULT.
OUT OF CURIOSITY...
...AND BOREDOM...
...I HURT...
...TWO PEOPLE.
KRNCH
OH.
KRNCH
KRNCH
KRNCH
...

UM...
YA-MORI...
SHP

KO...

I WANTED TO APOLOGIZE TO BOTH OF THEM.

BUT I DIDN'T KNOW HOW.

WHAT IF IT JUST MADE THEM FEEL AWKWARD?

THE MORE I THOUGHT ABOUT IT, THE MORE PARALYZED I GOT.

AND THEN...

...KO STOPPED COMING TO SCHOOL.

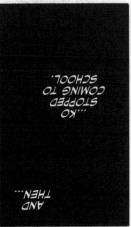

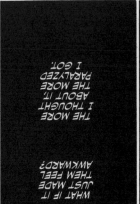

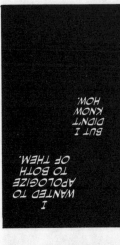

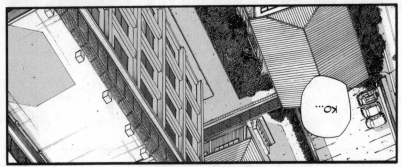

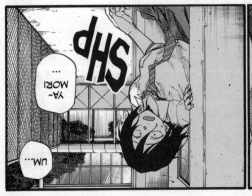

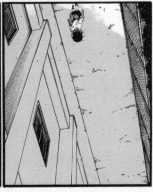

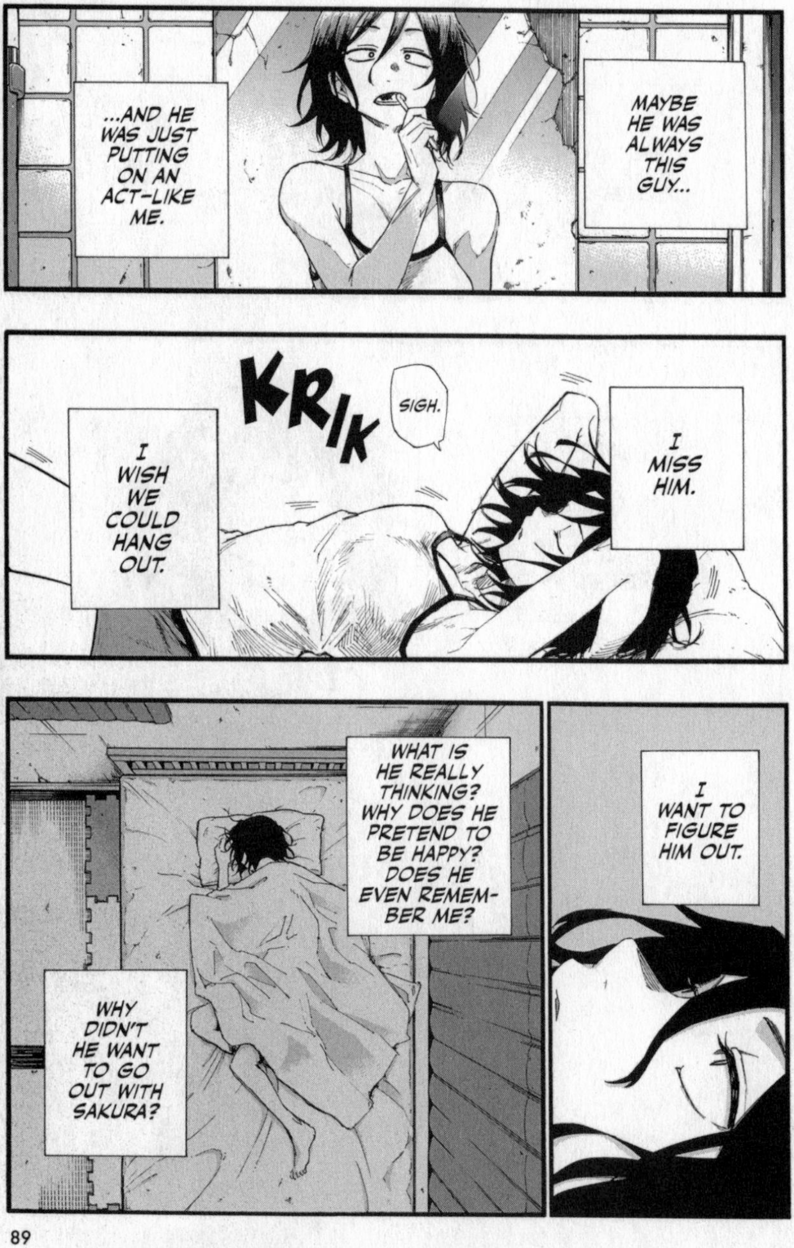
MAYBE HE WAS ALWAYS THIS GUY...
...AND HE WAS JUST PUTTING ON AN ACT-LIKE ME.
I MISS HIM.
SIGH.
KRIK
I WISH WE COULD HANG OUT.
I WANT TO FIGURE HIM OUT.
WHAT IS HE REALLY THINKING? WHY DOES HE PRETEND TO BE HAPPY? DOES HE EVEN REMEMBER ME?
WHY DIDN'T HE WANT TO GO OUT WITH SAKURA?

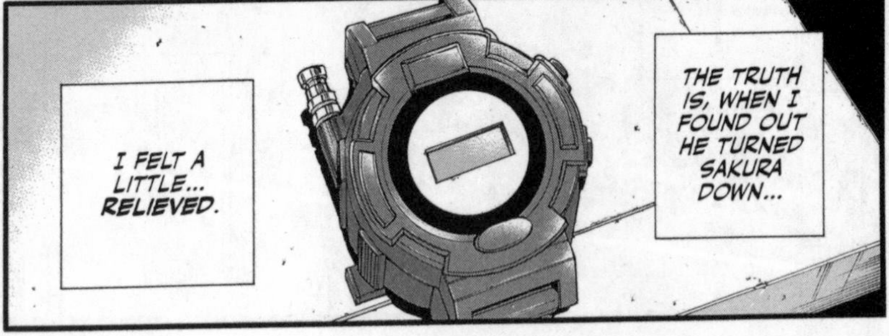
THE TRUTH IS, WHEN I FOUND OUT HE TURNED SAKURA DOWN...
I FELT A LITTLE... RELIEVED.

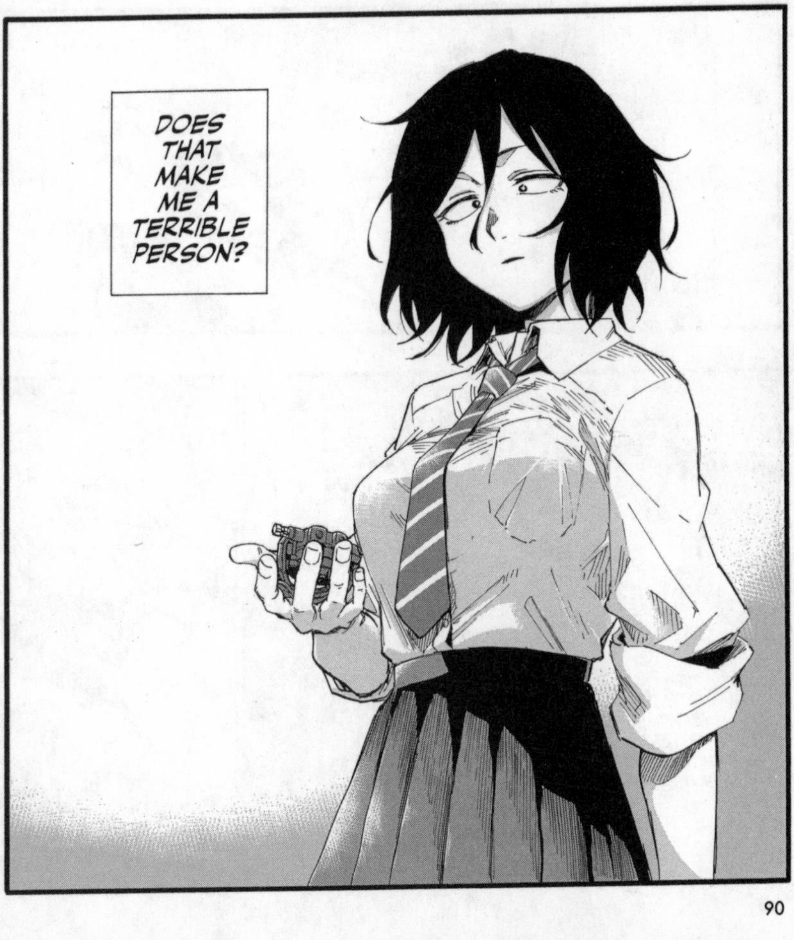
DOES THAT MAKE ME A TERRIBLE PERSON?

Call of the Night

Call of the Night

NIGHT 35: NOT MY FAVORITE TEACHER

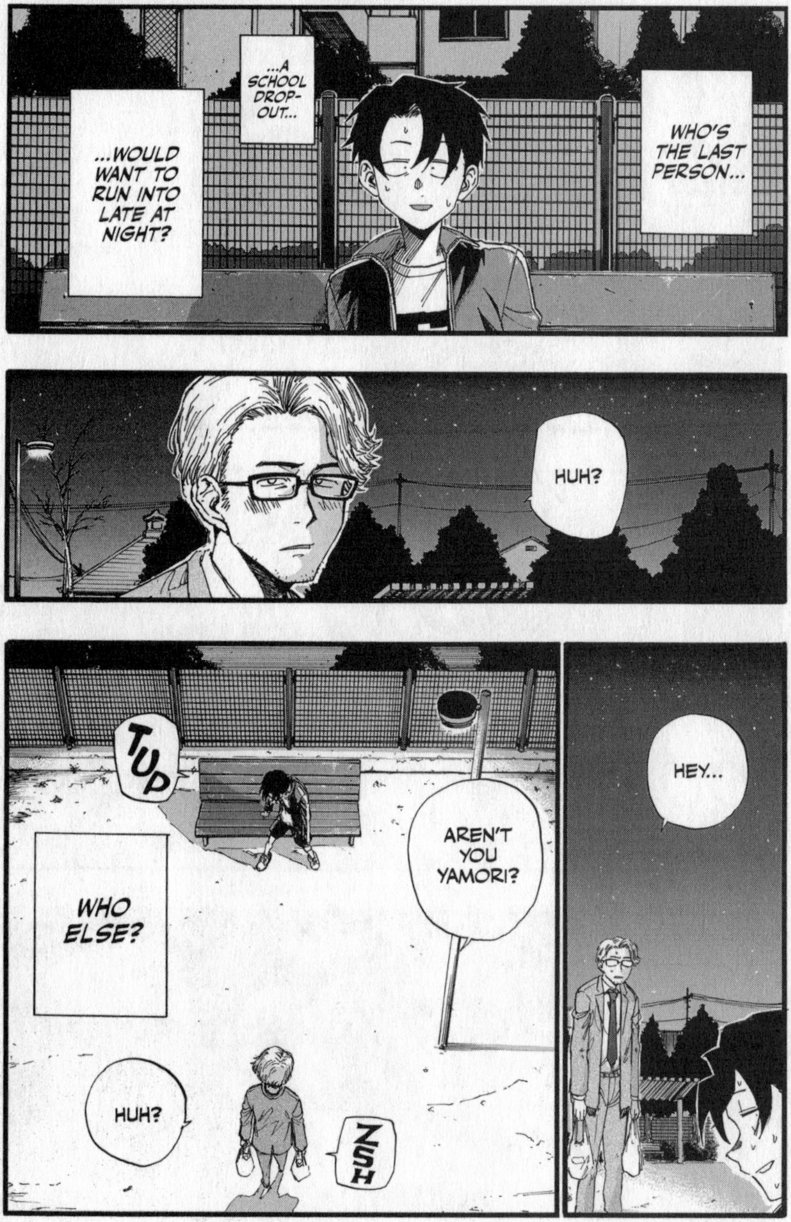
WHO'S THE LAST PERSON...
...A SCHOOL DROP-OUT...
...WOULD WANT TO RUN INTO LATE AT NIGHT?
HUH?
HEY...
AREN'T YOU YAMORI?
TUP
WHO ELSE?
HUH?
ZSH

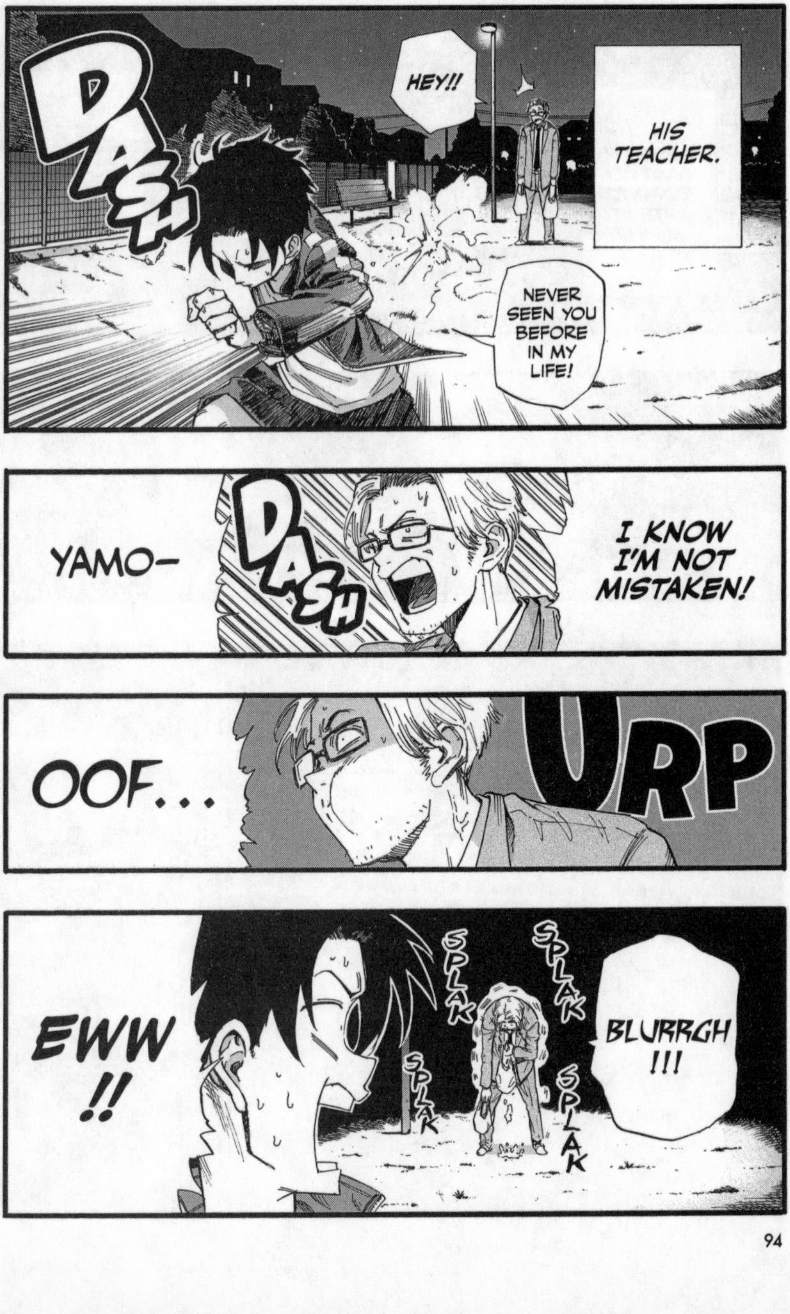
HIS TEACHER.
HEY!!
DASH
NEVER SEEN YOU BEFORE IN MY LIFE!
I KNOW I'M NOT MISTAKEN!
DASH
YAMO-
URP
OOF...
BLURRGH !!!
SPLAK
SPLAK
SPLAK
SPLAK
EWW !!

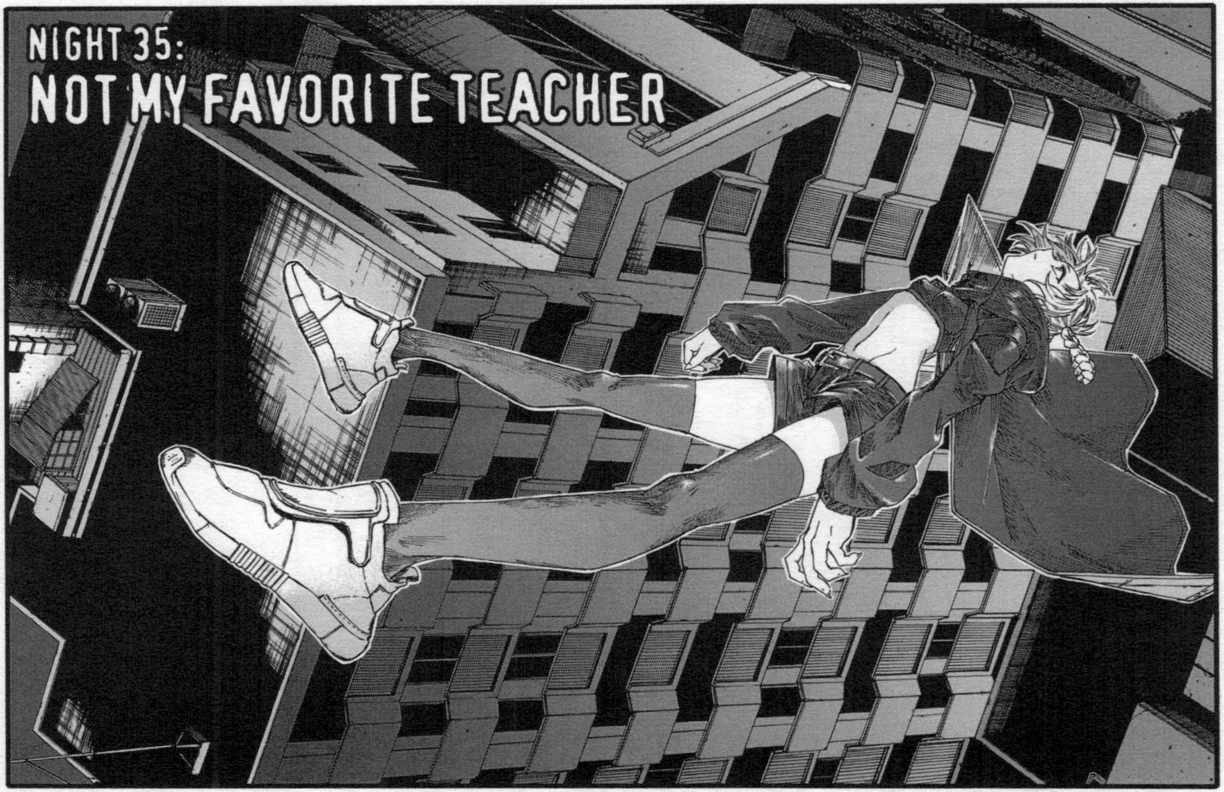
NIGHT 35:
NOT MY FAVORITE TEACHER

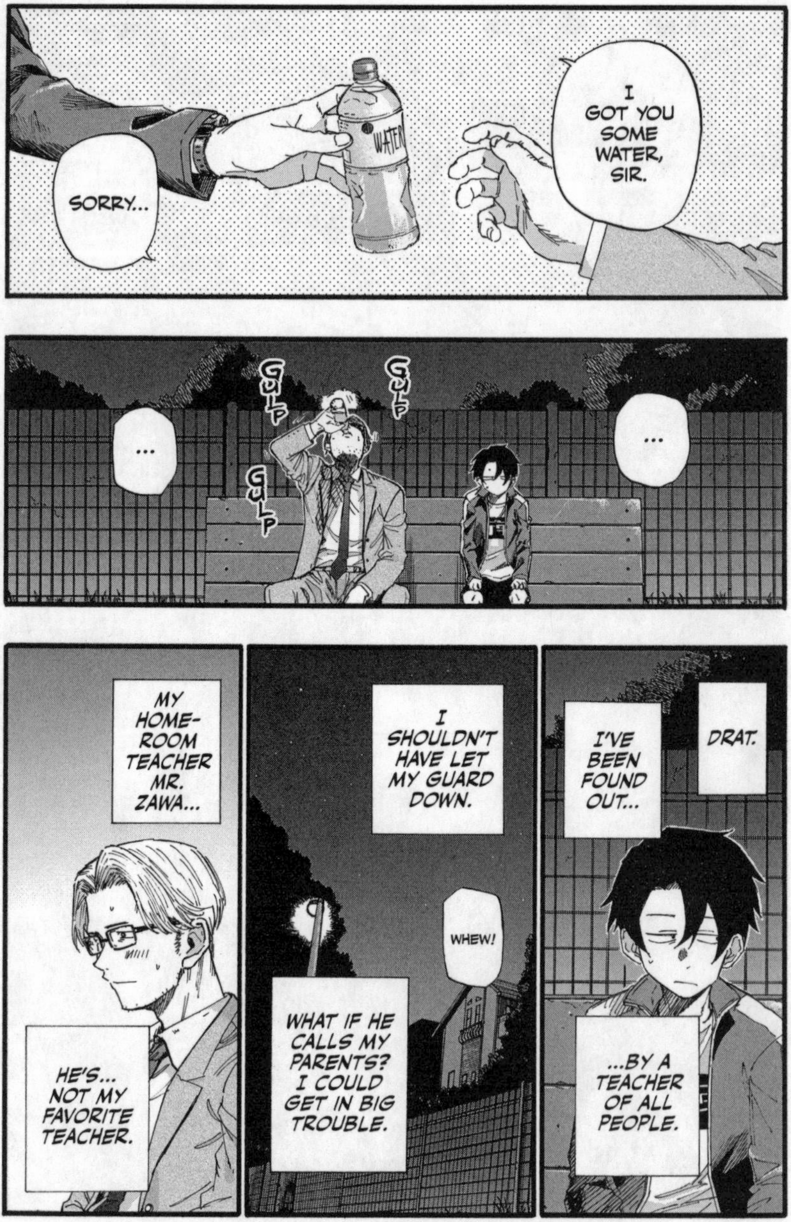
I GOT YOU SOME WATER, SIR.
SORRY...
...
GULP
GULP
GULP
...
DRAT.
I'VE BEEN FOUND OUT...
...BY A TEACHER OF ALL PEOPLE.
I SHOULDN'T HAVE LET MY GUARD DOWN.
WHEW!
WHAT IF HE CALLS MY PARENTS? I COULD GET IN BIG TROUBLE.
MY HOME-ROOM TEACHER MR. ZAWA...
HE'S... NOT MY FAVORITE TEACHER.

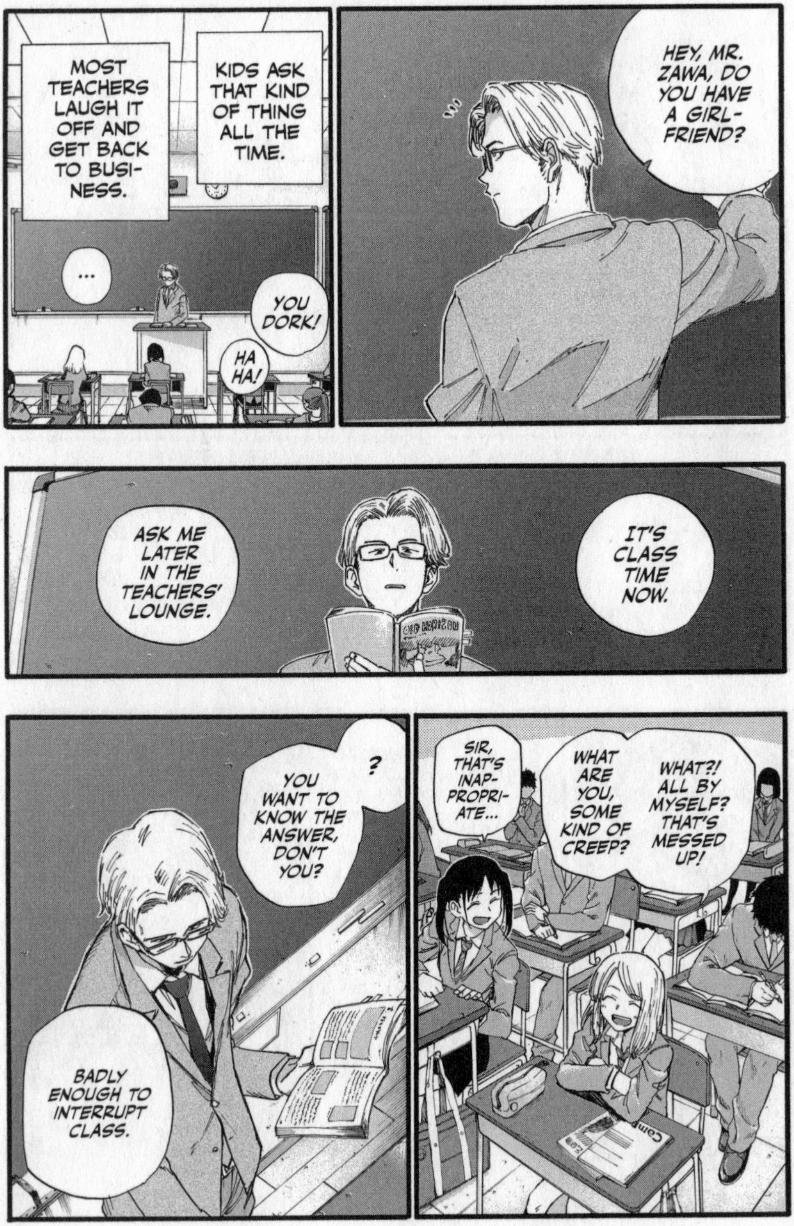
HEY, MR. ZAWA, DO YOU HAVE A GIRL-FRIEND?
KIDS ASK THAT KIND OF THING ALL THE TIME.
MOST TEACHERS LAUGH IT OFF AND GET BACK TO BUSI-NESS.
YOU DORK!
HA HA!
...
IT'S CLASS TIME NOW.
ASK ME LATER IN THE TEACHERS' LOUNGE.
WHAT?! ALL BY MYSELF? THAT'S MESSED UP!
WHAT ARE YOU, SOME KIND OF CREEP?
SIR, THAT'S INAP-PROPRI-ATE...
?
YOU WANT TO KNOW THE ANSWER, DON'T YOU?
BADLY ENOUGH TO INTERRUPT CLASS.

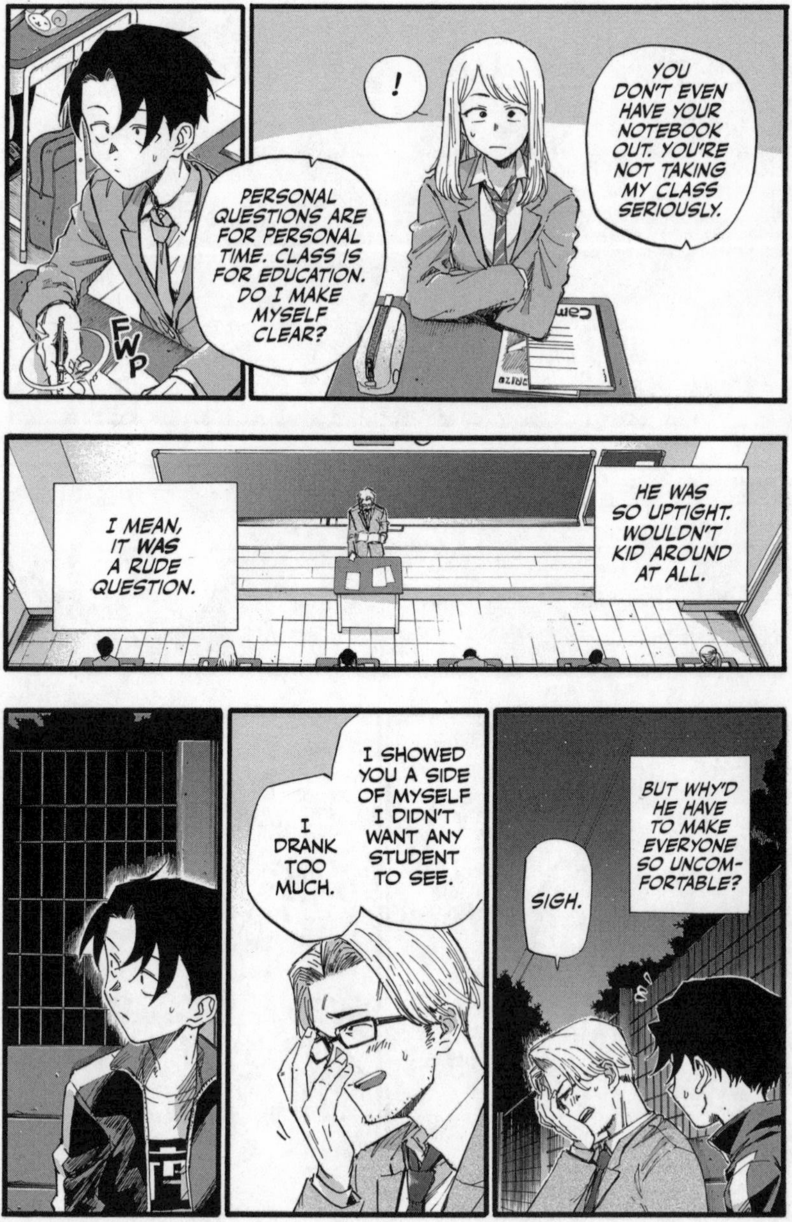
YOU DON'T EVEN HAVE YOUR NOTEBOOK OUT. YOU'RE NOT TAKING MY CLASS SERIOUSLY.
!
PERSONAL QUESTIONS ARE FOR PERSONAL TIME. CLASS IS FOR EDUCATION. DO I MAKE MYSELF CLEAR?
FWP
HE WAS SO UPTIGHT. WOULDN'T KID AROUND AT ALL.
I MEAN, IT WAS A RUDE QUESTION.
BUT WHY'D HE HAVE TO MAKE EVERYONE SO UNCOMFORTABLE?
SIGH.
I SHOWED YOU A SIDE OF MYSELF I DIDN'T WANT ANY STUDENT TO SEE.
I DRANK TOO MUCH.

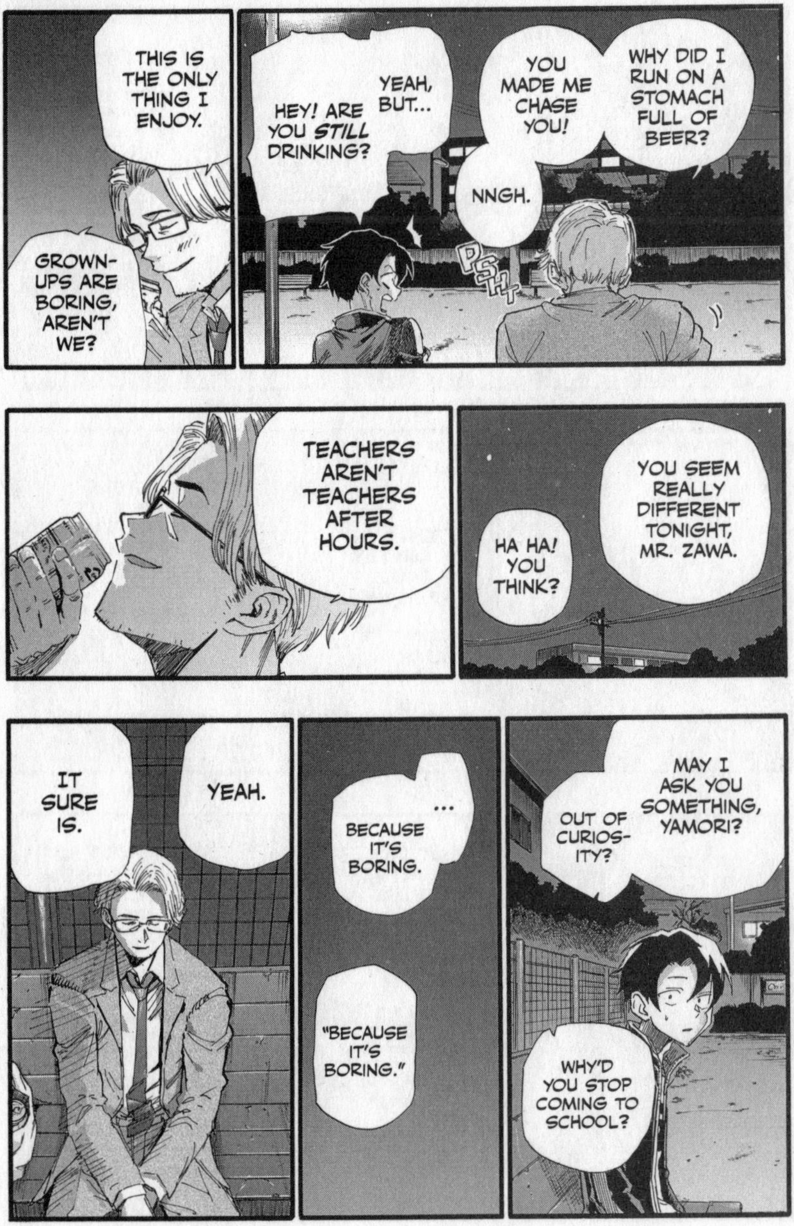
WHY DID I RUN ON A STOMACH FULL OF BEER?
YOU MADE ME CHASE YOU!
NNGH.
PSHT
YEAH, BUT...
HEY! ARE YOU STILL DRINKING?
THIS IS THE ONLY THING I ENJOY.
GROWN-UPS ARE BORING, AREN'T WE?
YOU SEEM REALLY DIFFERENT TONIGHT, MR. ZAWA.
HA HA! YOU THINK?
TEACHERS AREN'T TEACHERS AFTER HOURS.
MAY I ASK YOU SOMETHING, YAMORI?
OUT OF CURIOS-ITY?
WHY'D YOU STOP COMING TO SCHOOL?
...
BECAUSE IT'S BORING.
"BECAUSE IT'S BORING."
YEAH.
IT SURE IS.

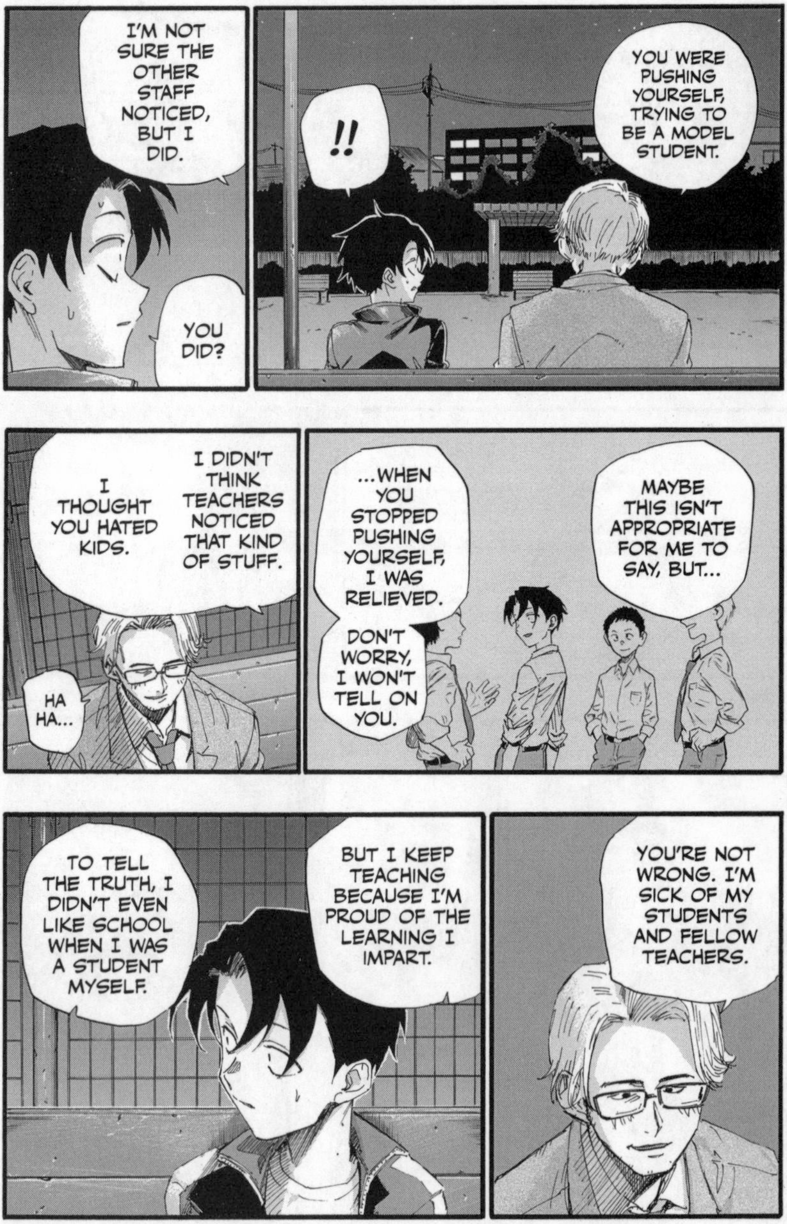
YOU WERE PUSHING YOURSELF, TRYING TO BE A MODEL STUDENT.
!!
I'M NOT SURE THE OTHER STAFF NOTICED, BUT I DID.
YOU DID?
MAYBE THIS ISN'T APPROPRIATE FOR ME TO SAY, BUT...
...WHEN YOU STOPPED PUSHING YOURSELF, I WAS RELIEVED.
DON'T WORRY, I WON'T TELL ON YOU.
I DIDN'T THINK TEACHERS NOTICED THAT KIND OF STUFF.
I THOUGHT YOU HATED KIDS.
HA HA...
YOU'RE NOT WRONG. I'M SICK OF MY STUDENTS AND FELLOW TEACHERS.
BUT I KEEP TEACHING BECAUSE I'M PROUD OF THE LEARNING I IMPART.
TO TELL THE TRUTH, I DIDN'T EVEN LIKE SCHOOL WHEN I WAS A STUDENT MYSELF.

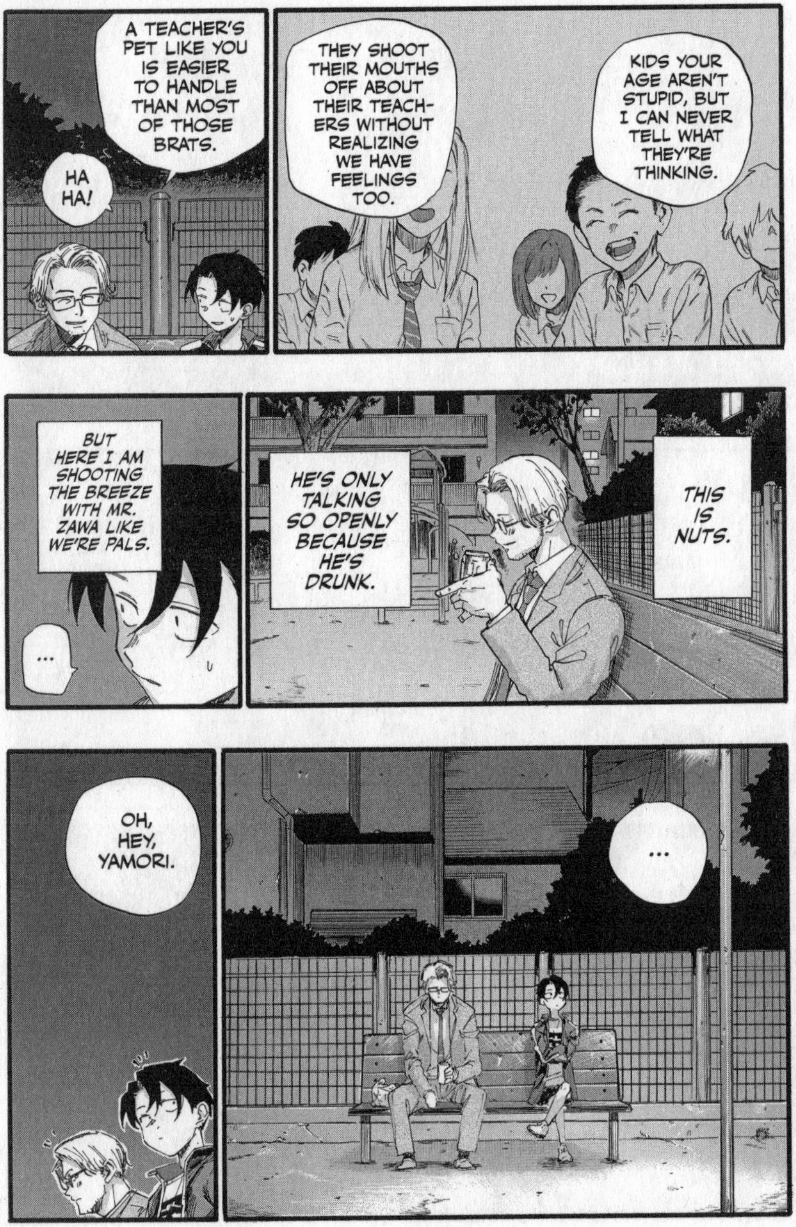
KIDS YOUR AGE AREN'T STUPID, BUT I CAN NEVER TELL WHAT THEY'RE THINKING.
THEY SHOOT THEIR MOUTHS OFF ABOUT THEIR TEACHERS WITHOUT REALIZING WE HAVE FEELINGS TOO.
A TEACHER'S PET LIKE YOU IS EASIER TO HANDLE THAN MOST OF THOSE BRATS.
HA HA!
THIS IS NUTS.
HE'S ONLY TALKING SO OPENLY BECAUSE HE'S DRUNK.
BUT HERE I AM SHOOTING THE BREEZE WITH MR. ZAWA LIKE WE'RE PALS.
...
...
OH, HEY, YAMORI.

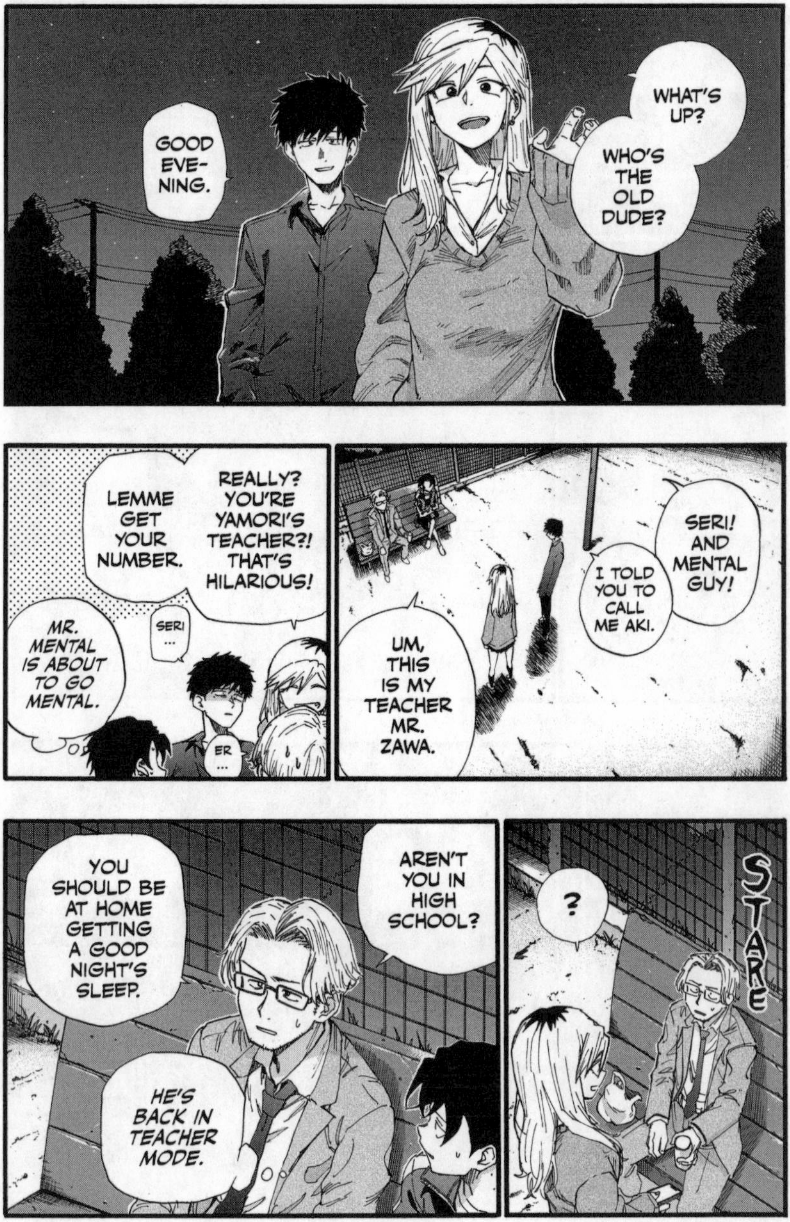
WHAT'S UP?
WHO'S THE OLD DUDE?
GOOD EVE-NING.
SERI! AND MENTAL GUY!
I TOLD YOU TO CALL ME AKI.
UM, THIS IS MY TEACHER MR. ZAWA.
REALLY? YOU'RE YAMORI'S TEACHER?! THAT'S HILARIOUS!
LEMME GET YOUR NUMBER.
SERI ...
MR. MENTAL IS ABOUT TO GO MENTAL.
ER ...
STARE
?
AREN'T YOU IN HIGH SCHOOL?
YOU SHOULD BE AT HOME GETTING A GOOD NIGHT'S SLEEP.
HE'S BACK IN TEACHER MODE.

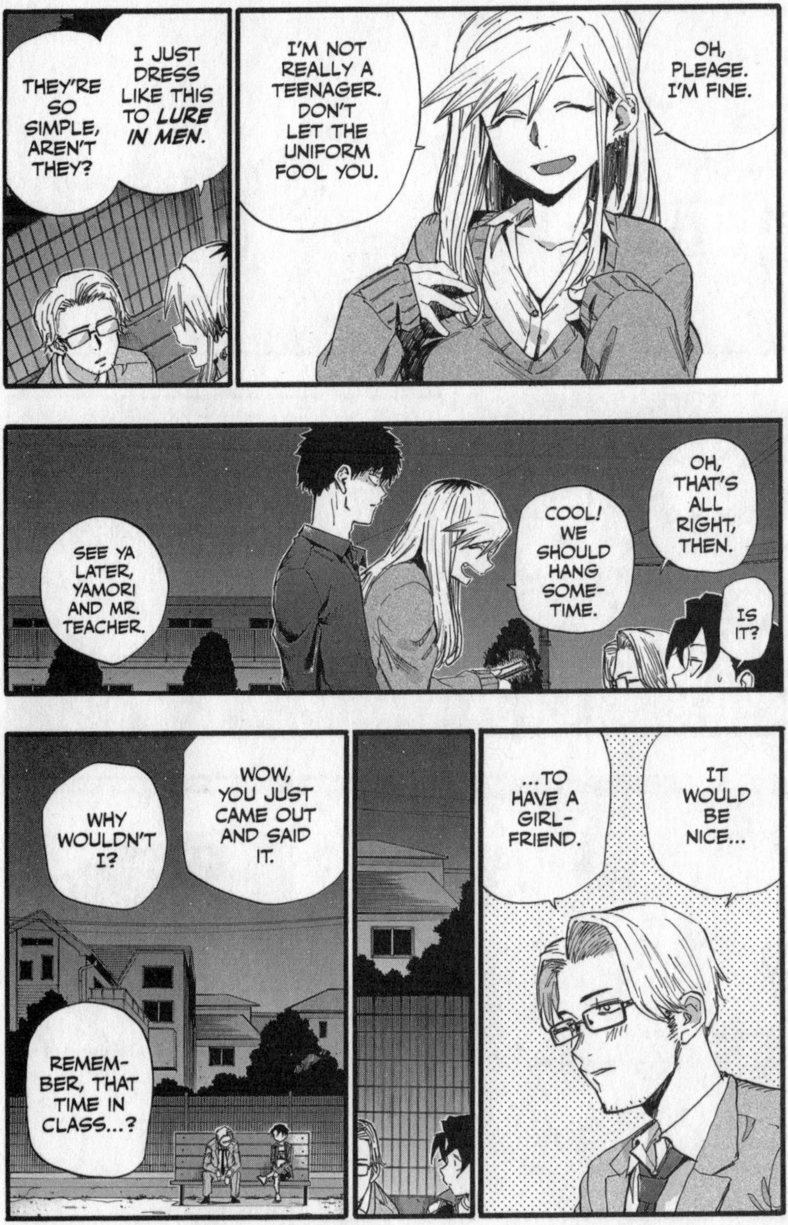
OH, PLEASE. I'M FINE.
I'M NOT REALLY A TEENAGER. DON'T LET THE UNIFORM FOOL YOU.
I JUST DRESS LIKE THIS TO ***LURE IN MEN***.
THEY'RE SO SIMPLE, AREN'T THEY?
OH, THAT'S ALL RIGHT, THEN.
IS IT?
COOL! WE SHOULD HANG SOME-TIME.
SEE YA LATER, YAMORI AND MR. TEACHER.
IT WOULD BE NICE...
...TO HAVE A GIRL-FRIEND.
WOW, YOU JUST CAME OUT AND SAID IT.
WHY WOULDN'T I?
REMEM-BER, THAT TIME IN CLASS...?

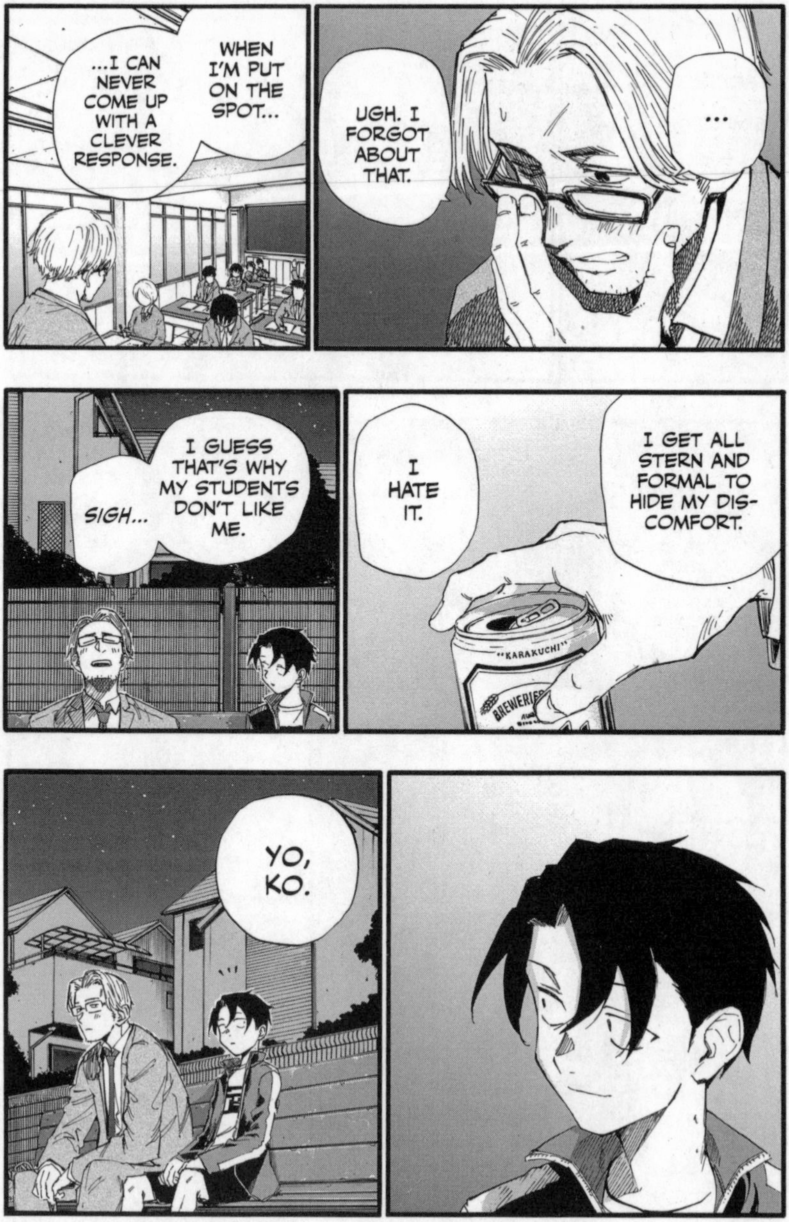
...
UGH. I FORGOT ABOUT THAT.
WHEN I'M PUT ON THE SPOT...
...I CAN NEVER COME UP WITH A CLEVER RESPONSE.
I GET ALL STERN AND FORMAL TO HIDE MY DIS-COMFORT.
I HATE IT.
"KARAKUCHI"
BREWERIES
I GUESS THAT'S WHY MY STUDENTS DON'T LIKE ME.
SIGH...
YO, KO.

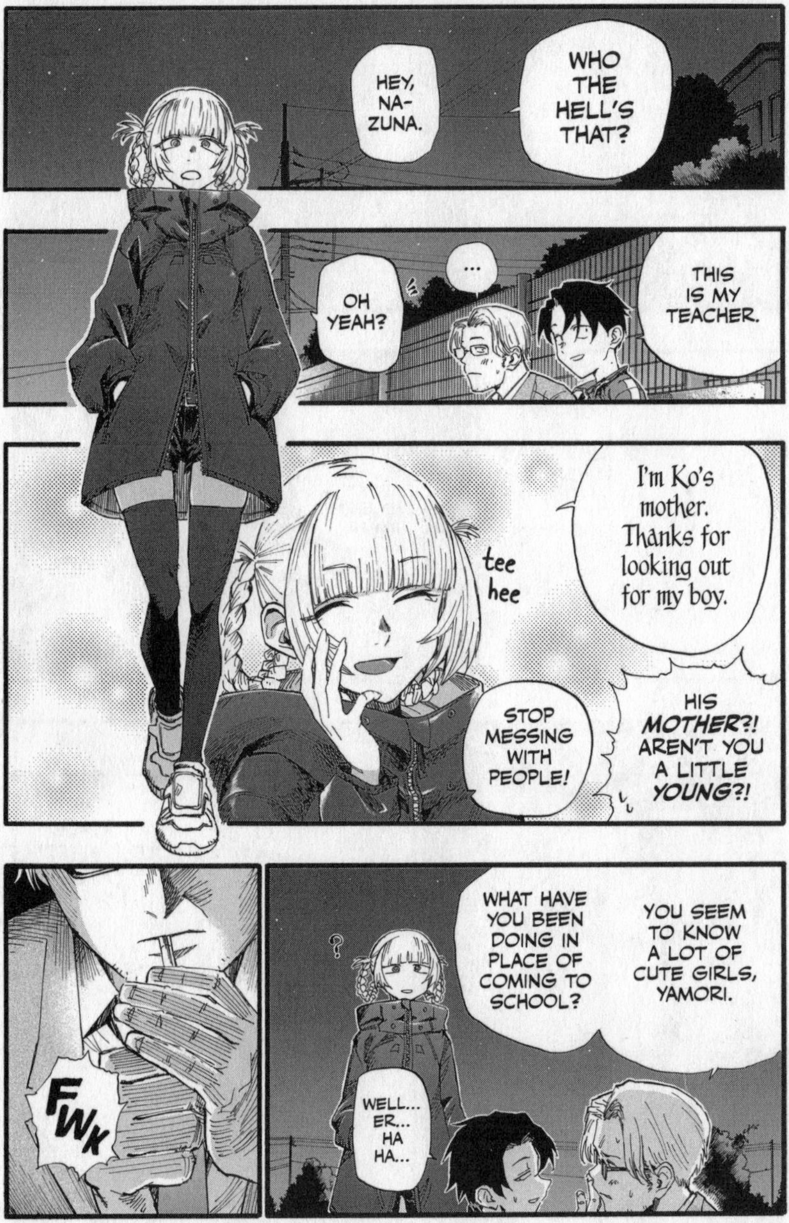
WHO THE HELL'S THAT?
HEY, NA-ZUNA.
THIS IS MY TEACHER.
...
OH YEAH?
I'm Ko's mother. Thanks for looking out for my boy.
tee hee
HIS *MOTHER?!* AREN'T YOU A LITTLE *YOUNG?!*
STOP MESSING WITH PEOPLE!
YOU SEEM TO KNOW A LOT OF CUTE GIRLS, YAMORI.
WHAT HAVE YOU BEEN DOING IN PLACE OF COMING TO SCHOOL?
?
WELL... ER... HA HA...
FWK

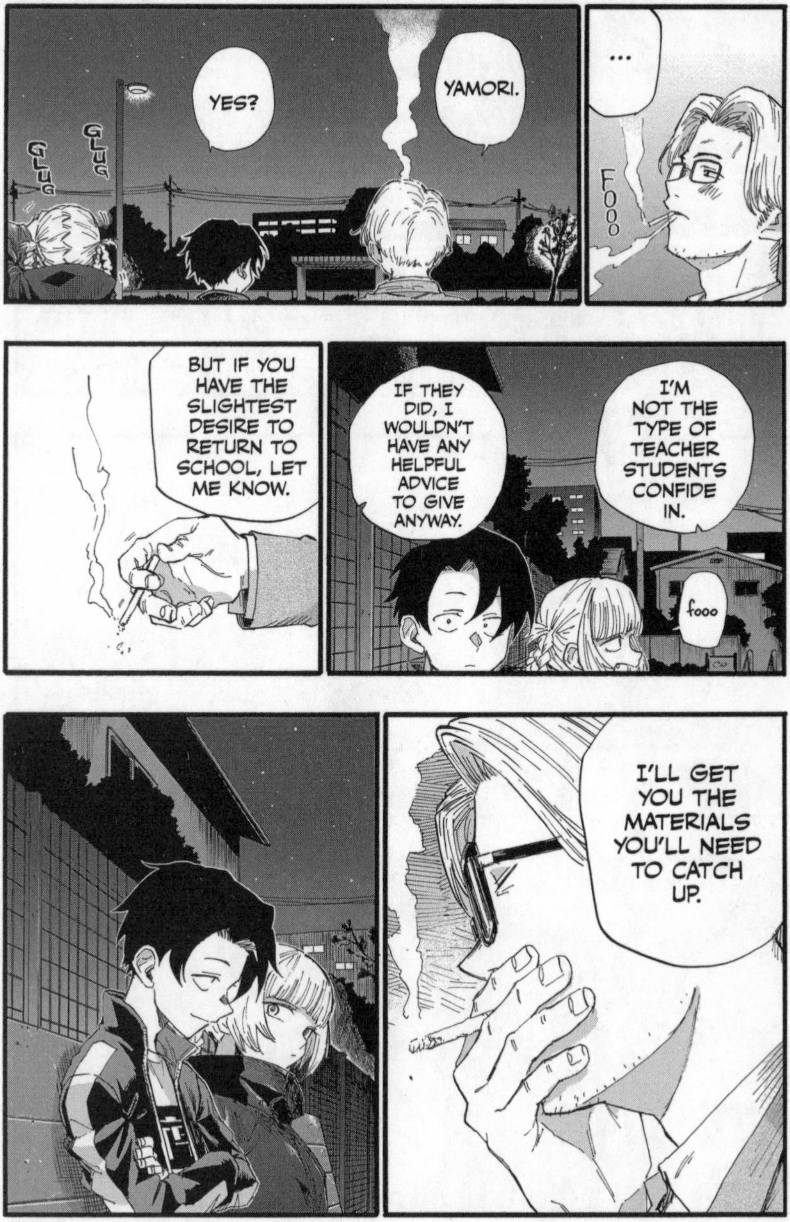
...
FOOO
YAMORI.
YES?
GLUG
GLUG
I'M NOT THE TYPE OF TEACHER STUDENTS CONFIDE IN.
IF THEY DID, I WOULDN'T HAVE ANY HELPFUL ADVICE TO GIVE ANYWAY.
fooo
BUT IF YOU HAVE THE SLIGHTEST DESIRE TO RETURN TO SCHOOL, LET ME KNOW.
I'LL GET YOU THE MATERIALS YOU'LL NEED TO CATCH UP.

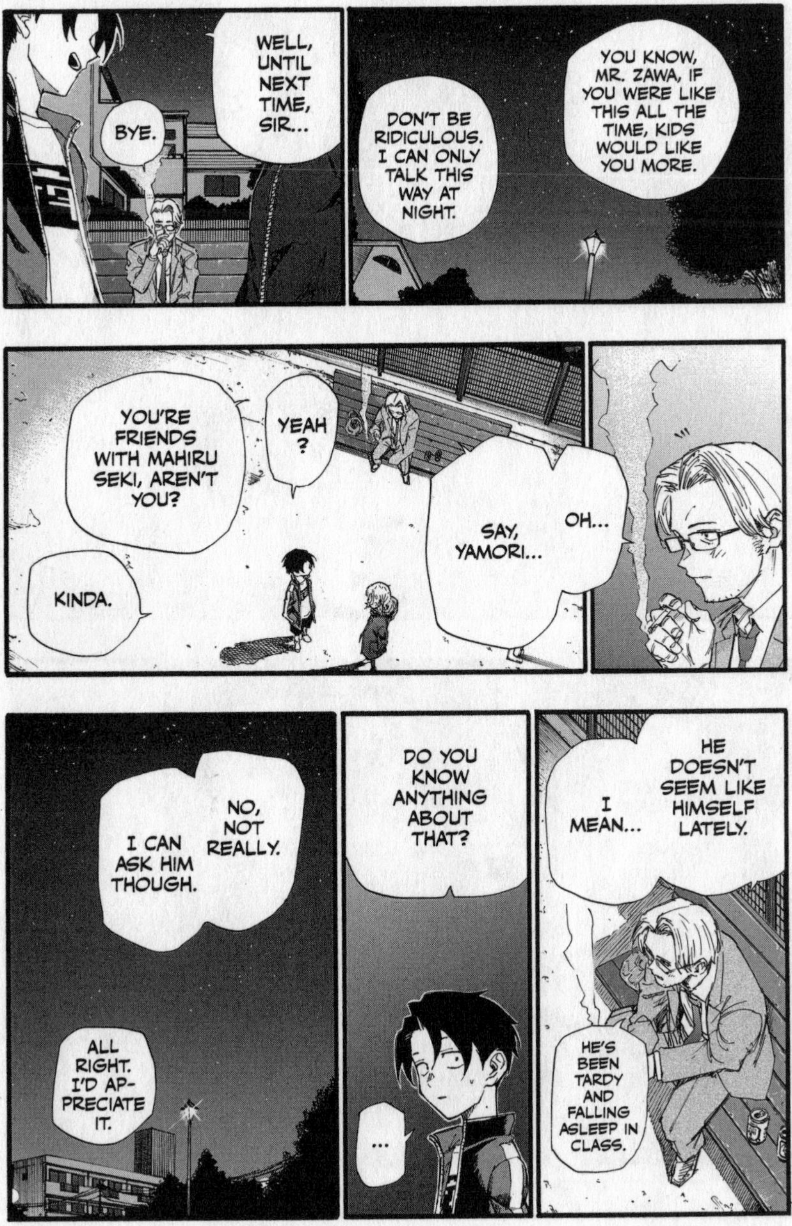
YOU KNOW, MR. ZAWA, IF YOU WERE LIKE THIS ALL THE TIME, KIDS WOULD LIKE YOU MORE.
DON'T BE RIDICULOUS. I CAN ONLY TALK THIS WAY AT NIGHT.
WELL, UNTIL NEXT TIME, SIR...
BYE.
...
OH...
SAY, YAMORI...
YEAH?
YOU'RE FRIENDS WITH MAHIRU SEKI, AREN'T YOU?
KINDA.
HE DOESN'T SEEM LIKE HIMSELF LATELY.
I MEAN...
HE'S BEEN TARDY AND FALLING ASLEEP IN CLASS.
DO YOU KNOW ANYTHING ABOUT THAT?
...
NO, NOT REALLY.
I CAN ASK HIM THOUGH.
ALL RIGHT. I'D AP-PRECIATE IT.

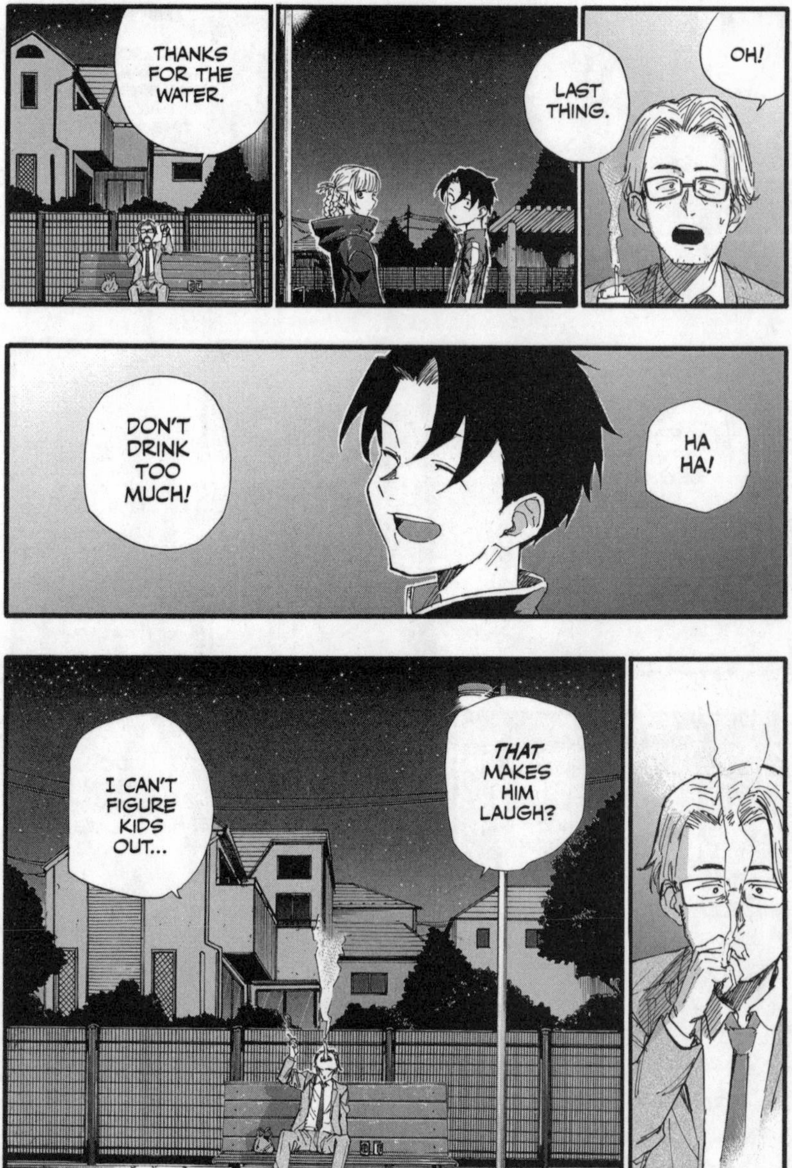
OH!
LAST THING.
THANKS FOR THE WATER.
HA HA!
DON'T DRINK TOO MUCH!
THAT MAKES HIM LAUGH?
I CAN'T FIGURE KIDS OUT...

Call of the Night

Call of the Night

NIGHT 36: MWA HA HA! I'M DRIVING DRUNK!

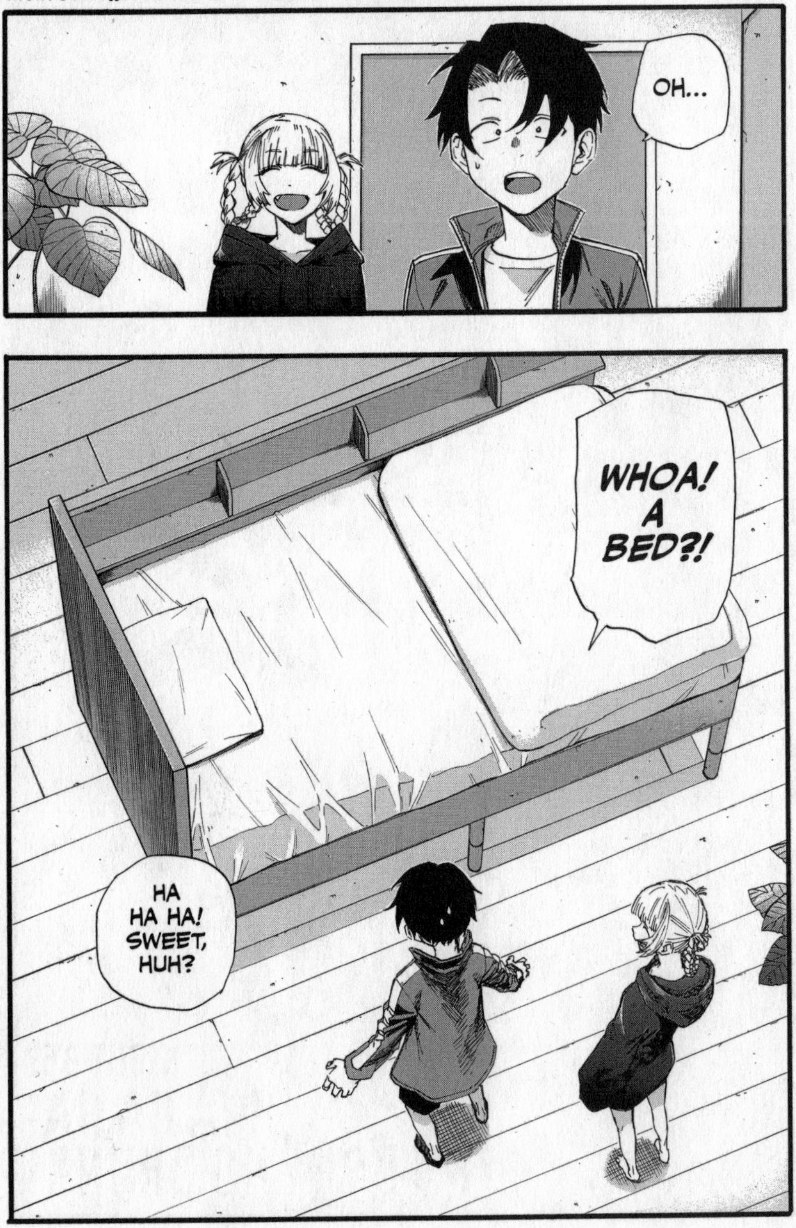
OH...
WHOA! A BED?!
HA HA HA! SWEET, HUH?

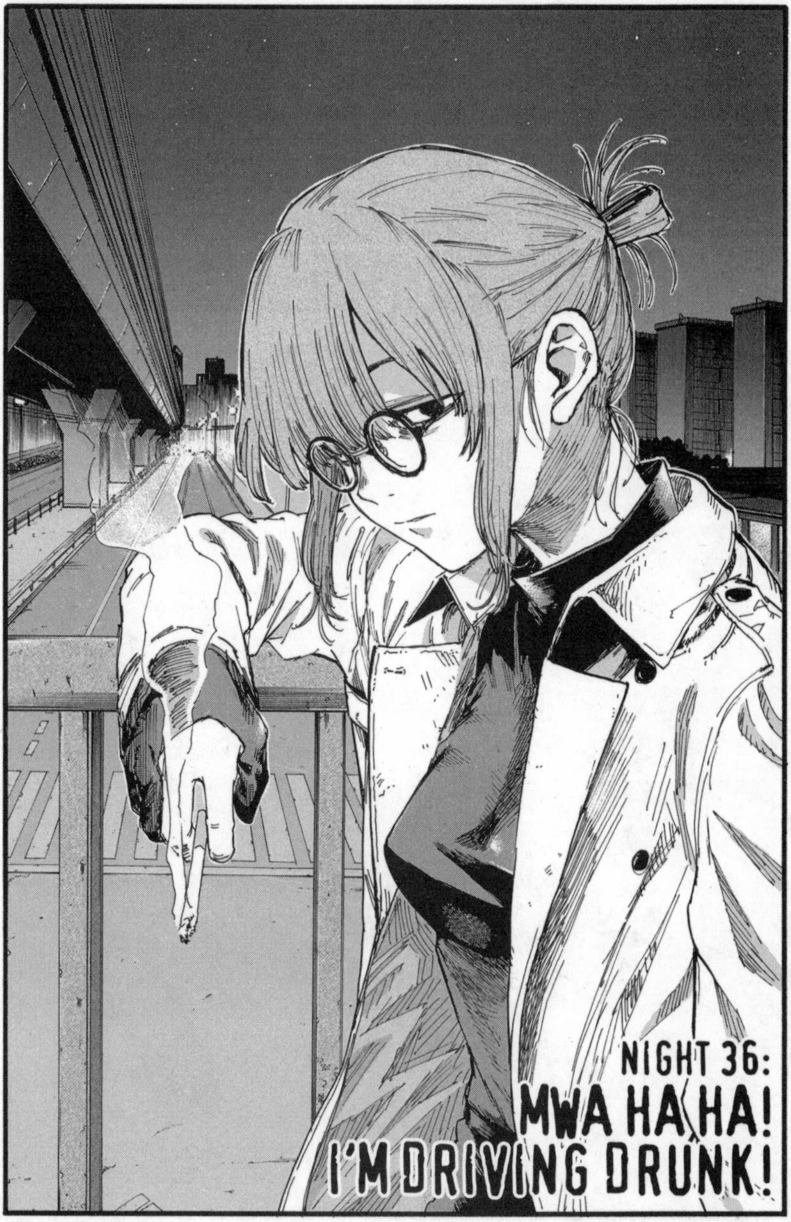
NIGHT 36:
MWA HA HA!
I'M DRIVING DRUNK!

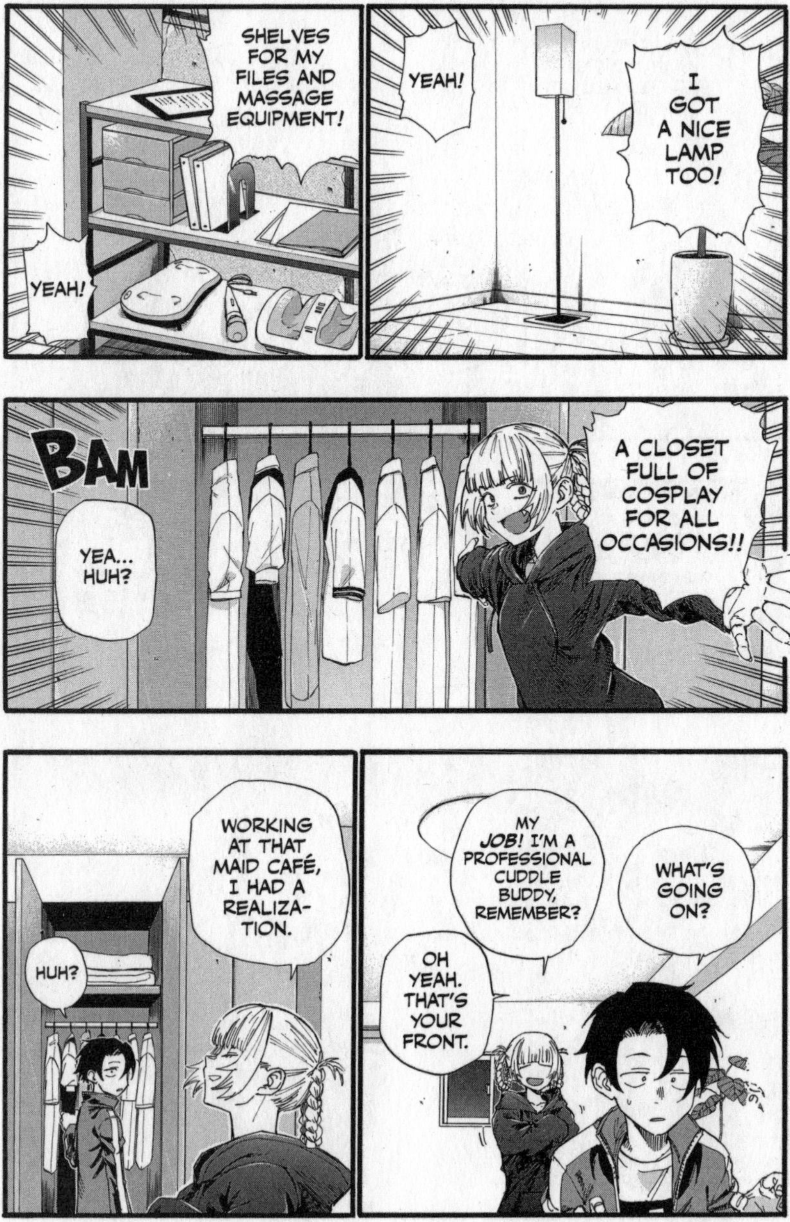
I GOT A NICE LAMP TOO!
YEAH!
SHELVES FOR MY FILES AND MASSAGE EQUIPMENT!
YEAH!
A CLOSET FULL OF COSPLAY FOR ALL OCCASIONS!!
BAM
YEA... HUH?
WHAT'S GOING ON?
MY *JOB!* I'M A PROFESSIONAL CUDDLE BUDDY, REMEMBER?
OH YEAH. THAT'S YOUR FRONT.
WORKING AT THAT MAID CAFÉ, I HAD A REALIZA-TION.
HUH?

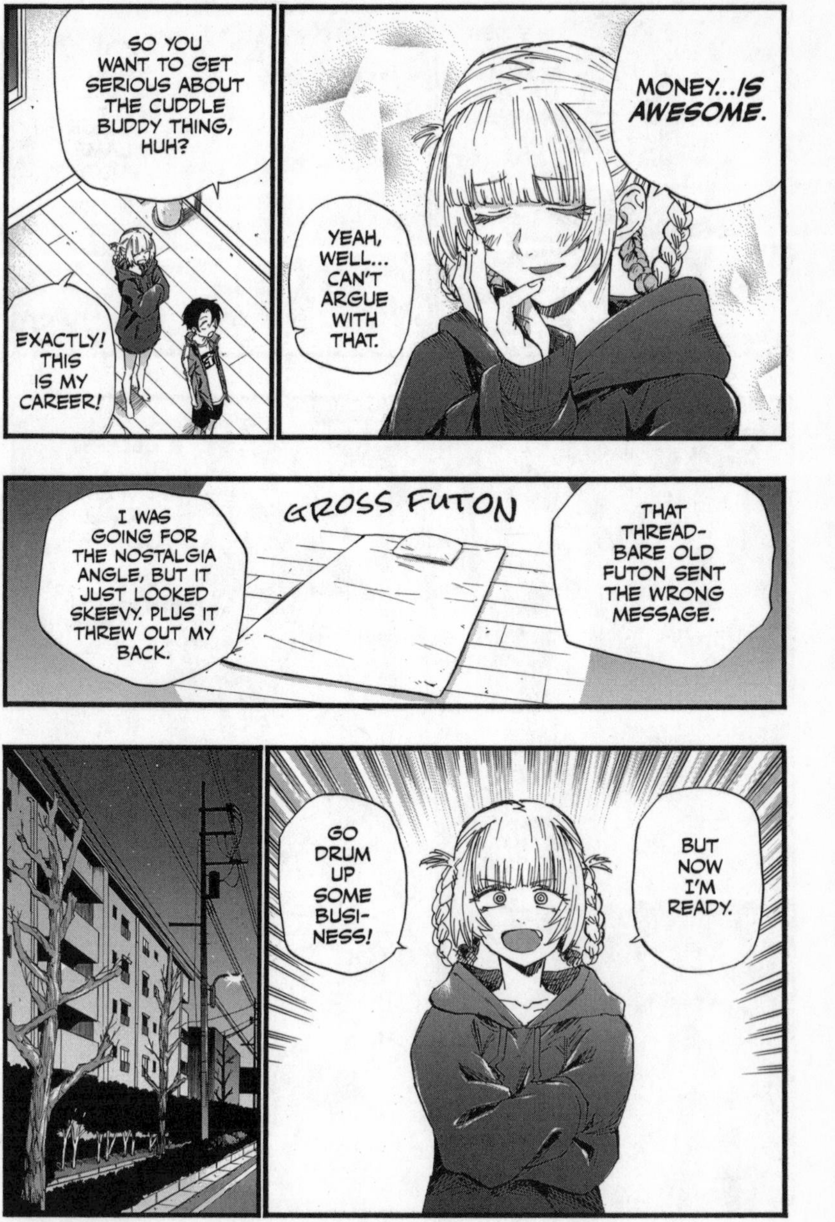
MONEY...IS AWESOME.
YEAH, WELL... CAN'T ARGUE WITH THAT.
SO YOU WANT TO GET SERIOUS ABOUT THE CUDDLE BUDDY THING, HUH?
EXACTLY! THIS IS MY CAREER!
THAT THREAD-BARE OLD FUTON SENT THE WRONG MESSAGE.
GROSS FUTON
I WAS GOING FOR THE NOSTALGIA ANGLE, BUT IT JUST LOOKED SKEEVY. PLUS IT THREW OUT MY BACK.
BUT NOW I'M READY.
GO DRUM UP SOME BUSI-NESS!

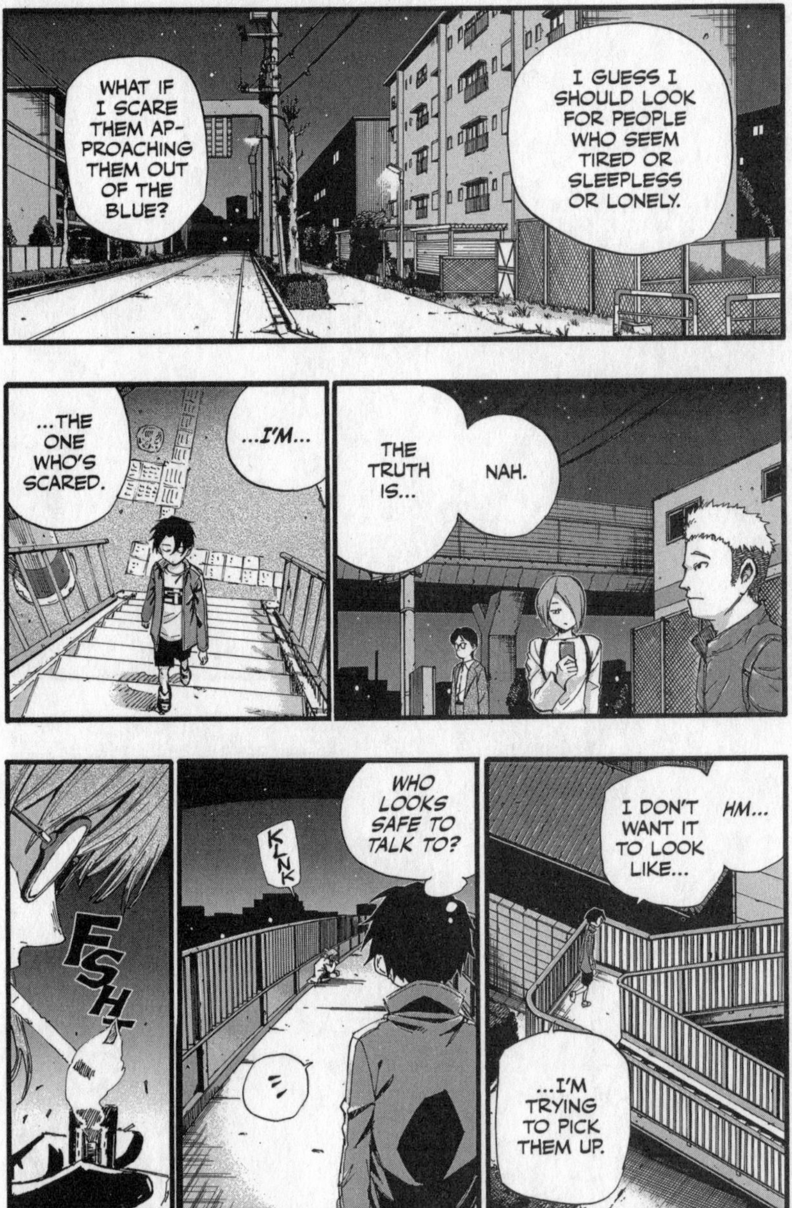
I GUESS I SHOULD LOOK FOR PEOPLE WHO SEEM TIRED OR SLEEPLESS OR LONELY.
WHAT IF I SCARE THEM AP-PROACHING THEM OUT OF THE BLUE?
NAH.
THE TRUTH IS...
...I'M...
...THE ONE WHO'S SCARED.
HM...
I DON'T WANT IT TO LOOK LIKE...
...I'M TRYING TO PICK THEM UP.
WHO LOOKS SAFE TO TALK TO?
KLNK
FSH

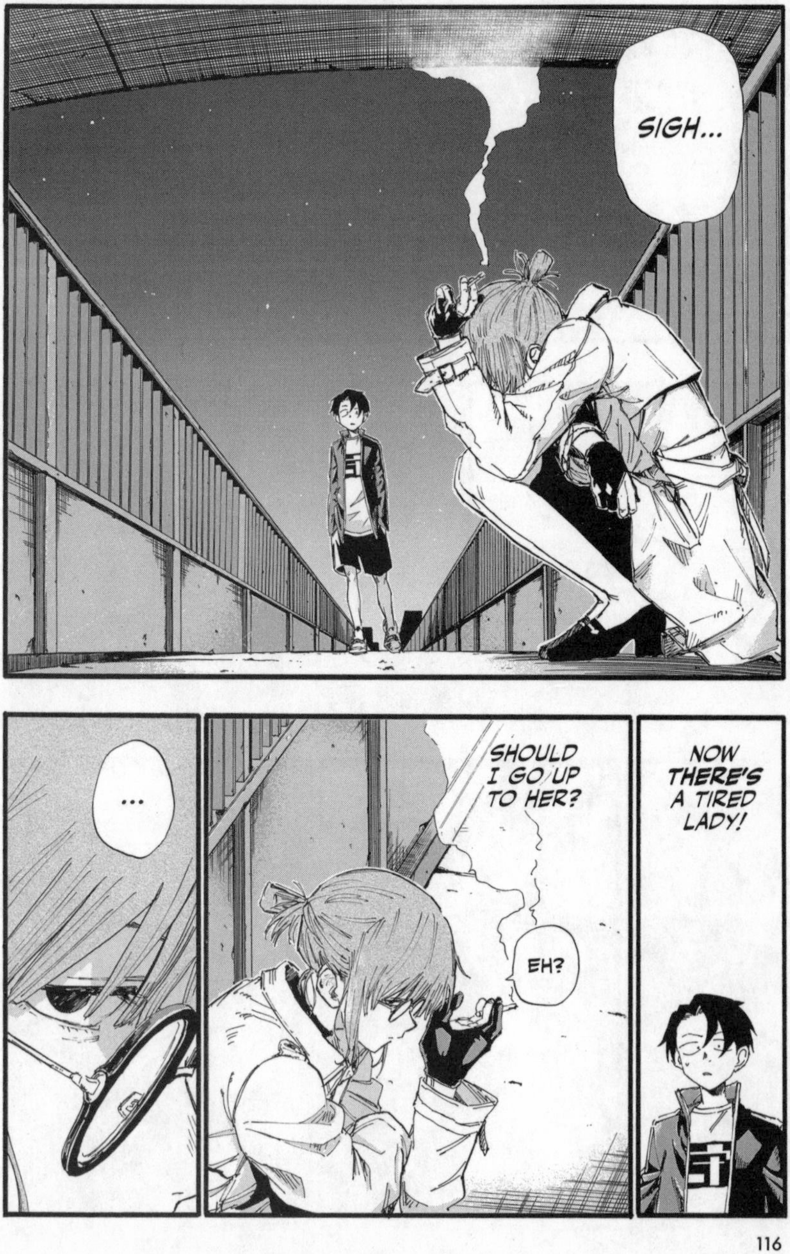
SIGH...
NOW THERE'S A TIRED LADY!
SHOULD I GO UP TO HER?
EH?
...

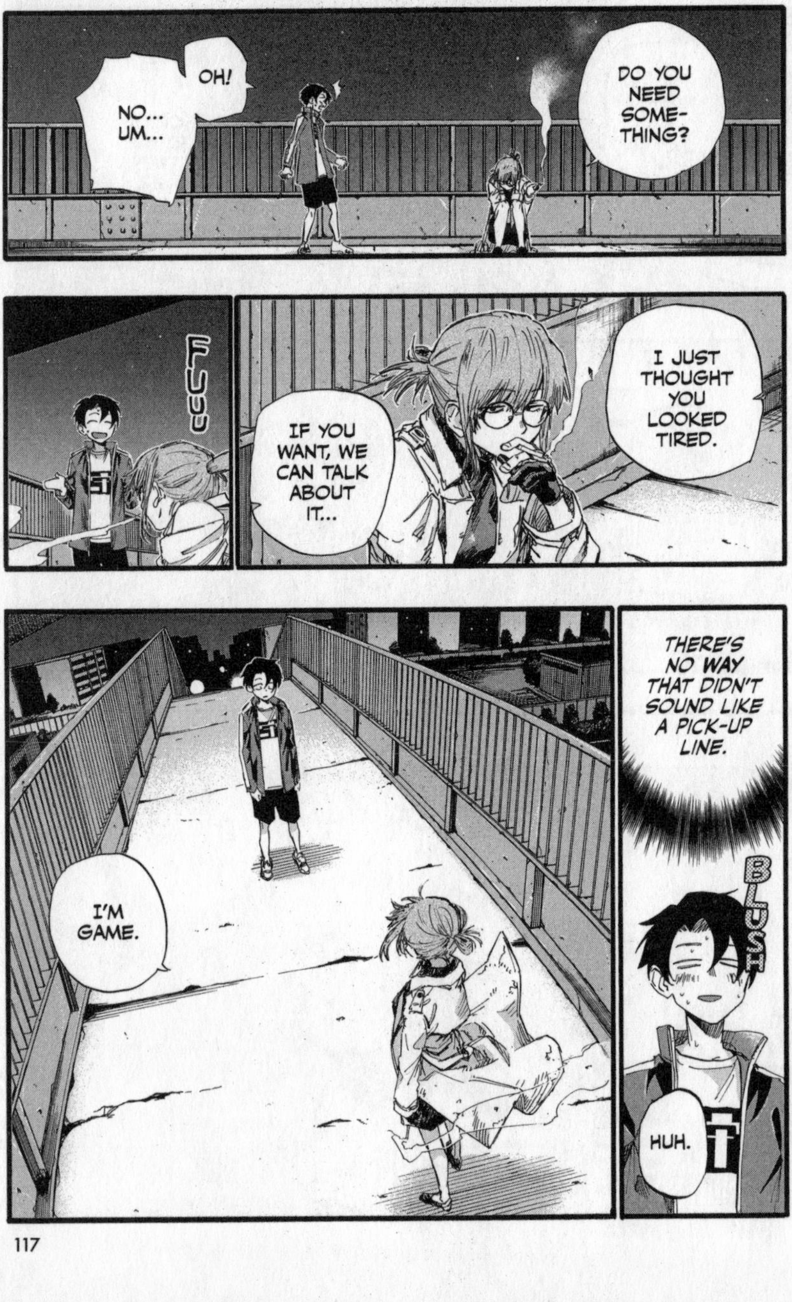
DO YOU NEED SOME-THING?
OH!
NO... UM...
I JUST THOUGHT YOU LOOKED TIRED.
IF YOU WANT, WE CAN TALK ABOUT IT...
FLUUU
THERE'S NO WAY THAT DIDN'T SOUND LIKE A PICK-UP LINE.
BLUSH
HUH.
I'M GAME.

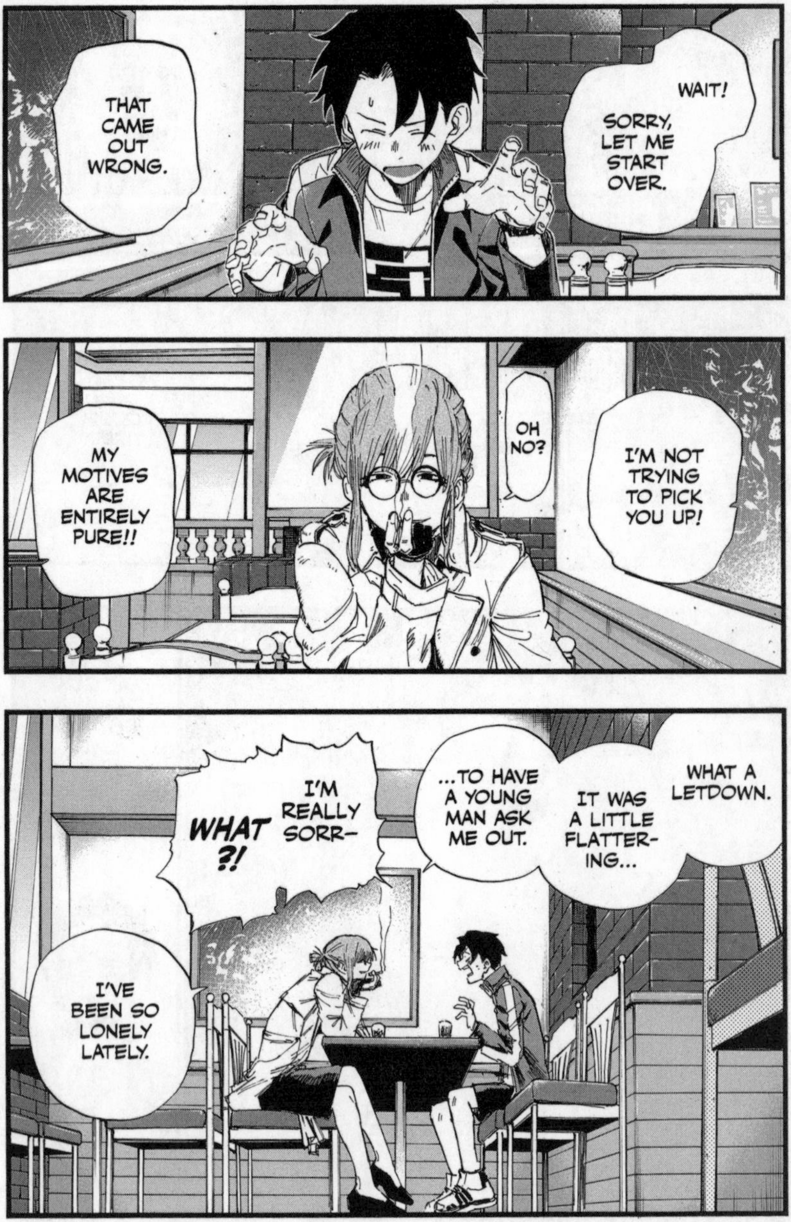
WAIT!
SORRY, LET ME START OVER.
THAT CAME OUT WRONG.
I'M NOT TRYING TO PICK YOU UP!
OH NO?
MY MOTIVES ARE ENTIRELY PURE!!
WHAT A LETDOWN.
IT WAS A LITTLE FLATTERING...
...TO HAVE A YOUNG MAN ASK ME OUT.
I'M REALLY SORR-
WHAT ?!
I'VE BEEN SO LONELY LATELY.

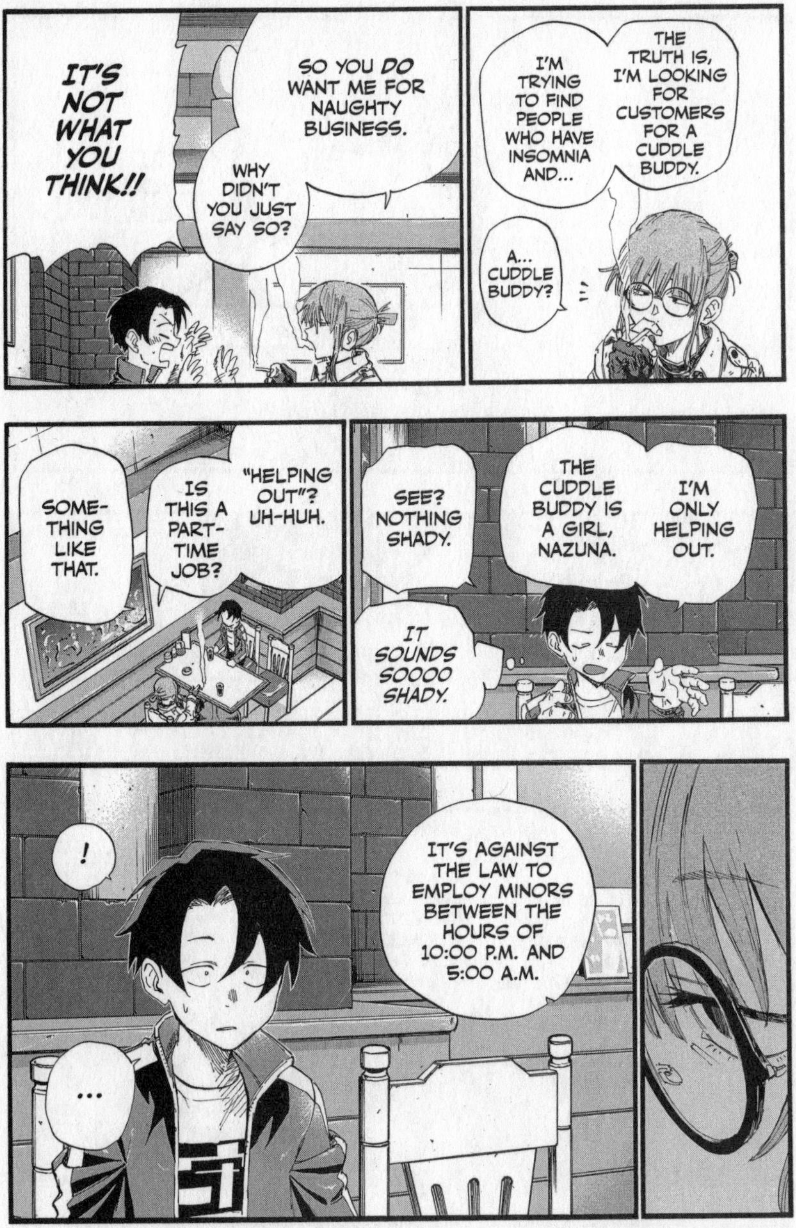
THE TRUTH IS, I'M LOOKING FOR CUSTOMERS FOR A CUDDLE BUDDY.
I'M TRYING TO FIND PEOPLE WHO HAVE INSOMNIA AND...
A... CUDDLE BUDDY?
SO YOU DO WANT ME FOR NAUGHTY BUSINESS.
WHY DIDN'T YOU JUST SAY SO?
IT'S NOT WHAT YOU THINK!!
I'M ONLY HELPING OUT.
THE CUDDLE BUDDY IS A GIRL, NAZUNA.
SEE? NOTHING SHADY.
IT SOUNDS SOOOO SHADY.
"HELPING OUT"? UH-HUH.
IS THIS A PART-TIME JOB?
SOME-THING LIKE THAT.
IT'S AGAINST THE LAW TO EMPLOY MINORS BETWEEN THE HOURS OF 10:00 P.M. AND 5:00 A.M.
!
...

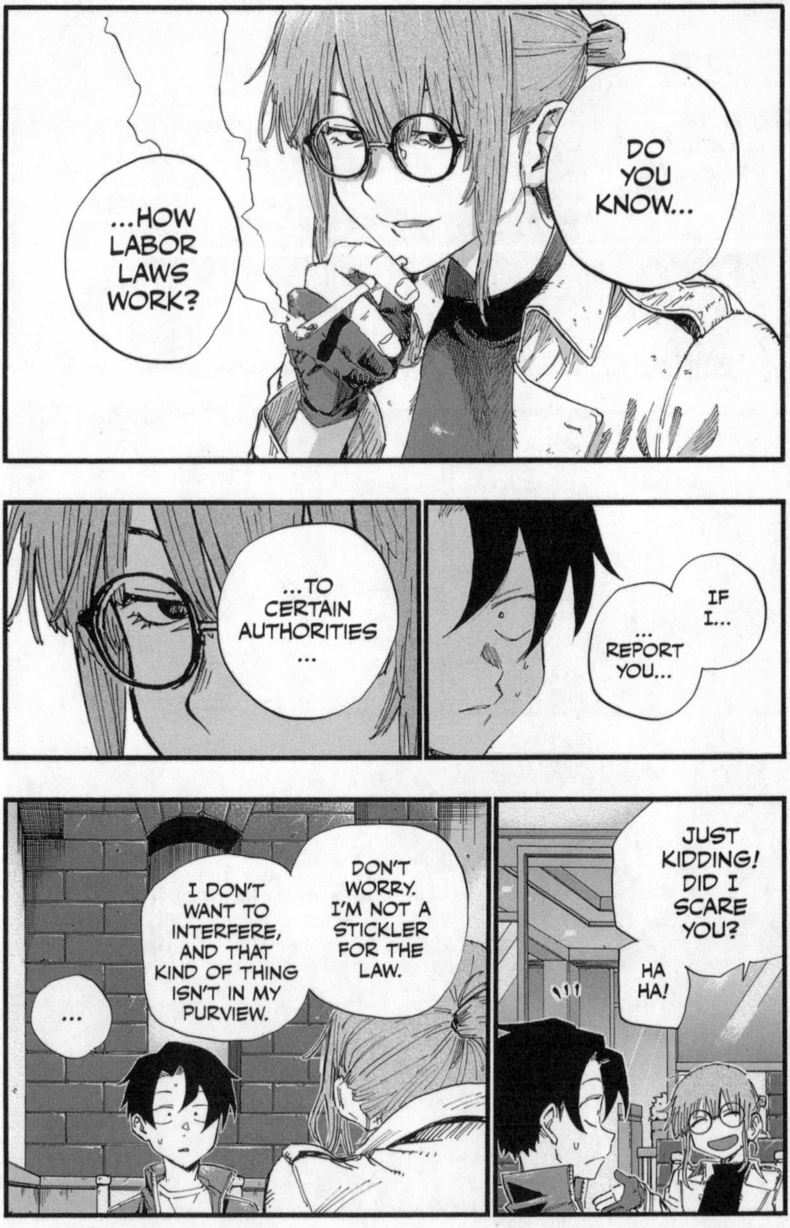
DO YOU KNOW...
...HOW LABOR LAWS WORK?
IF I... ...REPORT YOU...
...TO CERTAIN AUTHORITIES ...
JUST KIDDING! DID I SCARE YOU?
HA HA!
DON'T WORRY. I'M NOT A STICKLER FOR THE LAW.
I DON'T WANT TO INTERFERE, AND THAT KIND OF THING ISN'T IN MY PURVIEW.
...

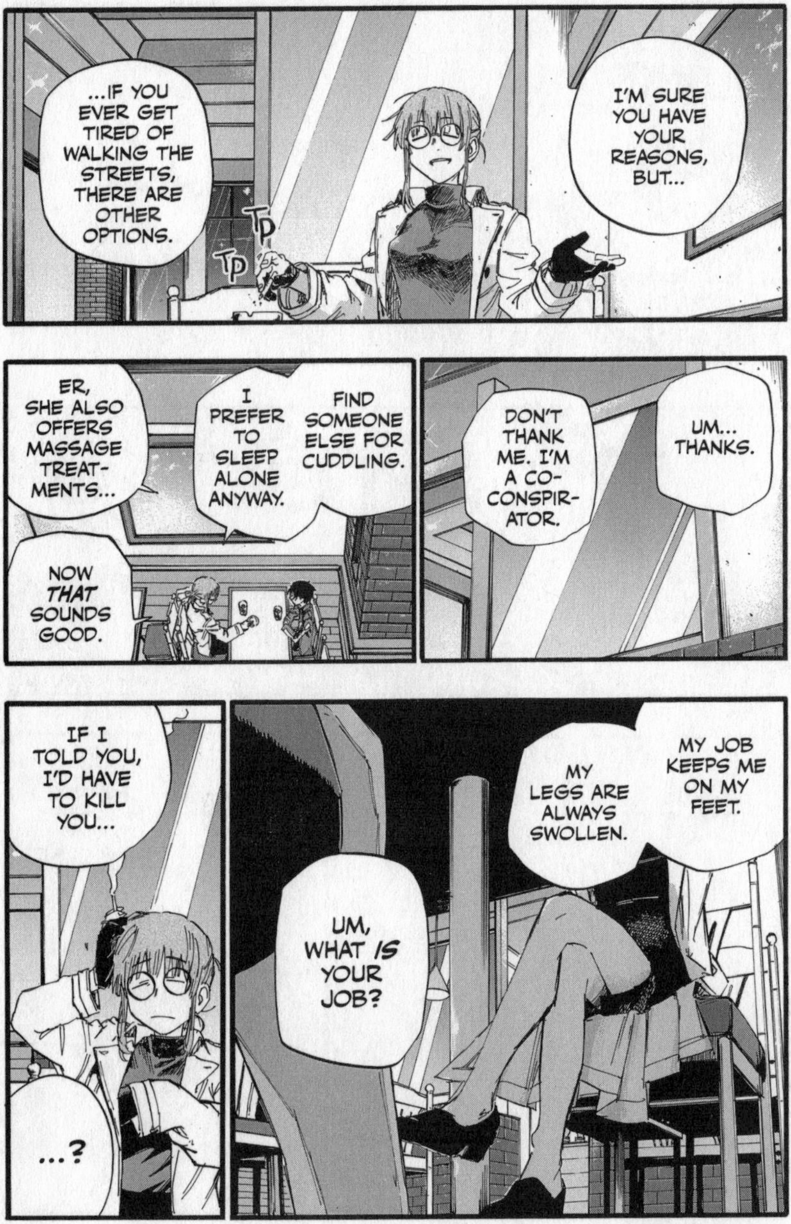
I'M SURE YOU HAVE YOUR REASONS, BUT...
...IF YOU EVER GET TIRED OF WALKING THE STREETS, THERE ARE OTHER OPTIONS.
TP
TP
UM... THANKS.
DON'T THANK ME. I'M A CO-CONSPIR-ATOR.
FIND SOMEONE ELSE FOR CUDDLING.
I PREFER TO SLEEP ALONE ANYWAY.
ER, SHE ALSO OFFERS MASSAGE TREAT-MENTS...
NOW *THAT* SOUNDS GOOD.
MY JOB KEEPS ME ON MY FEET.
MY LEGS ARE ALWAYS SWOLLEN.
UM, WHAT *IS* YOUR JOB?
IF I TOLD YOU, I'D HAVE TO KILL YOU...
...?

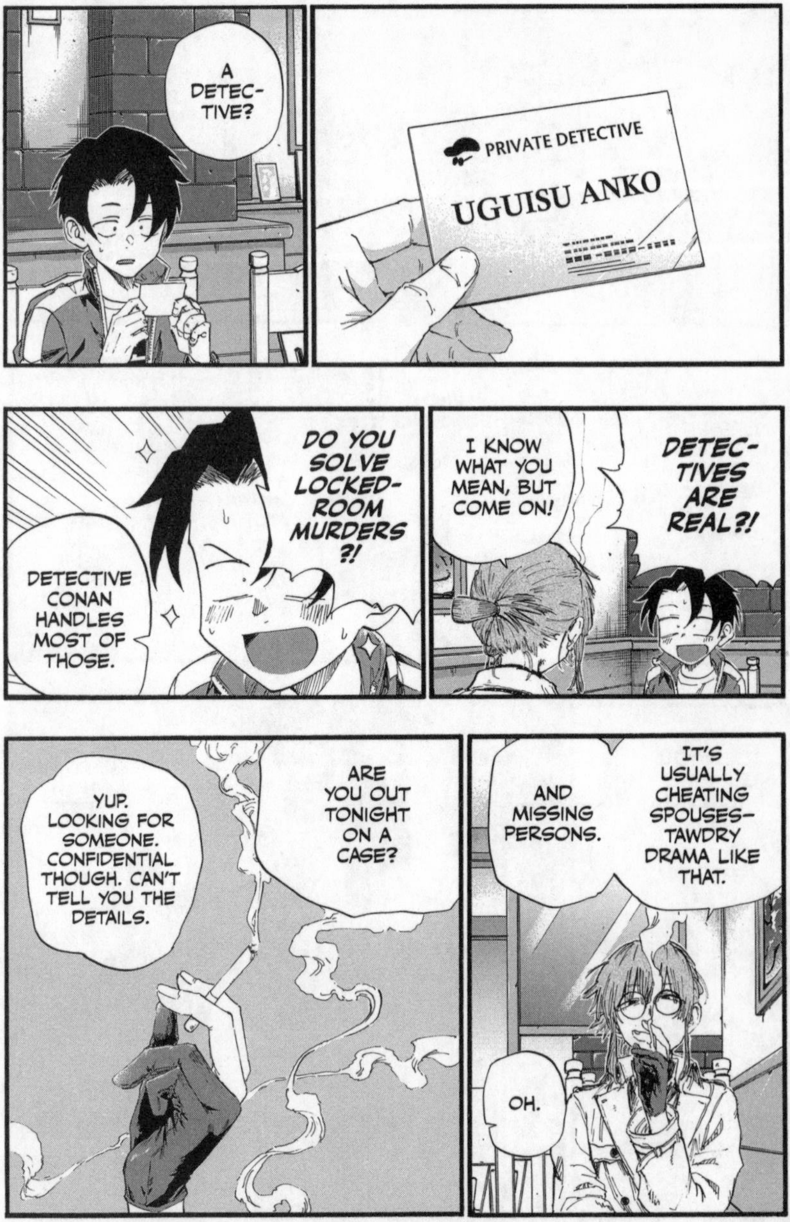
PRIVATE DETECTIVE
UGUISU ANKO
A DETECTIVE?
DETECTIVES ARE REAL?!
I KNOW WHAT YOU MEAN, BUT COME ON!
DO YOU SOLVE LOCKED-ROOM MURDERS?!
DETECTIVE CONAN HANDLES MOST OF THOSE.
IT'S USUALLY CHEATING SPOUSES—TAWDRY DRAMA LIKE THAT.
AND MISSING PERSONS.
OH.
ARE YOU OUT TONIGHT ON A CASE?
YUP. LOOKING FOR SOMEONE. CONFIDENTIAL THOUGH. CAN'T TELL YOU THE DETAILS.

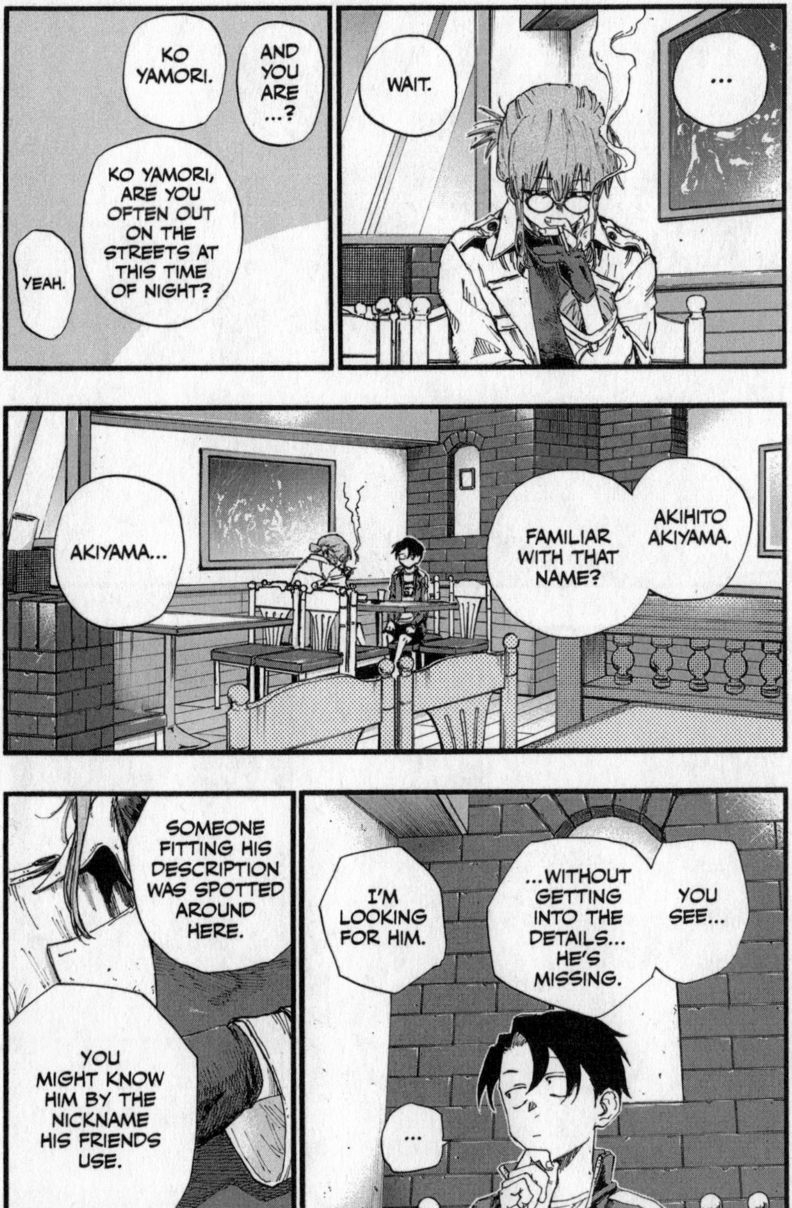
...
WAIT.
AND YOU ARE ...?
KO YAMORI.
KO YAMORI, ARE YOU OFTEN OUT ON THE STREETS AT THIS TIME OF NIGHT?
YEAH.
AKIHITO AKIYAMA.
FAMILIAR WITH THAT NAME?
AKIYAMA...
YOU SEE...
...WITHOUT GETTING INTO THE DETAILS... HE'S MISSING.
I'M LOOKING FOR HIM.
...
SOMEONE FITTING HIS DESCRIPTION WAS SPOTTED AROUND HERE.
YOU MIGHT KNOW HIM BY THE NICKNAME HIS FRIENDS USE.

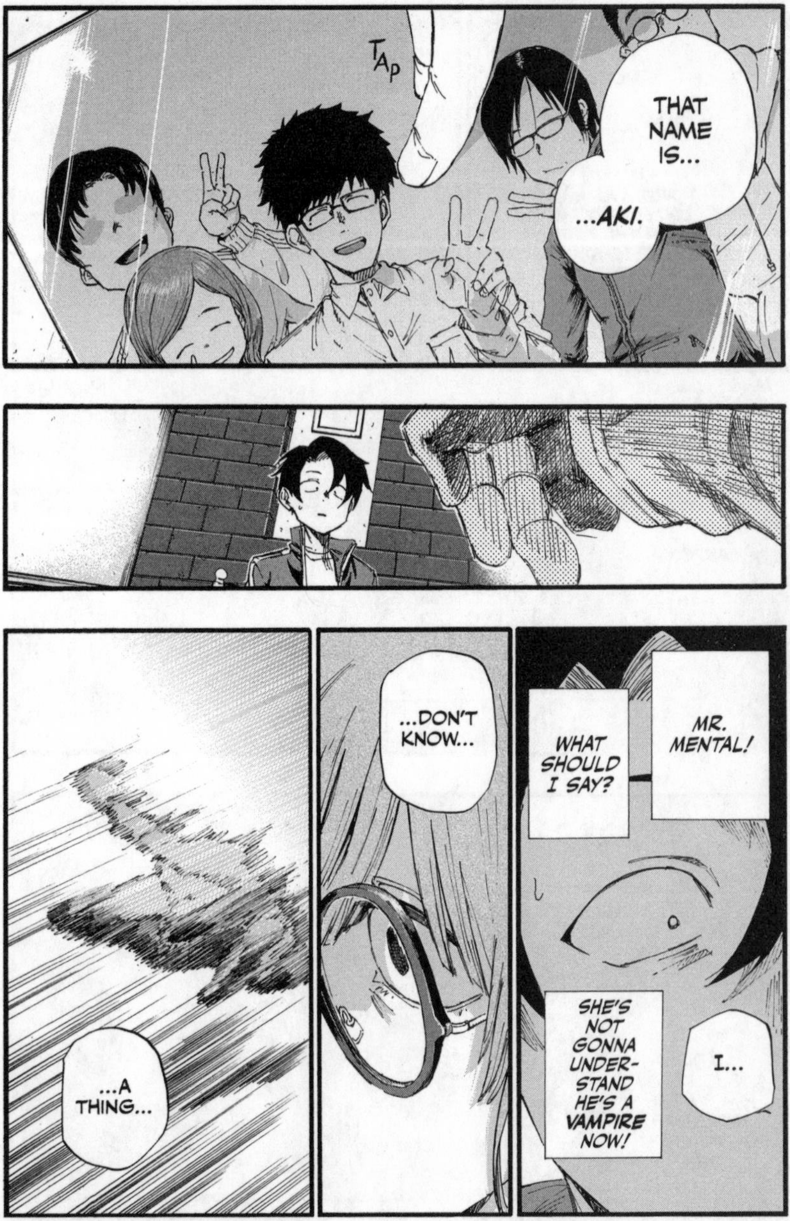
THAT NAME IS...
...AKI.
TAP
MR. MENTAL!
WHAT SHOULD I SAY?
SHE'S NOT GONNA UNDER-STAND HE'S A VAMPIRE NOW!
I...
...DON'T KNOW...
...A THING...

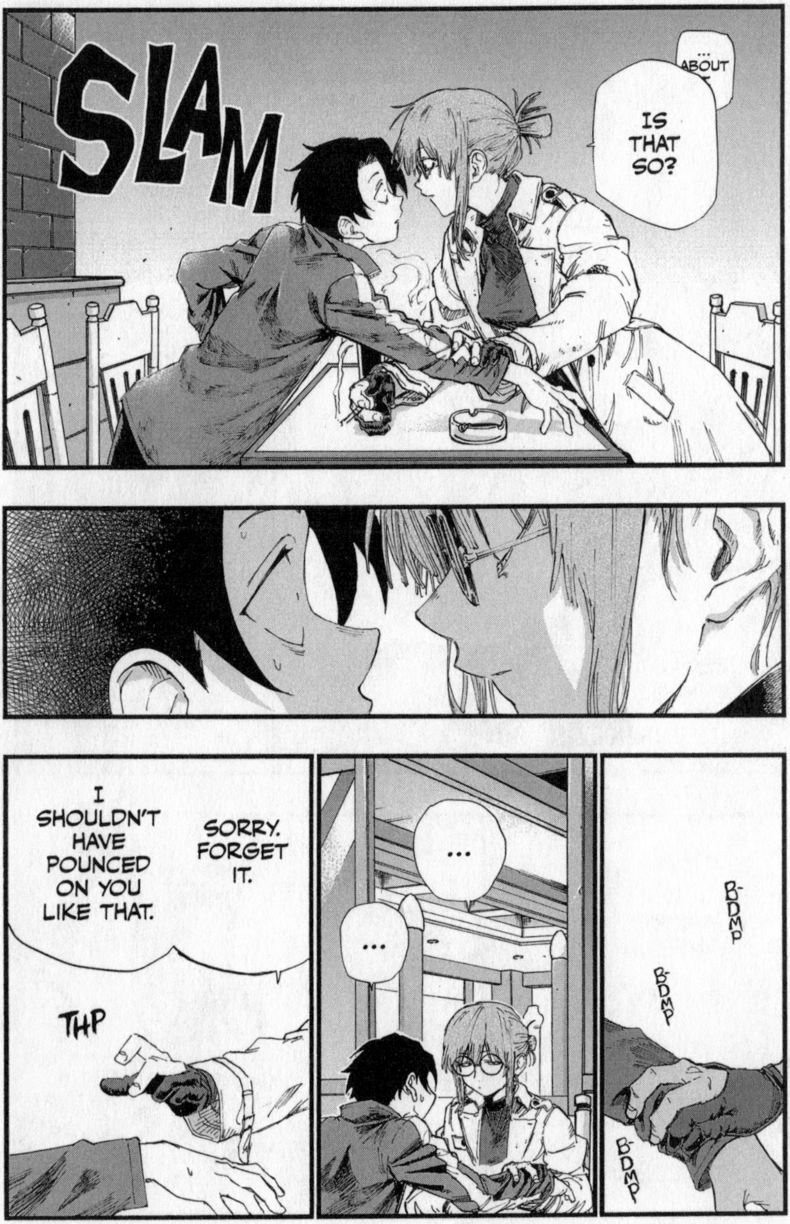

... ABOUT
IS THAT SO?
SLAM
B-DMP
B-DMP
B-DMP
...
...
SORRY. FORGET IT.
I SHOULDN'T HAVE POUNCED ON YOU LIKE THAT.
THP

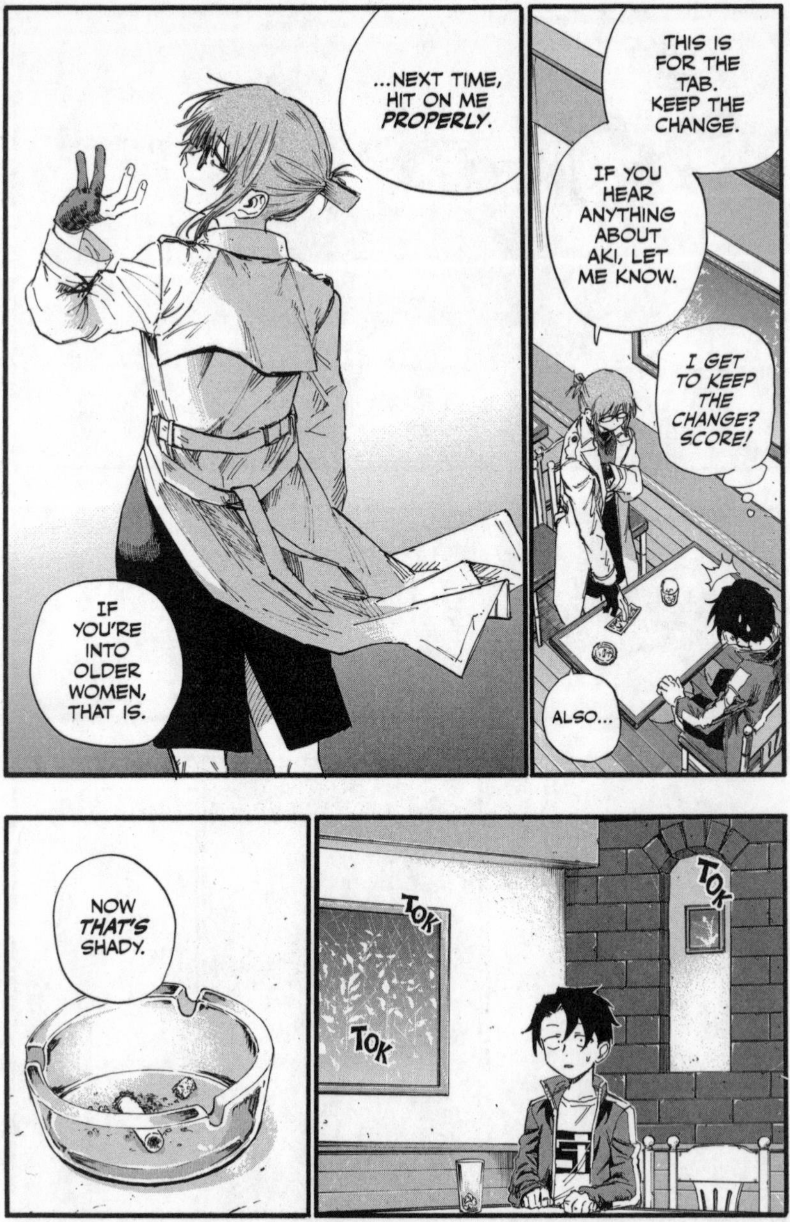
THIS IS FOR THE TAB. KEEP THE CHANGE.
IF YOU HEAR ANYTHING ABOUT AKI, LET ME KNOW.
I GET TO KEEP THE CHANGE? SCORE!
ALSO...
...NEXT TIME, HIT ON ME *PROPERLY*.
IF YOU'RE INTO OLDER WOMEN, THAT IS.
TOK
TOK
TOK
NOW *THAT'S* SHADY.

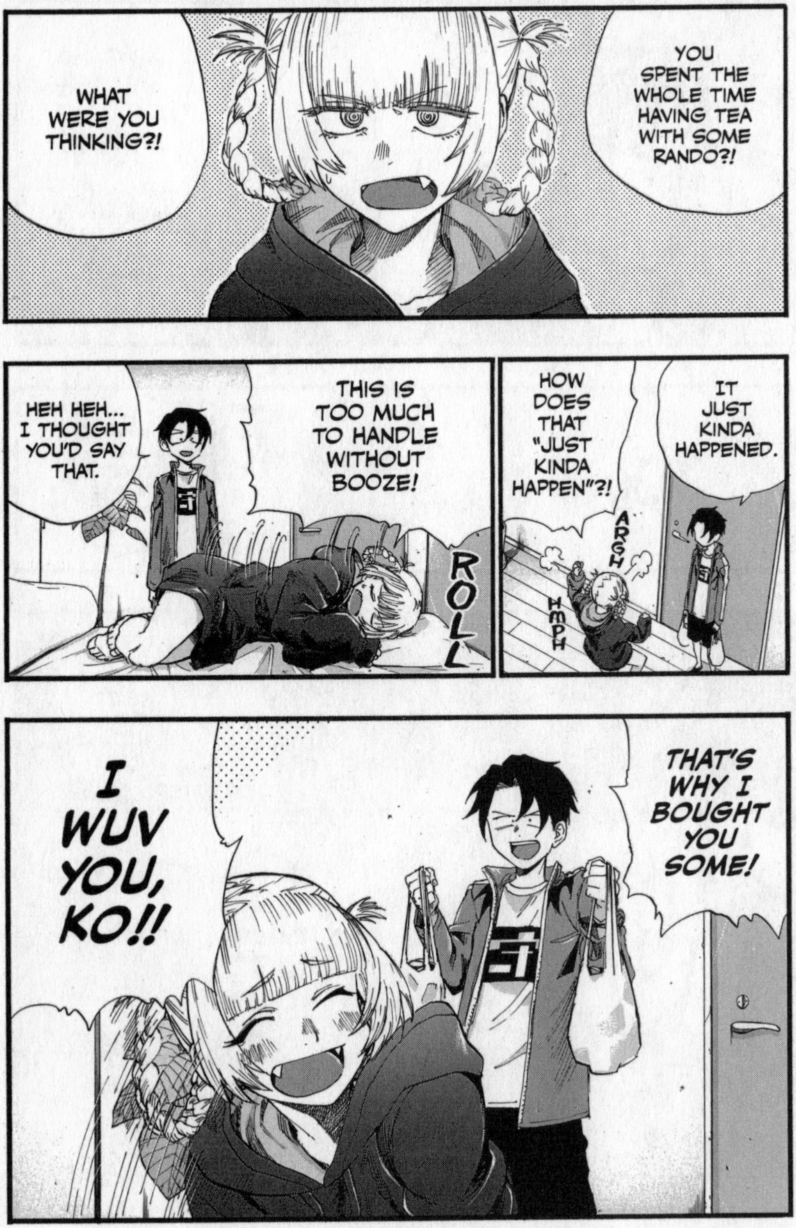
YOU SPENT THE WHOLE TIME HAVING TEA WITH SOME RANDO?!
WHAT WERE YOU THINKING?!
IT JUST KINDA HAPPENED.
HOW DOES THAT "JUST KINDA HAPPEN"?!
ARGH
HMPH
THIS IS TOO MUCH TO HANDLE WITHOUT BOOZE!
ROLL
HEH HEH... I THOUGHT YOU'D SAY THAT.
THAT'S WHY I BOUGHT YOU SOME!
I WUV YOU, KO!!

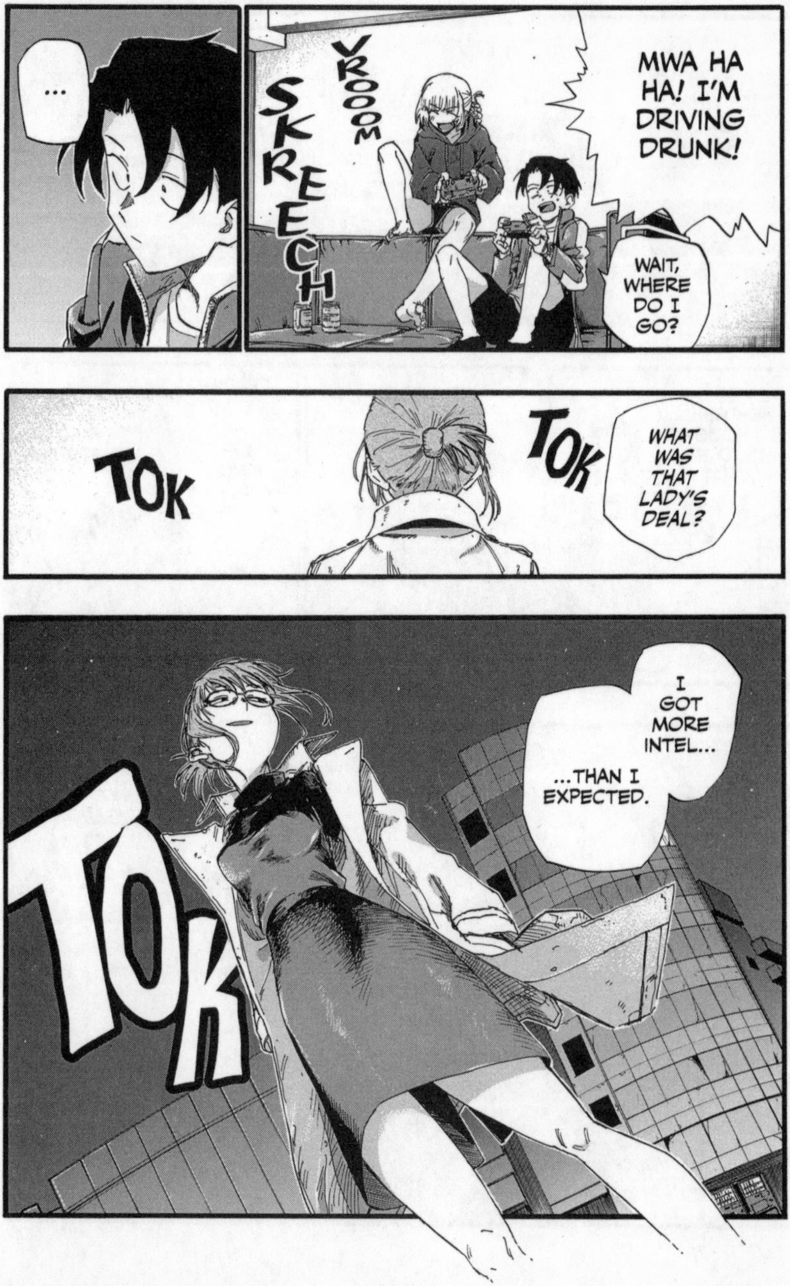
MWA HA HA! I'M DRIVING DRUNK!
WAIT, WHERE DO I GO?
VROOOM
SKREEECH
...
TOK
WHAT WAS THAT LADY'S DEAL?
TOK
I GOT MORE INTEL...
...THAN I EXPECTED.
TOK

NIGHT 37: TOO DARK TO SEE

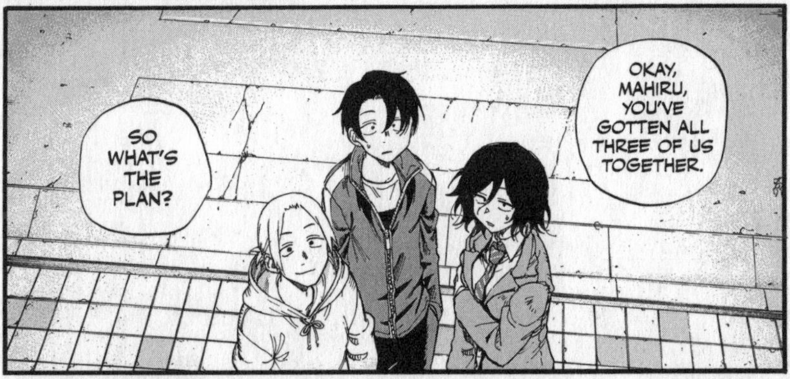
OKAY, MAHIRU, YOU'VE GOTTEN ALL THREE OF US TOGETHER.
SO WHAT'S THE PLAN?

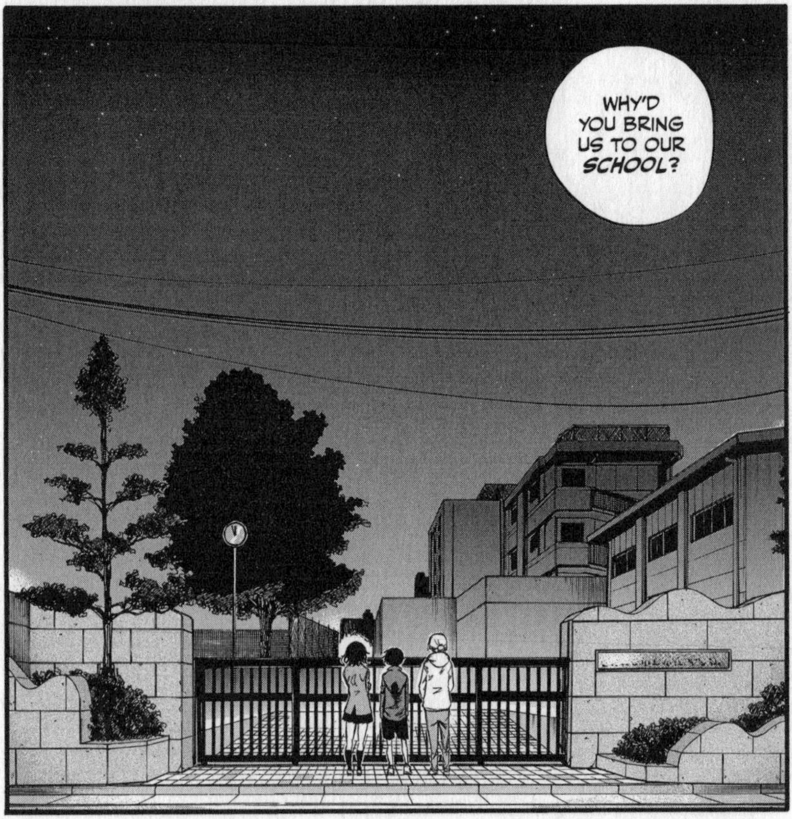
WHY'D YOU BRING US TO OUR *SCHOOL*?

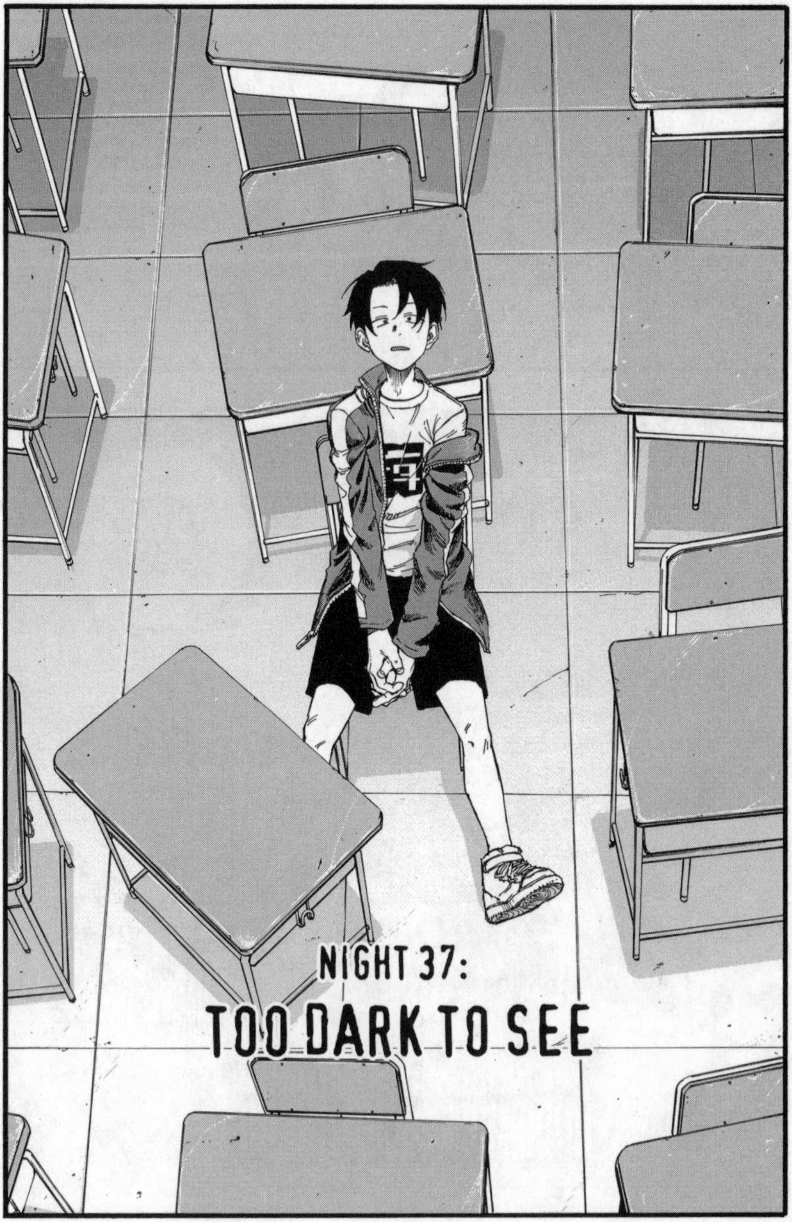
NIGHT 37:
TOO DARK TO SEE

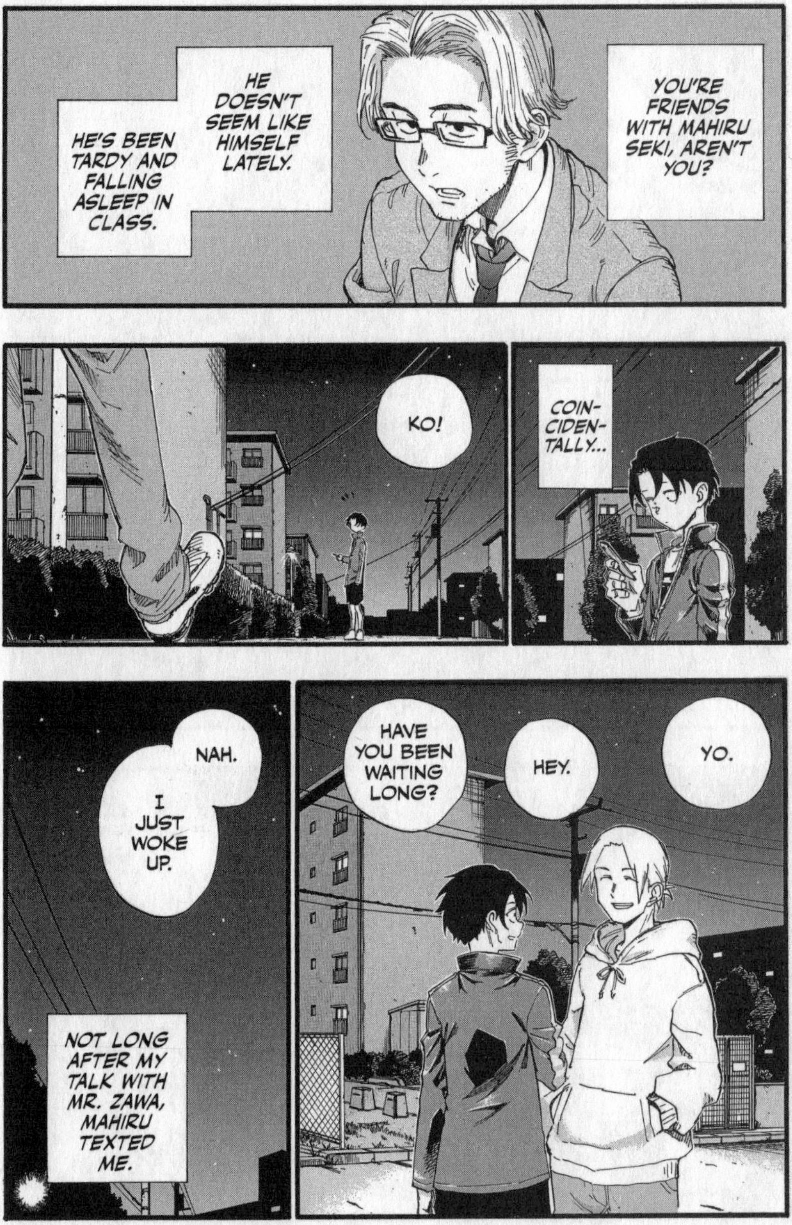
YOU'RE FRIENDS WITH MAHIRU SEKI, AREN'T YOU?
HE DOESN'T SEEM LIKE HIMSELF LATELY.
HE'S BEEN TARDY AND FALLING ASLEEP IN CLASS.
COIN-CIDEN-TALLY...
KO!
YO.
HEY.
HAVE YOU BEEN WAITING LONG?
NAH.
I JUST WOKE UP.
NOT LONG AFTER MY TALK WITH MR. ZAWA, MAHIRU TEXTED ME.

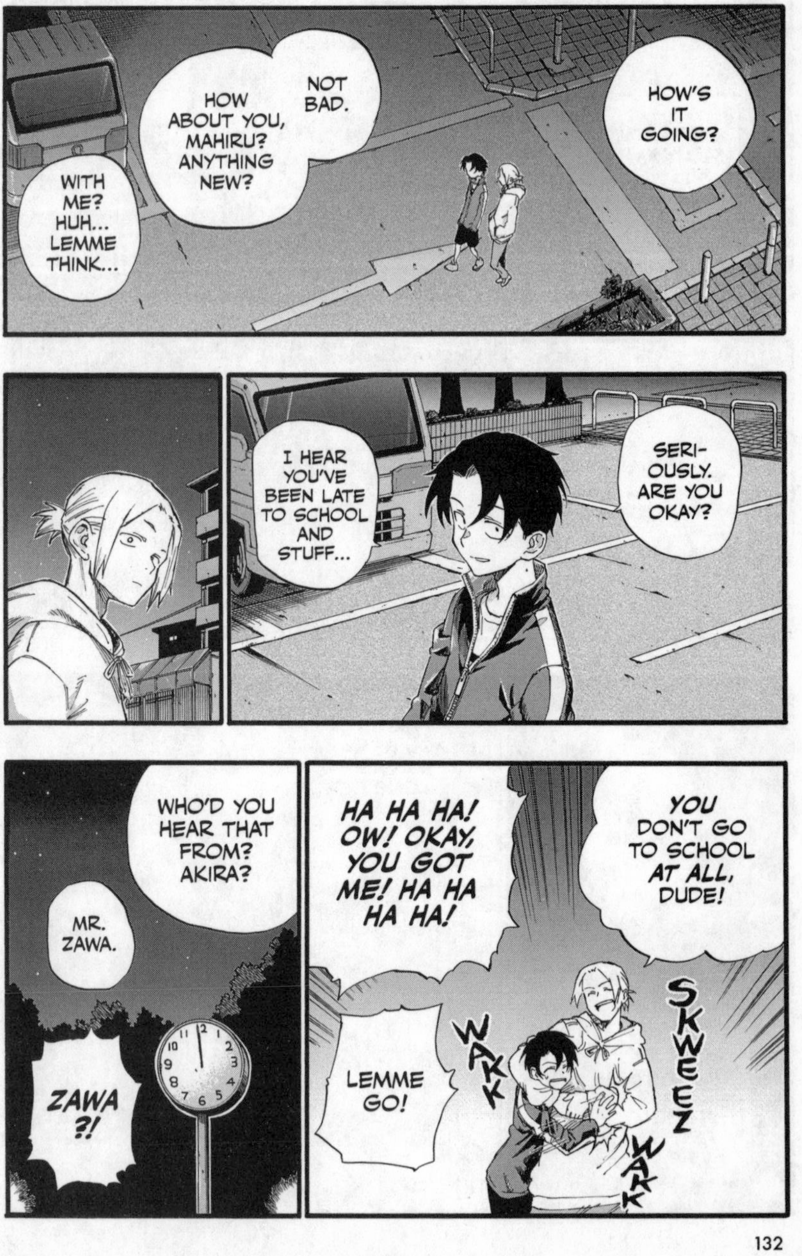
HOW'S IT GOING?
NOT BAD.
HOW ABOUT YOU, MAHIRU? ANYTHING NEW?
WITH ME? HUH... LEMME THINK...
SERI-OUSLY. ARE YOU OKAY?
I HEAR YOU'VE BEEN LATE TO SCHOOL AND STUFF...
YOU DON'T GO TO SCHOOL AT ALL, DUDE!
SKWEEZ
HA HA HA! OW! OKAY, YOU GOT ME! HA HA HA HA!
WAKK
WAKK
LEMME GO!
WHO'D YOU HEAR THAT FROM? AKIRA?
MR. ZAWA.
ZAWA ?!

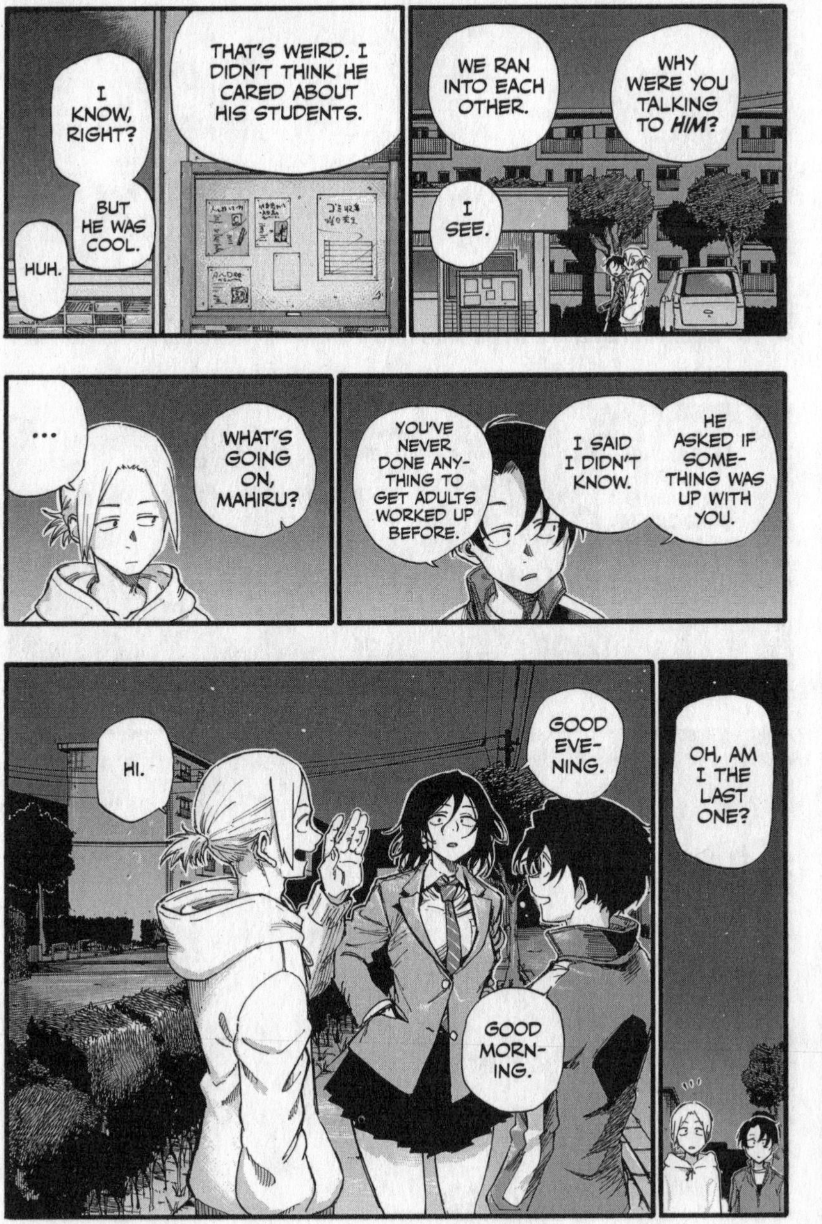
WHY WERE YOU TALKING TO *HIM*?
WE RAN INTO EACH OTHER.
I SEE.
THAT'S WEIRD. I DIDN'T THINK HE CARED ABOUT HIS STUDENTS.
I KNOW, RIGHT?
BUT HE WAS COOL.
HUH.
HE ASKED IF SOME-THING WAS UP WITH YOU.
I SAID I DIDN'T KNOW.
YOU'VE NEVER DONE ANY-THING TO GET ADULTS WORKED UP BEFORE.
WHAT'S GOING ON, MAHIRU?
...
OH, AM I THE LAST ONE?
GOOD EVE-NING.
GOOD MORN-ING.
HI.

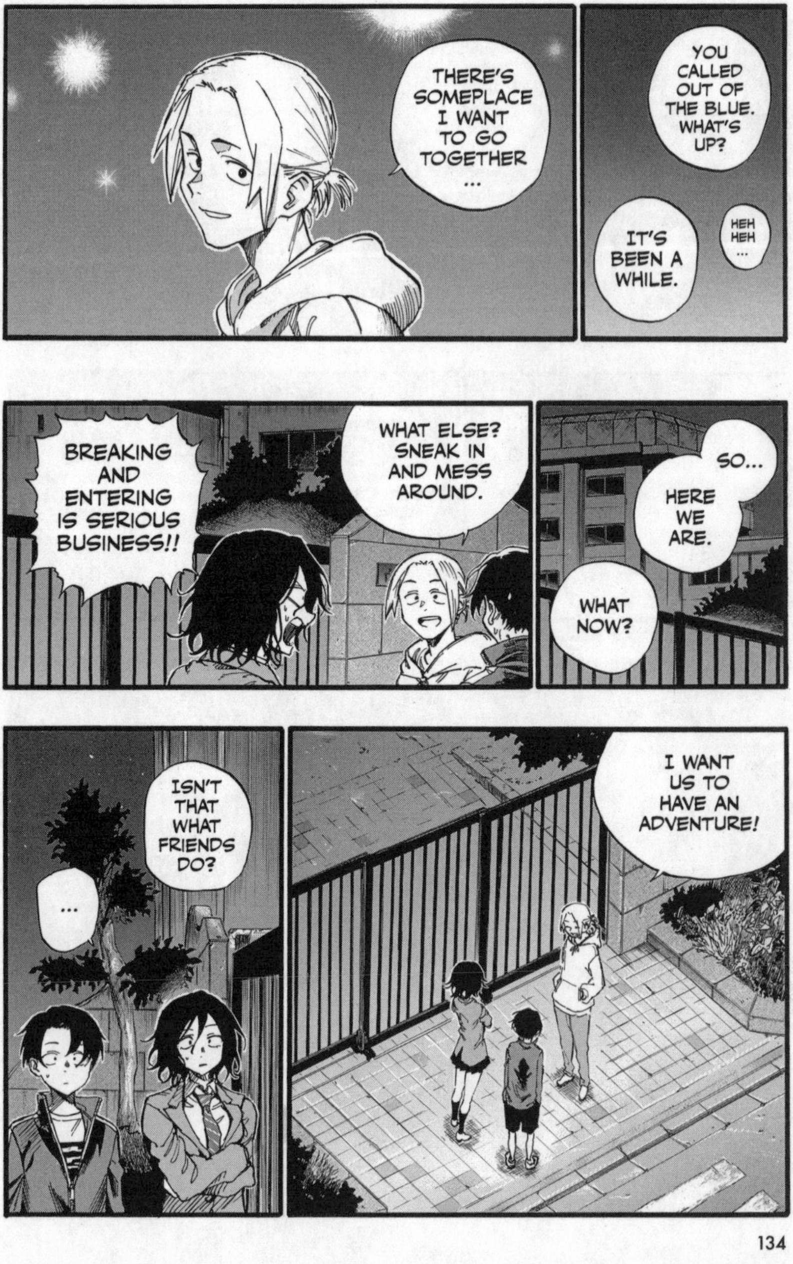
YOU CALLED OUT OF THE BLUE. WHAT'S UP?
HEH HEH ...
IT'S BEEN A WHILE.
THERE'S SOMEPLACE I WANT TO GO TOGETHER ...
SO...
HERE WE ARE.
WHAT NOW?
WHAT ELSE? SNEAK IN AND MESS AROUND.
BREAKING AND ENTERING IS SERIOUS BUSINESS!!
I WANT US TO HAVE AN ADVENTURE!
ISN'T THAT WHAT FRIENDS DO?
...

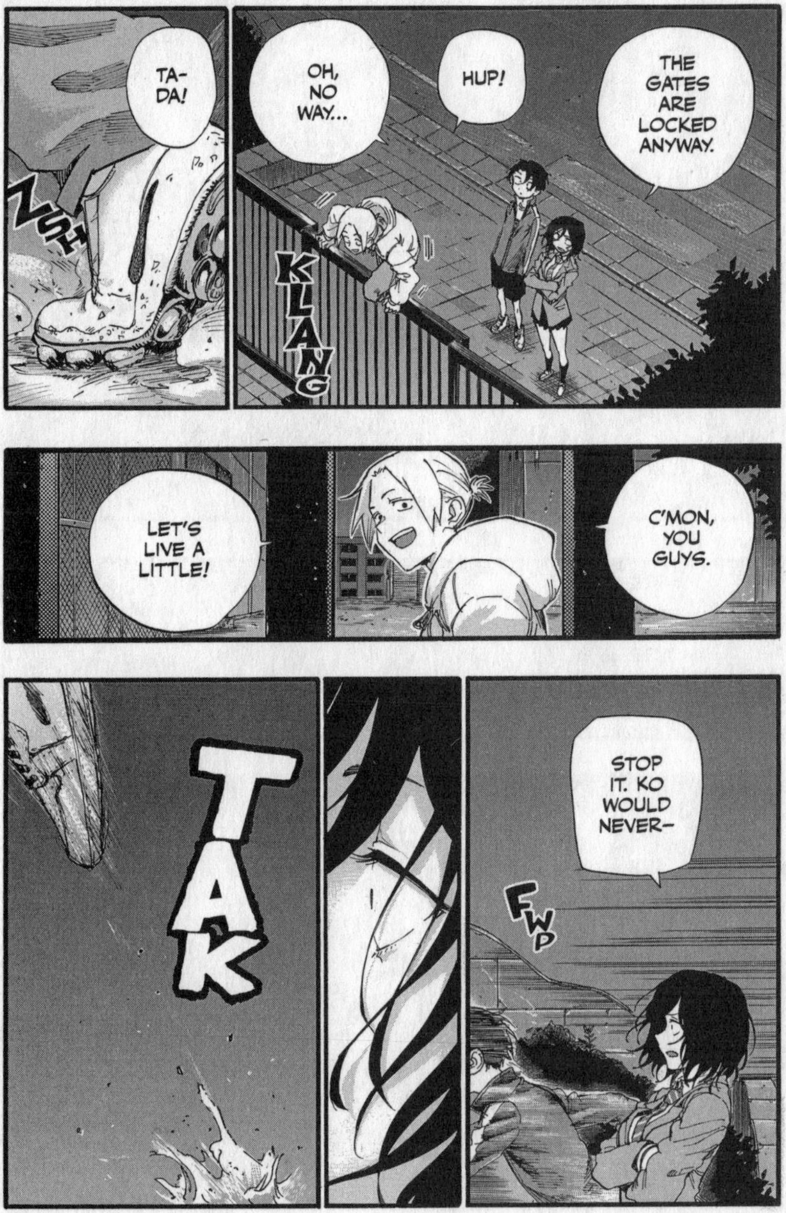
THE GATES ARE LOCKED ANYWAY.
HUP!
OH, NO WAY...
KLANG
TA-DA!
ZSH
C'MON, YOU GUYS.
LET'S LIVE A LITTLE!
STOP IT. KO WOULD NEVER–
FWP
TAK

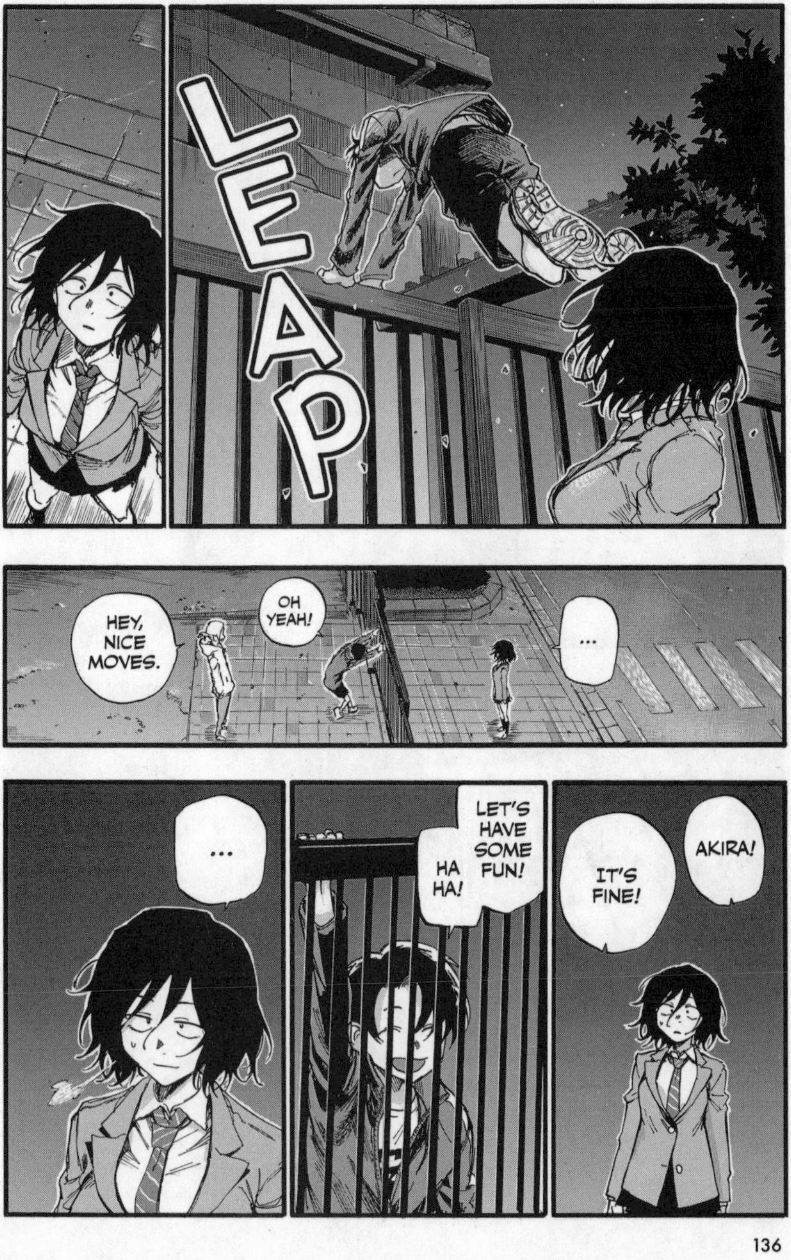
LEAP
...
OH YEAH!
HEY, NICE MOVES.
AKIRA!
IT'S FINE!
LET'S HAVE SOME FUN!
HA HA!
...

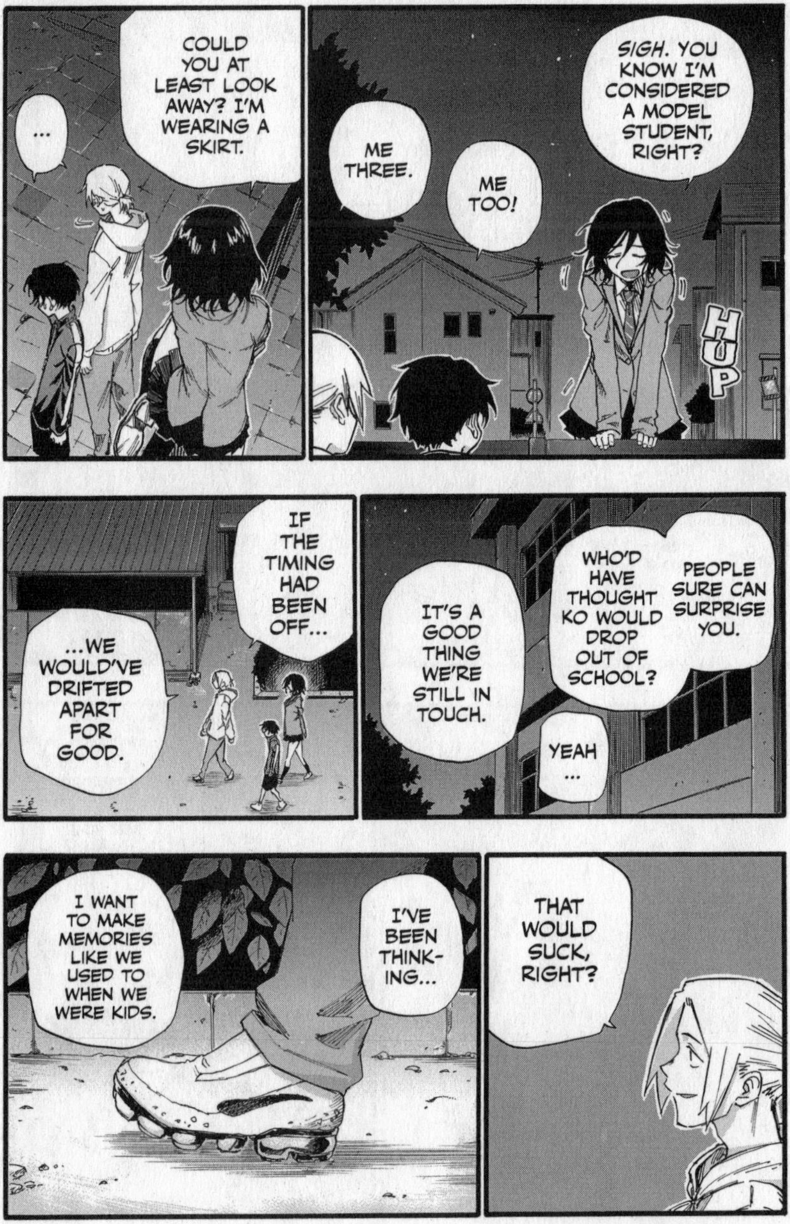
SIGH. YOU KNOW I'M CONSIDERED A MODEL STUDENT, RIGHT?
HUP
ME TOO!
ME THREE.
COULD YOU AT LEAST LOOK AWAY? I'M WEARING A SKIRT.
...
PEOPLE SURE CAN SURPRISE YOU.
WHO'D HAVE THOUGHT KO WOULD DROP OUT OF SCHOOL?
YEAH ...
IT'S A GOOD THING WE'RE STILL IN TOUCH.
IF THE TIMING HAD BEEN OFF...
...WE WOULD'VE DRIFTED APART FOR GOOD.
THAT WOULD SUCK, RIGHT?
I'VE BEEN THINKING...
I WANT TO MAKE MEMORIES LIKE WE USED TO WHEN WE WERE KIDS.

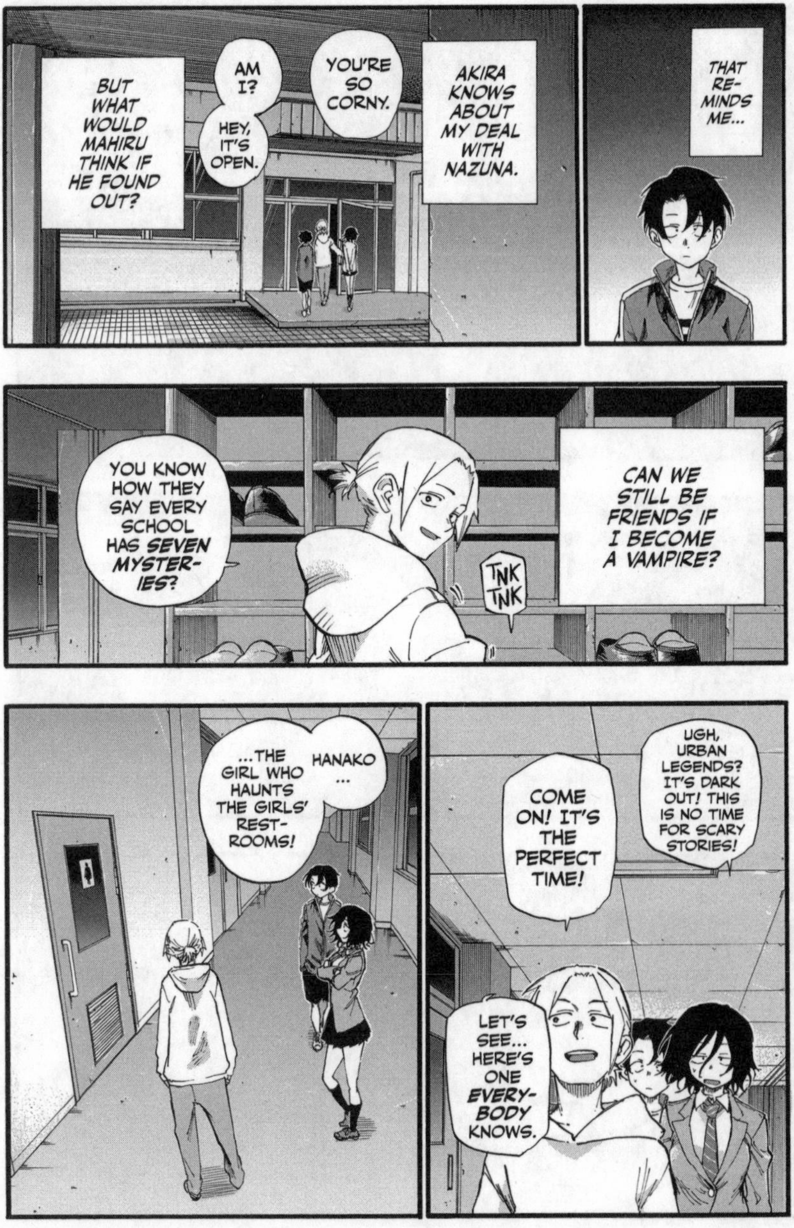
THAT RE-MINDS ME...
AKIRA KNOWS ABOUT MY DEAL WITH NAZUNA.
YOU'RE SO CORNY.
AM I?
HEY, IT'S OPEN.
BUT WHAT WOULD MAHIRU THINK IF HE FOUND OUT?
CAN WE STILL BE FRIENDS IF I BECOME A VAMPIRE?
TNK TNK
YOU KNOW HOW THEY SAY EVERY SCHOOL HAS SEVEN MYSTER-IES?
UGH, URBAN LEGENDS? IT'S DARK OUT! THIS IS NO TIME FOR SCARY STORIES!
COME ON! IT'S THE PERFECT TIME!
LET'S SEE... HERE'S ONE EVERY-BODY KNOWS.
HANAKO...
...THE GIRL WHO HAUNTS THE GIRLS' REST-ROOMS!

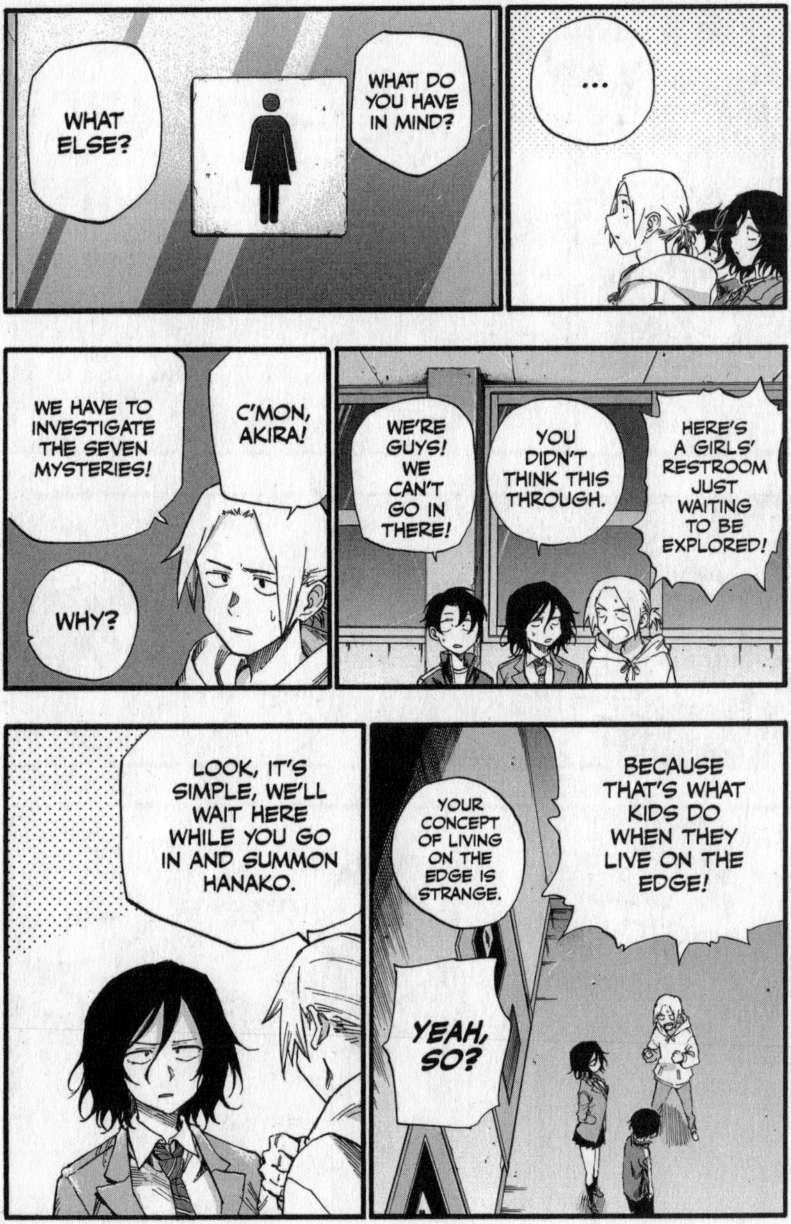
...
WHAT DO YOU HAVE IN MIND?
WHAT ELSE?
HERE'S A GIRLS' RESTROOM JUST WAITING TO BE EXPLORED!
YOU DIDN'T THINK THIS THROUGH.
WE'RE GUYS! WE CAN'T GO IN THERE!
C'MON, AKIRA!
WE HAVE TO INVESTIGATE THE SEVEN MYSTERIES!
WHY?
BECAUSE THAT'S WHAT KIDS DO WHEN THEY LIVE ON THE EDGE!
YOUR CONCEPT OF LIVING ON THE EDGE IS STRANGE.
YEAH, SO?
LOOK, IT'S SIMPLE, WE'LL WAIT HERE WHILE YOU GO IN AND SUMMON HANAKO.

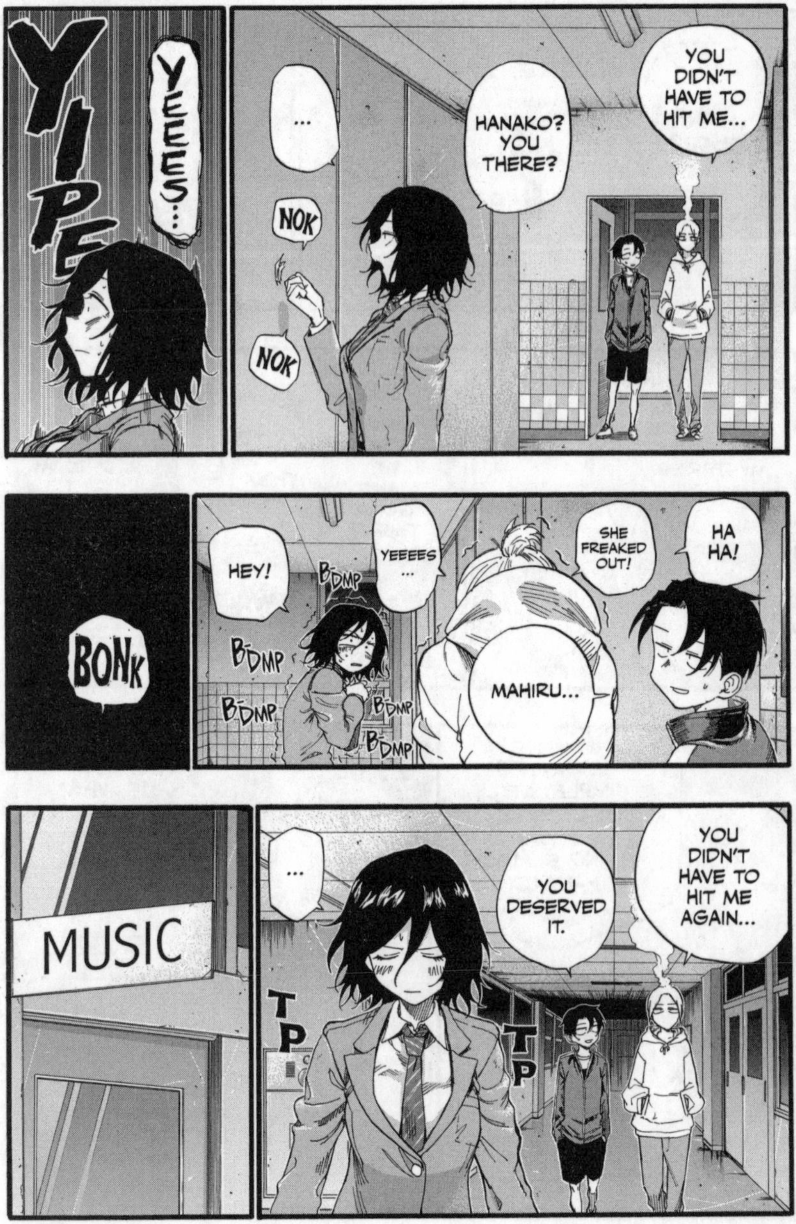
YOU DIDN'T HAVE TO HIT ME...
HANAKO? YOU THERE?
...
NOK
NOK
YEEES...
YIPE
HA HA!
SHE FREAKED OUT!
MAHIRU...
YEEEES ...
HEY!
B-DMP
B-DMP
B-DMP
B-DMP
B-DMP
BONK
YOU DIDN'T HAVE TO HIT ME AGAIN...
YOU DESERVED IT.
...
TP
TP
MUSIC

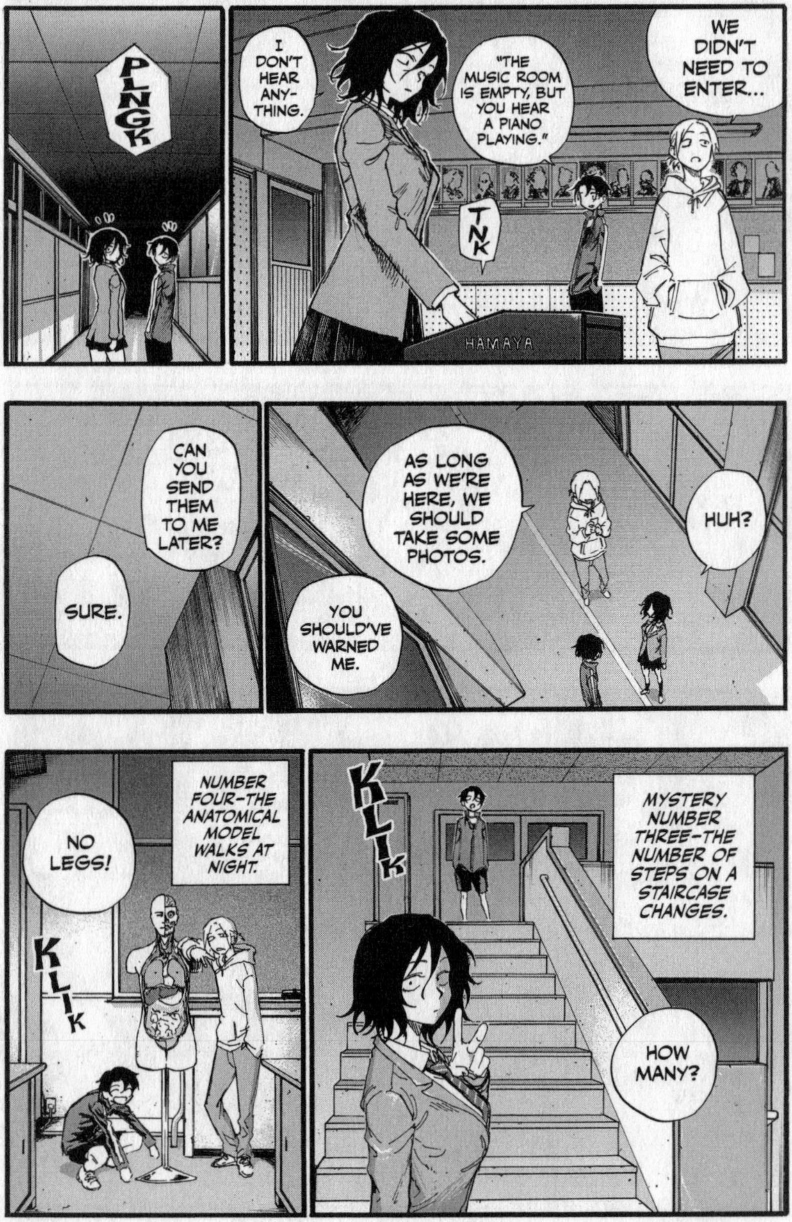
WE DIDN'T NEED TO ENTER...
"THE MUSIC ROOM IS EMPTY, BUT YOU HEAR A PIANO PLAYING."
I DON'T HEAR ANY-THING.
TNK
HAMAYA
PLNGK
HUH?
AS LONG AS WE'RE HERE, WE SHOULD TAKE SOME PHOTOS.
YOU SHOULD'VE WARNED ME.
CAN YOU SEND THEM TO ME LATER?
SURE.
MYSTERY NUMBER THREE—THE NUMBER OF STEPS ON A STAIRCASE CHANGES.
KLIK
HOW MANY?
NUMBER FOUR—THE ANATOMICAL MODEL WALKS AT NIGHT.
NO LEGS!
KLIK

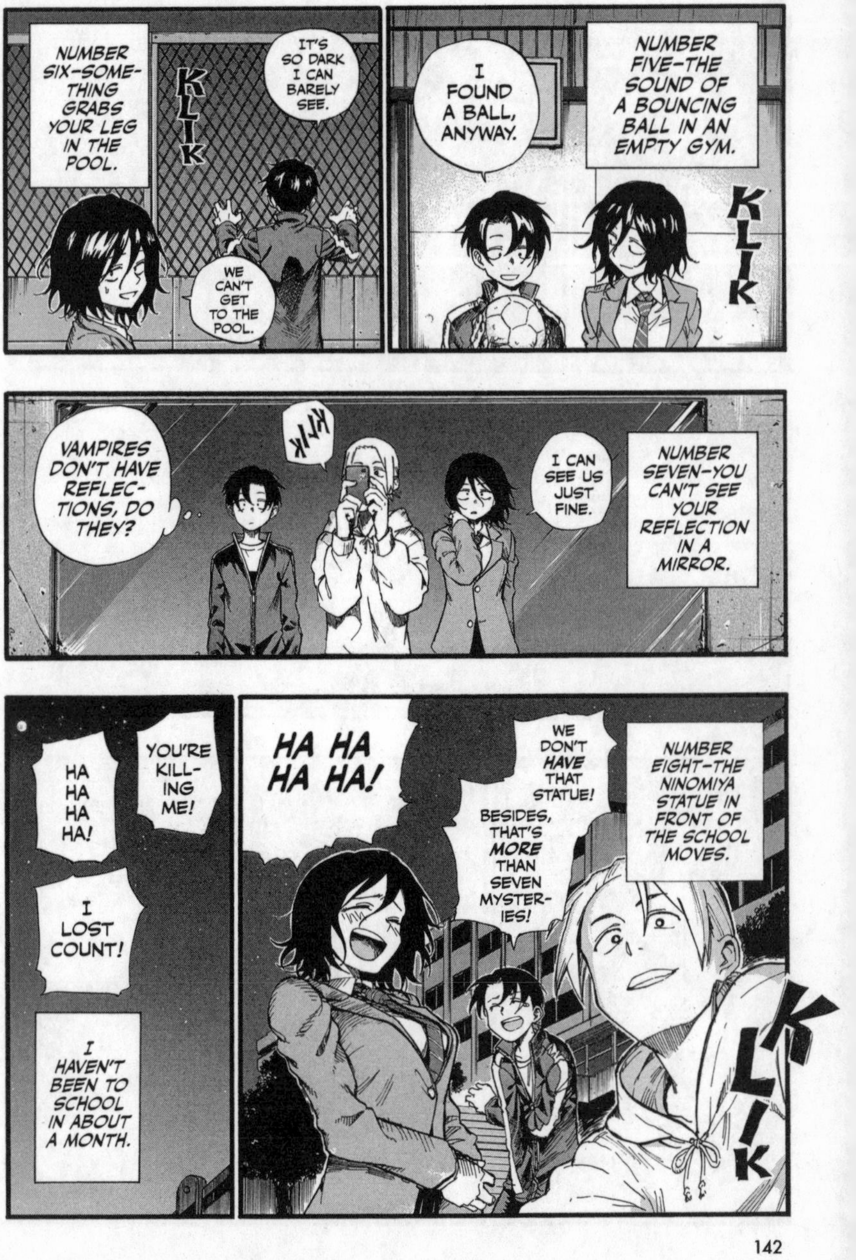
NUMBER FIVE—THE SOUND OF A BOUNCING BALL IN AN EMPTY GYM.
I FOUND A BALL, ANYWAY.
KLIK
NUMBER SIX—SOMETHING GRABS YOUR LEG IN THE POOL.
IT'S SO DARK I CAN BARELY SEE.
KLIK
WE CAN'T GET TO THE POOL.
NUMBER SEVEN—YOU CAN'T SEE YOUR REFLECTION IN A MIRROR.
I CAN SEE US JUST FINE.
KLIK
VAMPIRES DON'T HAVE REFLECTIONS, DO THEY?
NUMBER EIGHT—THE NINOMIYA STATUE IN FRONT OF THE SCHOOL MOVES.
WE DON'T HAVE THAT STATUE!
BESIDES, THAT'S MORE THAN SEVEN MYSTERIES!
HA HA HA HA!
KLIK
YOU'RE KILLING ME!
HA HA HA HA!
I LOST COUNT!
I HAVEN'T BEEN TO SCHOOL IN ABOUT A MONTH.

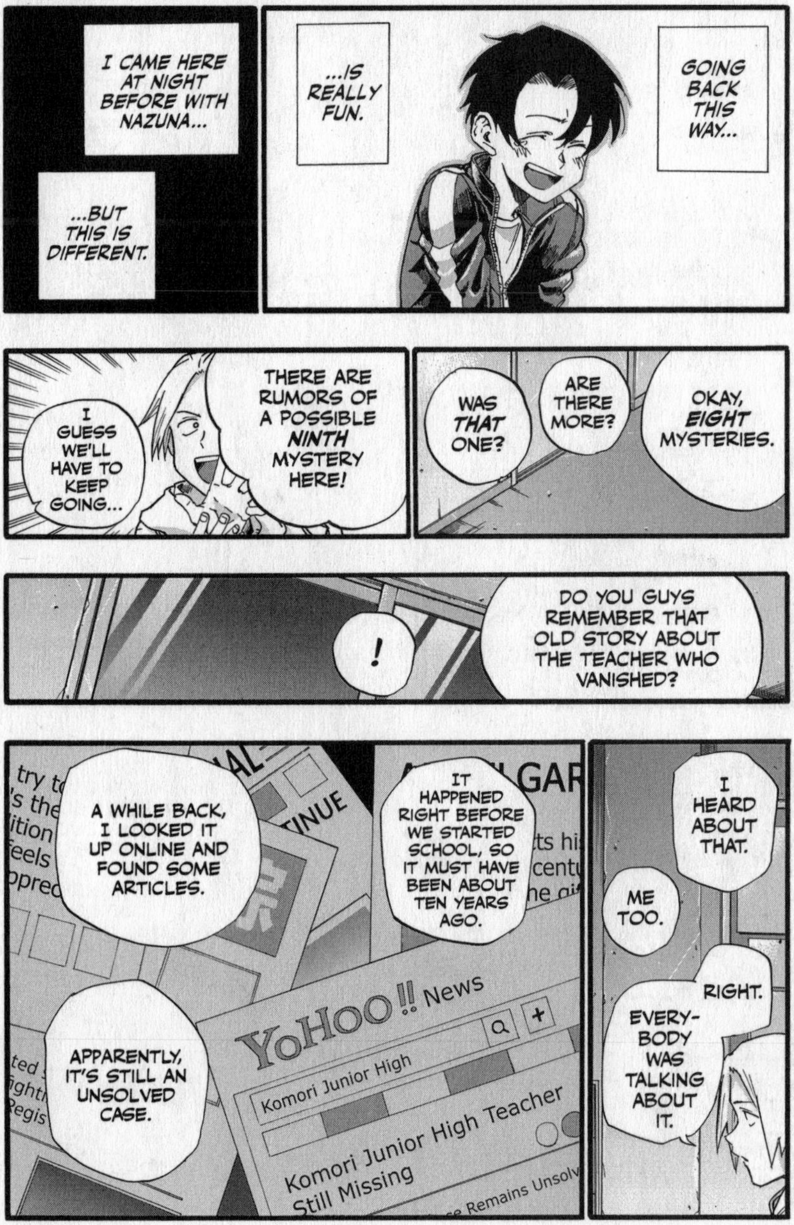
GOING BACK THIS WAY...
...IS REALLY FUN.
I CAME HERE AT NIGHT BEFORE WITH NAZUNA...
...BUT THIS IS DIFFERENT.
OKAY, EIGHT MYSTERIES.
ARE THERE MORE?
WAS THAT ONE?
THERE ARE RUMORS OF A POSSIBLE NINTH MYSTERY HERE!
I GUESS WE'LL HAVE TO KEEP GOING...
DO YOU GUYS REMEMBER THAT OLD STORY ABOUT THE TEACHER WHO VANISHED?
!
I HEARD ABOUT THAT.
ME TOO.
RIGHT.
EVERY-BODY WAS TALKING ABOUT IT.
IT HAPPENED RIGHT BEFORE WE STARTED SCHOOL, SO IT MUST HAVE BEEN ABOUT TEN YEARS AGO.
A WHILE BACK, I LOOKED IT UP ONLINE AND FOUND SOME ARTICLES.
YoHOO!! News
Komori Junior High
Komori Junior High Teacher Still Missing
APPARENTLY, IT'S STILL AN UNSOLVED CASE.

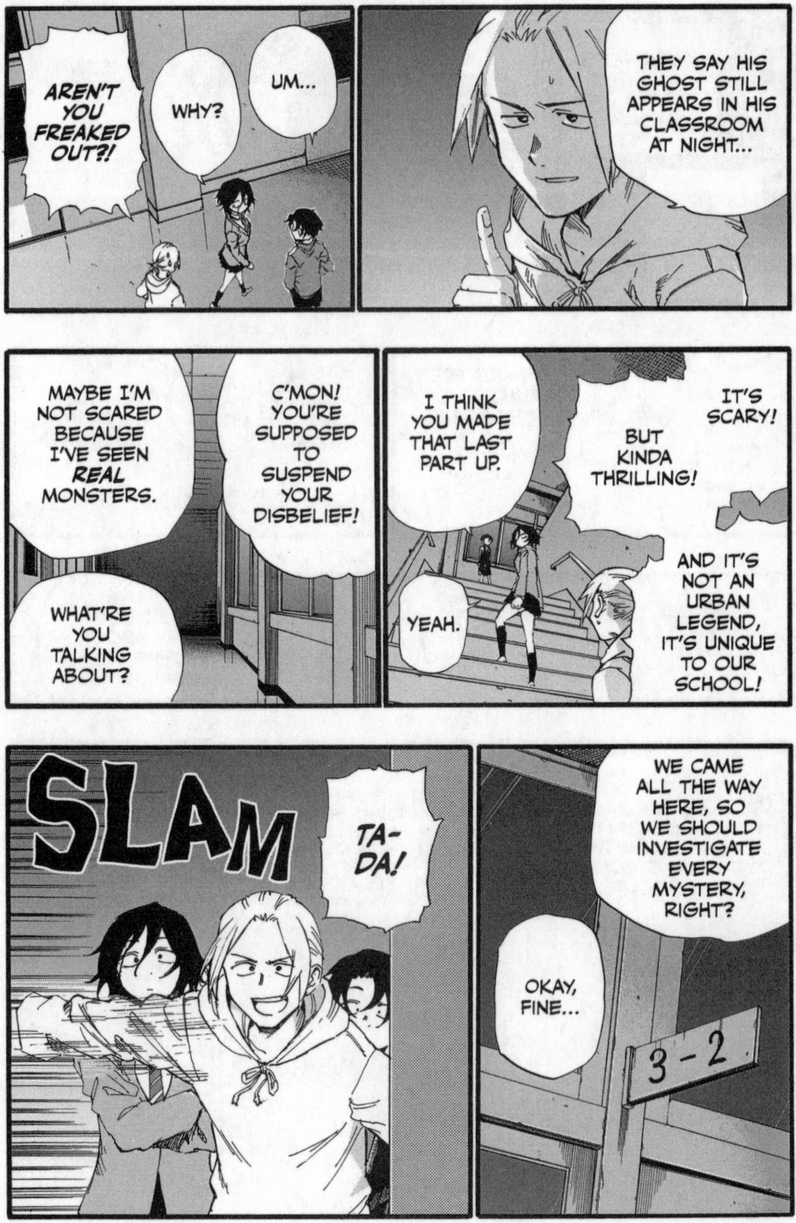
THEY SAY HIS GHOST STILL APPEARS IN HIS CLASSROOM AT NIGHT...
UM...
WHY?
AREN'T YOU FREAKED OUT?!
IT'S SCARY!
BUT KINDA THRILLING!
AND IT'S NOT AN URBAN LEGEND, IT'S UNIQUE TO OUR SCHOOL!
I THINK YOU MADE THAT LAST PART UP.
YEAH.
C'MON! YOU'RE SUPPOSED TO SUSPEND YOUR DISBELIEF!
MAYBE I'M NOT SCARED BECAUSE I'VE SEEN *REAL* MONSTERS.
WHAT'RE YOU TALKING ABOUT?
WE CAME ALL THE WAY HERE, SO WE SHOULD INVESTIGATE EVERY MYSTERY, RIGHT?
OKAY, FINE...
3-2
SLAM
TA-DA!

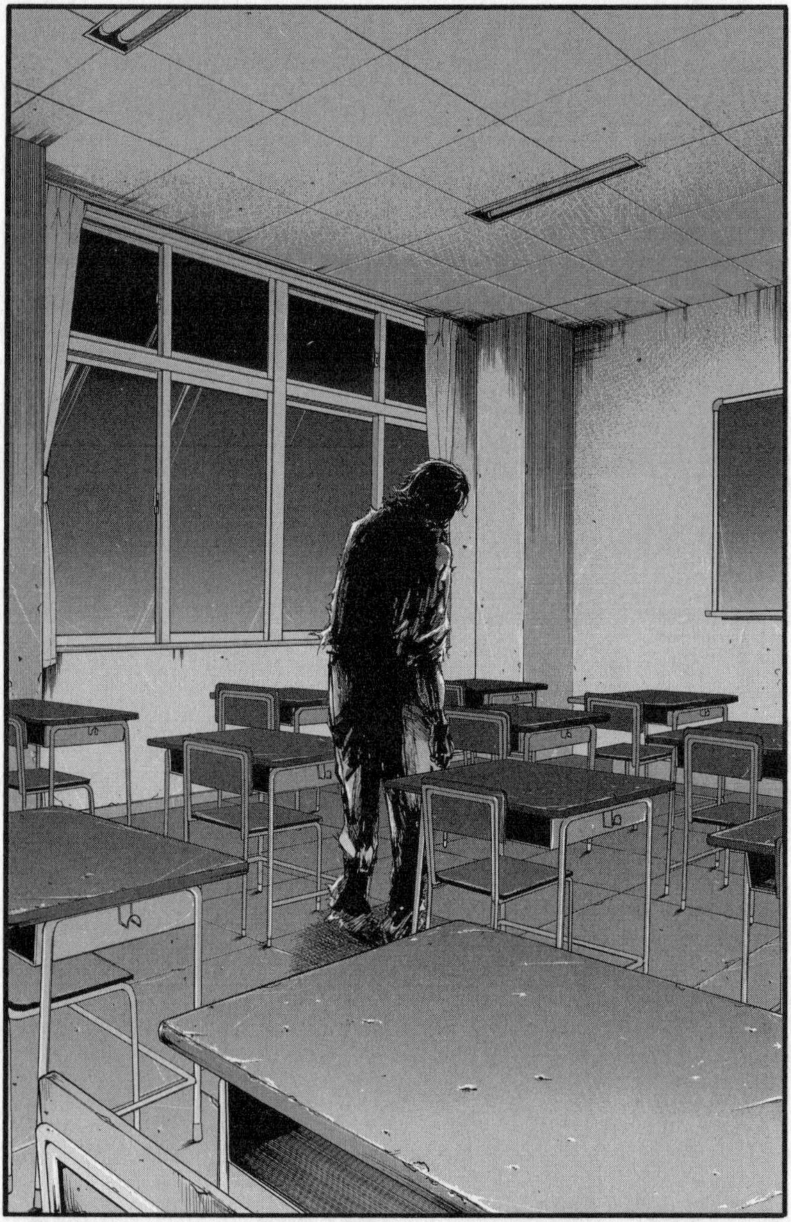

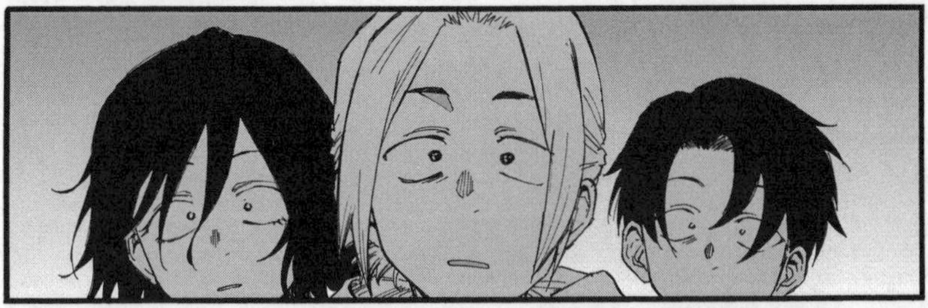

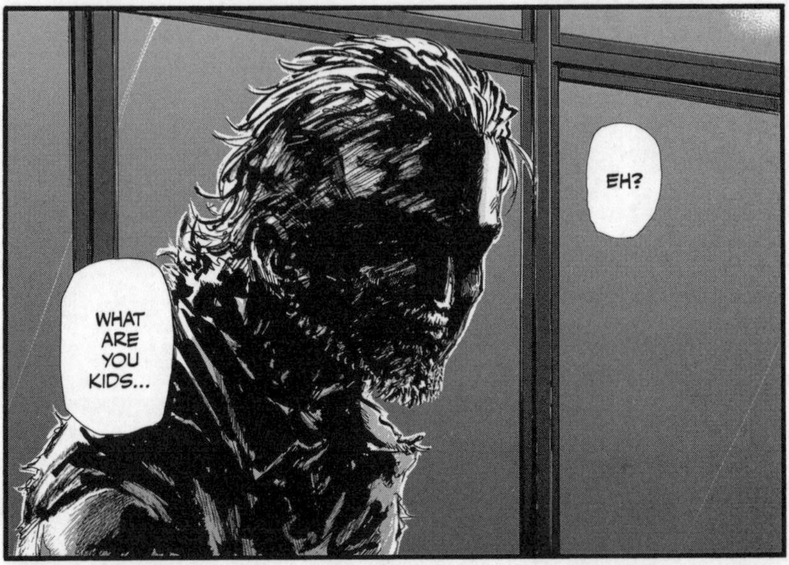
EH?
WHAT ARE YOU KIDS...

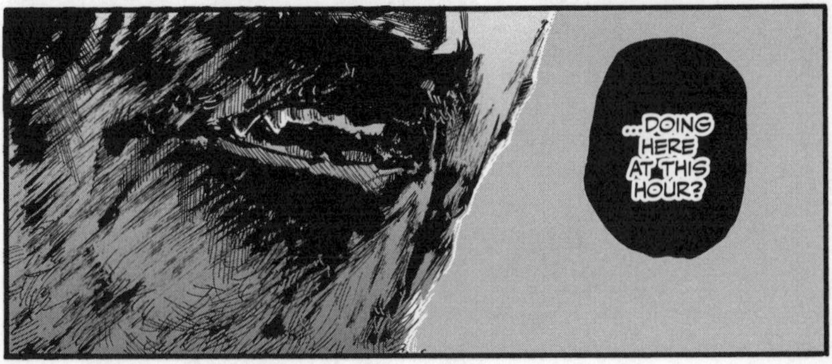
...DOING HERE AT THIS HOUR?

NIGHT 38: DO YOU KNOW WHAT A VAMPIRE IS?

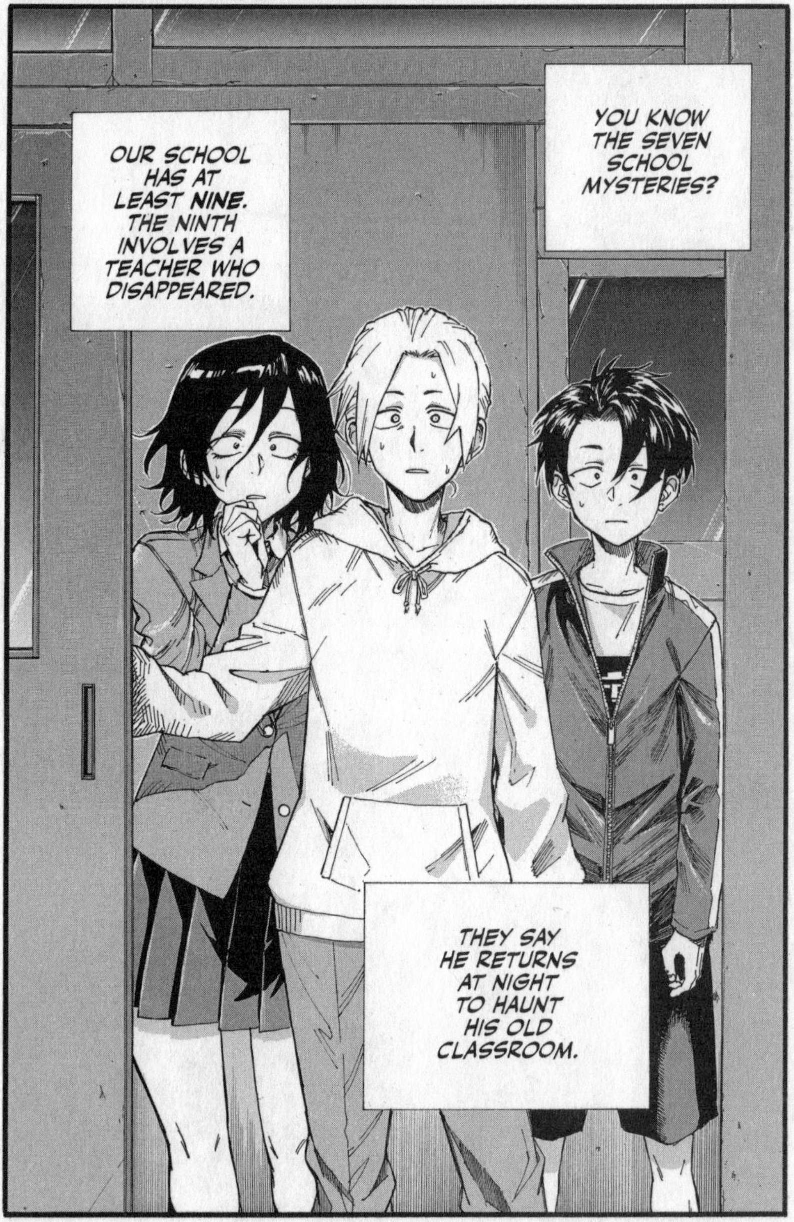
YOU KNOW THE SEVEN SCHOOL MYSTERIES?
OUR SCHOOL HAS AT LEAST NINE. THE NINTH INVOLVES A TEACHER WHO DISAPPEARED.
THEY SAY HE RETURNS AT NIGHT TO HAUNT HIS OLD CLASSROOM.

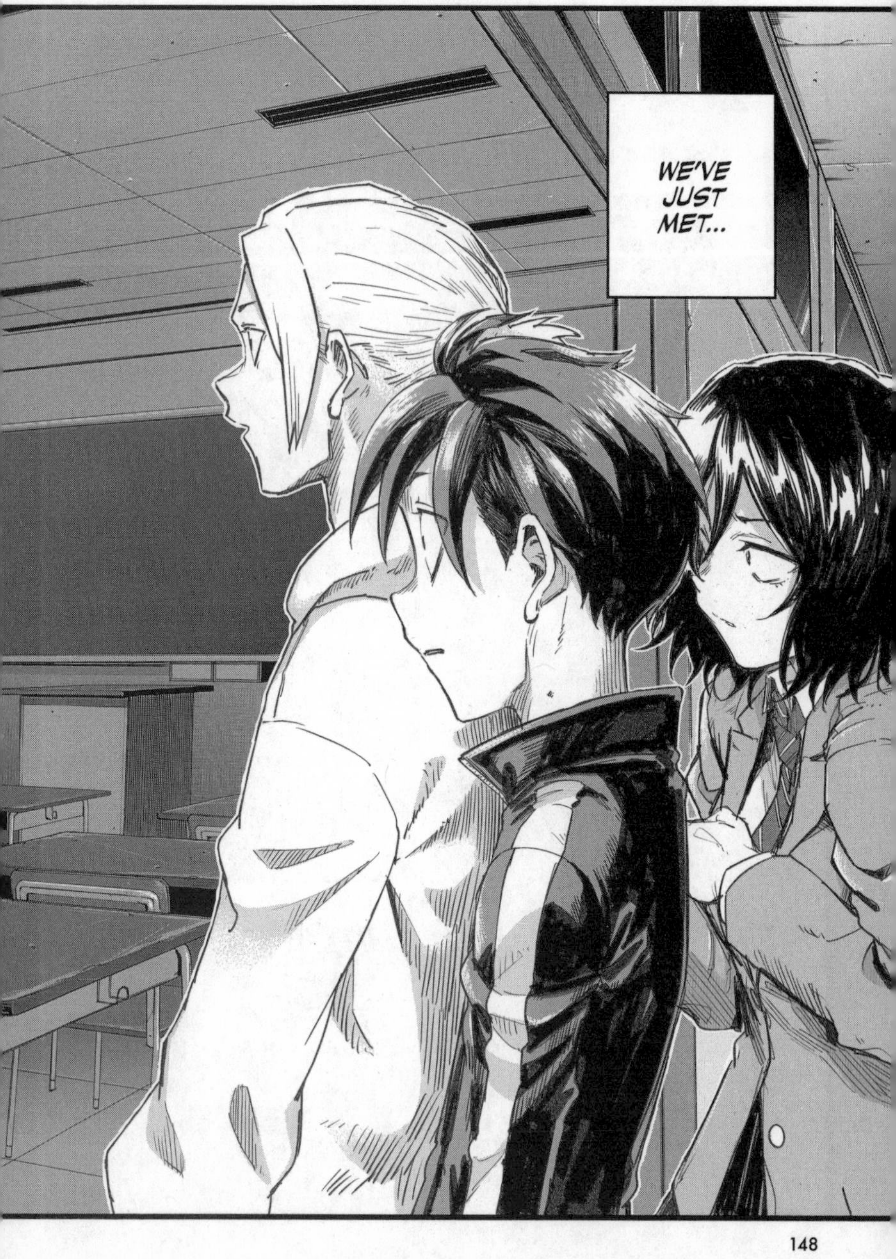
WE'VE JUST MET...

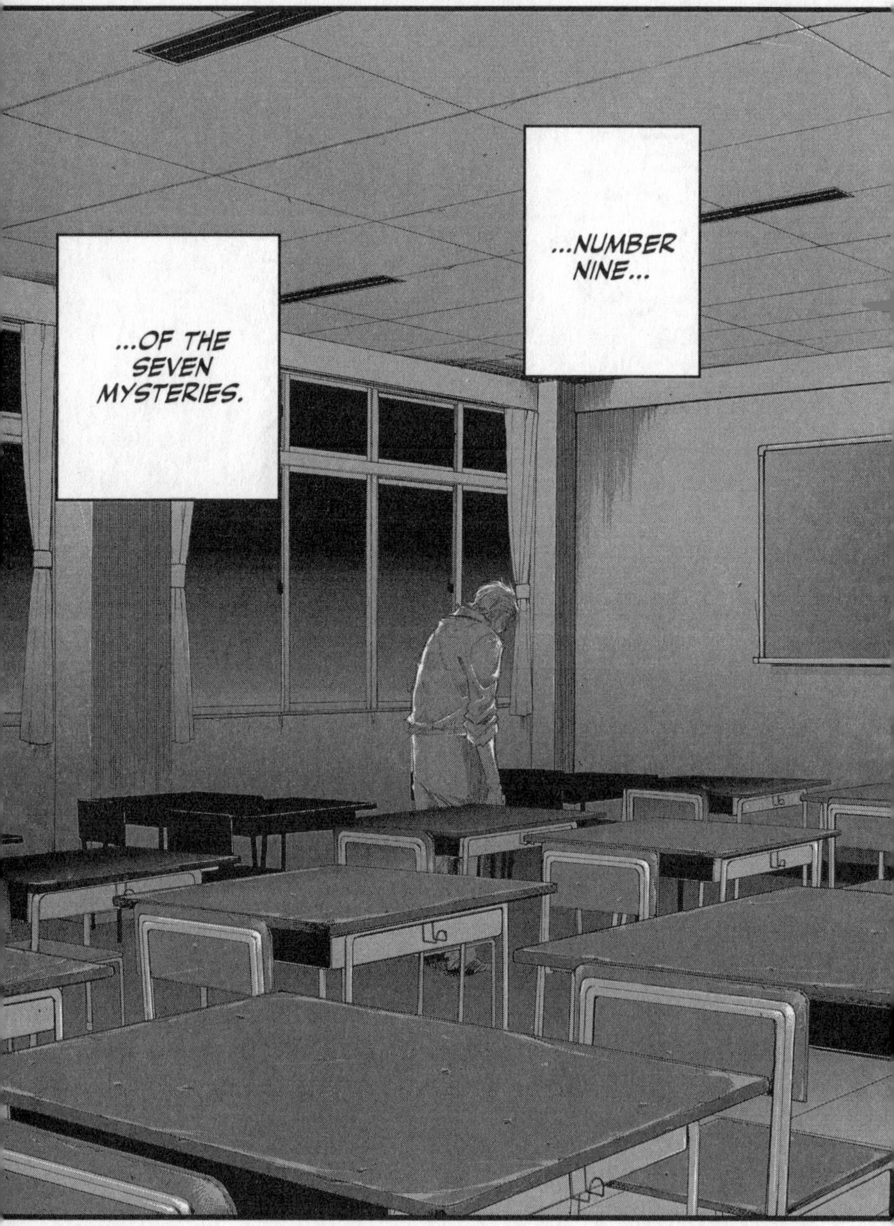
...NUMBER NINE...
...OF THE SEVEN MYSTERIES.

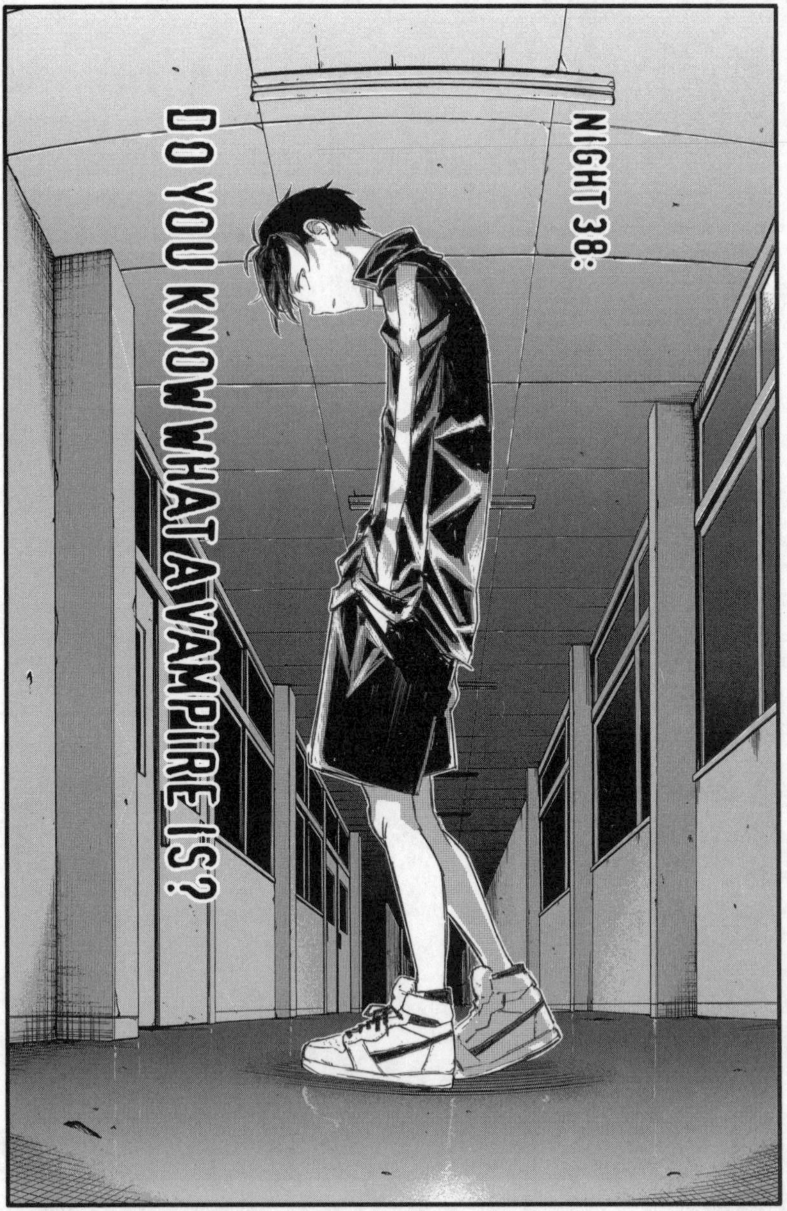
NIGHT 38:
DO YOU KNOW WHAT A VAMPIRE IS?

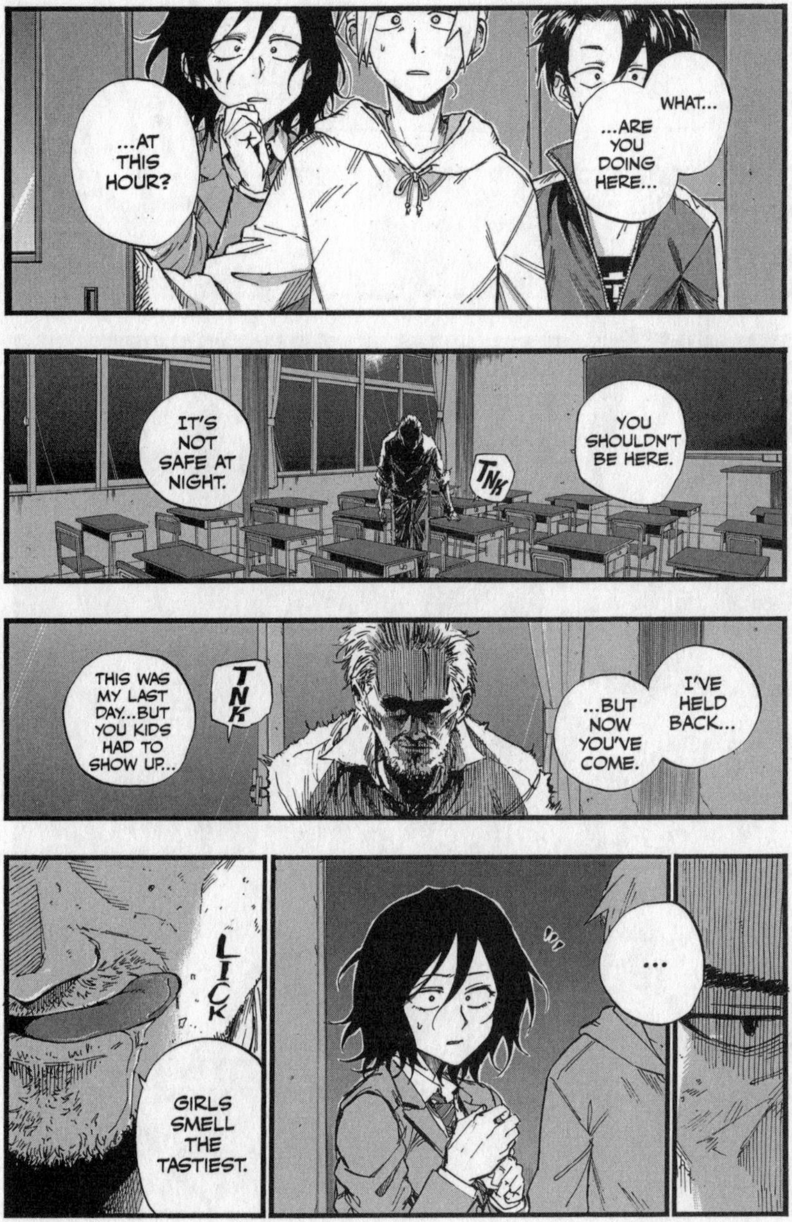
WHAT...
...ARE YOU DOING HERE...
...AT THIS HOUR?
YOU SHOULDN'T BE HERE.
TNK
IT'S NOT SAFE AT NIGHT.
I'VE HELD BACK...
...BUT NOW YOU'VE COME.
TNK
THIS WAS MY LAST DAY...BUT YOU KIDS HAD TO SHOW UP...
...
LICK
GIRLS SMELL THE TASTIEST.

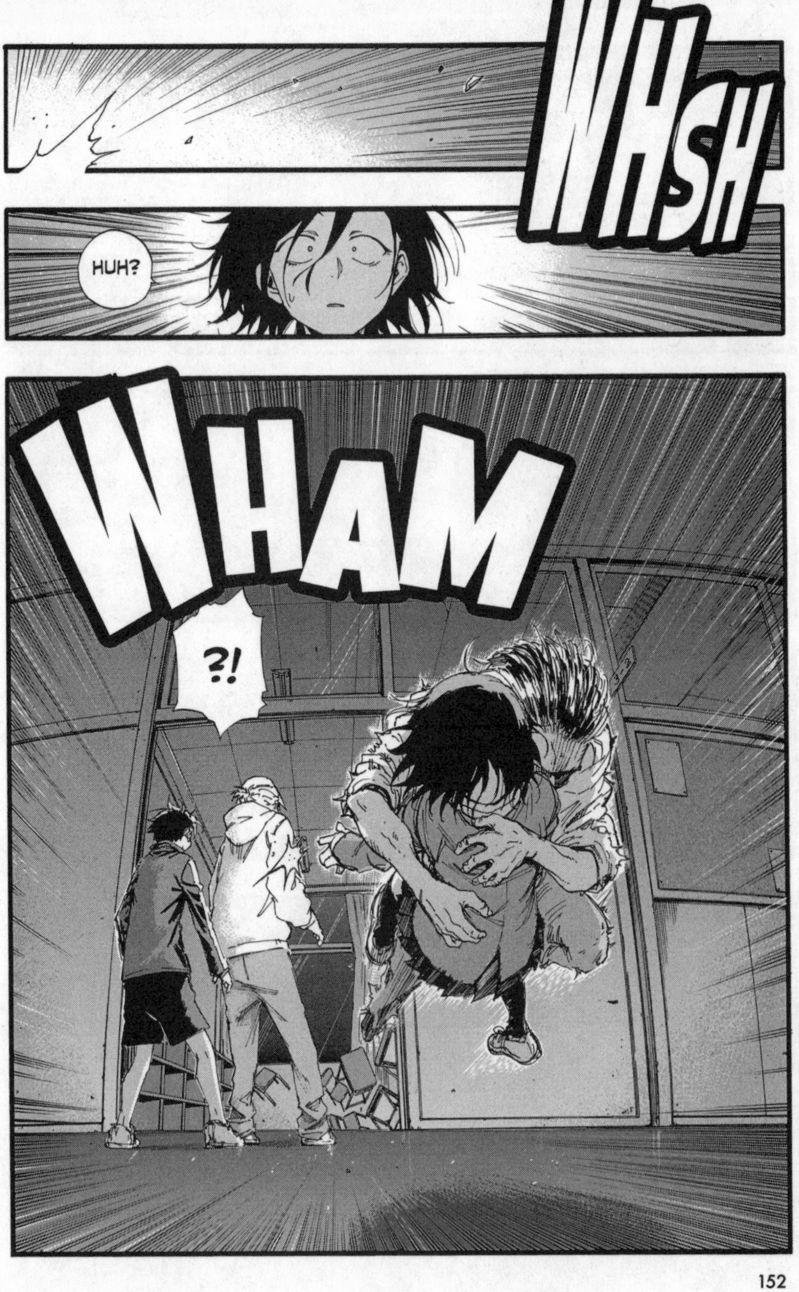
WHSH
HUH?
WHAM
?!

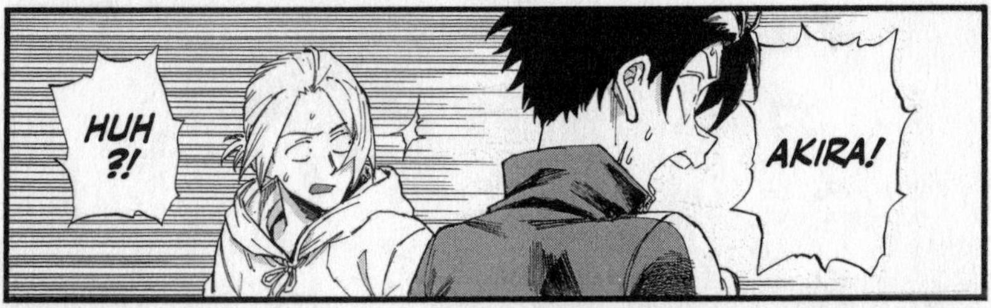
AKIRA!
HUH ?!
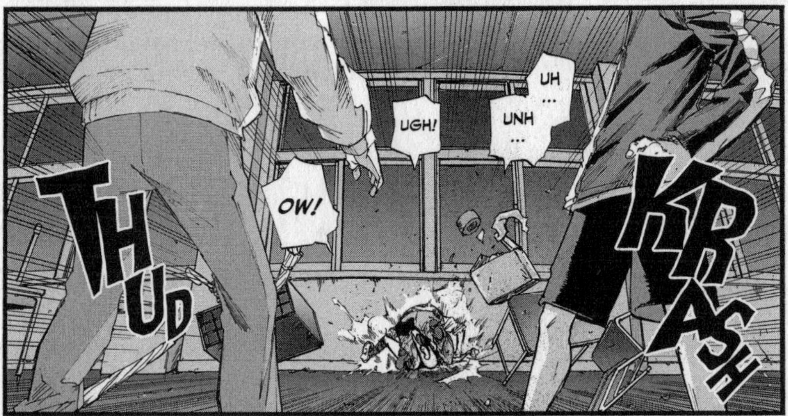
KRASH
UH ...
UNH ...
UGH!
OW!
THUD
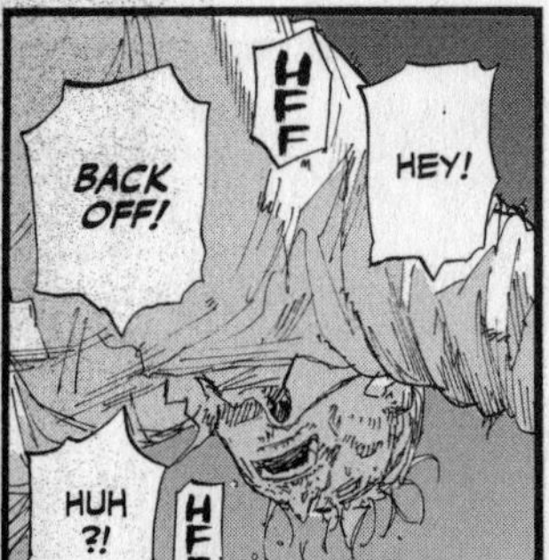
HEY!
HFF
BACK OFF!
HUH ?!
HFF
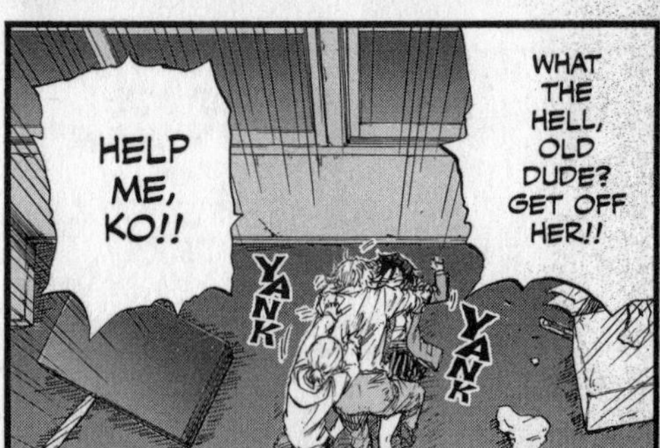
WHAT THE HELL, OLD DUDE? GET OFF HER!!
HELP ME, KO!!
YANK
YANK

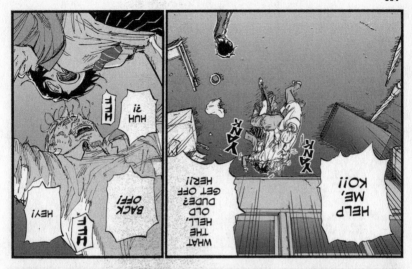

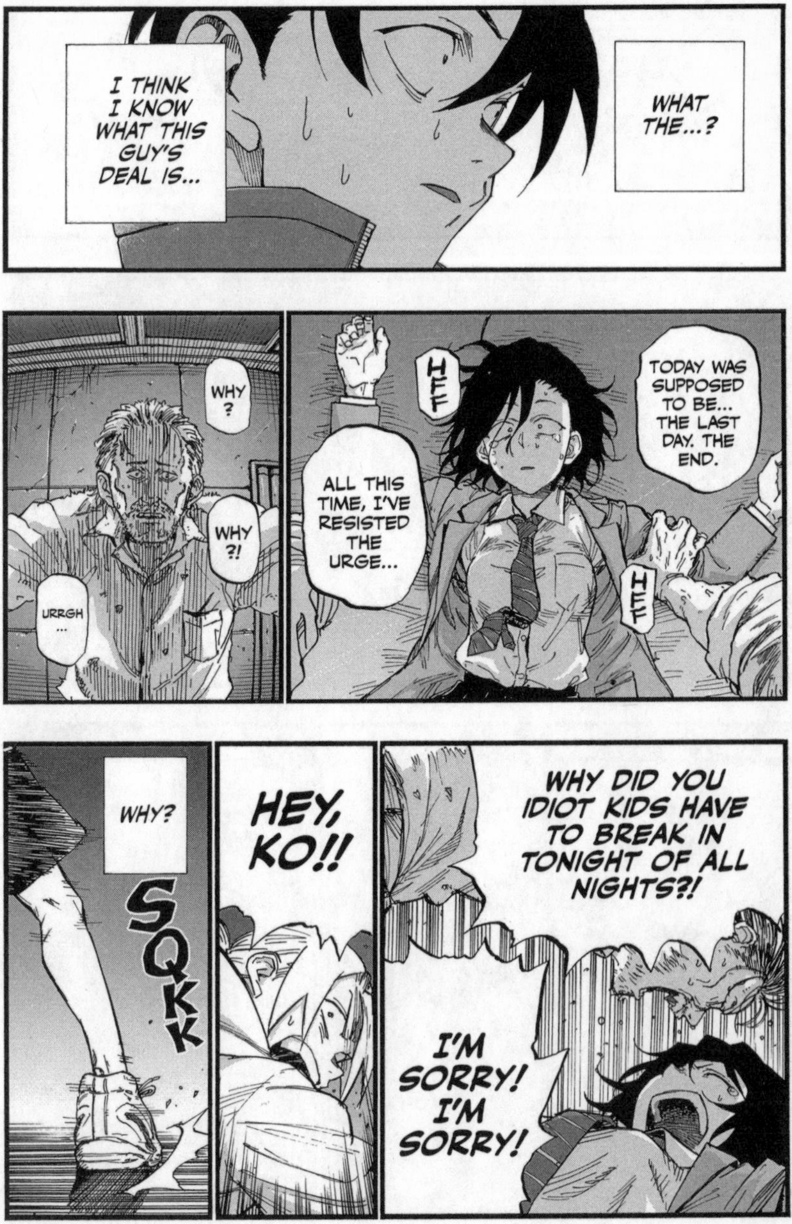
WHAT THE...?
I THINK I KNOW WHAT THIS GUY'S DEAL IS...
TODAY WAS SUPPOSED TO BE... THE LAST DAY. THE END.
HFF
ALL THIS TIME, I'VE RESISTED THE URGE...
HFF
WHY ?
WHY ?!
URRGH ...
WHY DID YOU IDIOT KIDS HAVE TO BREAK IN TONIGHT OF ALL NIGHTS?!
I'M SORRY! I'M SORRY!
HEY, KO!!
WHY?
SQKK

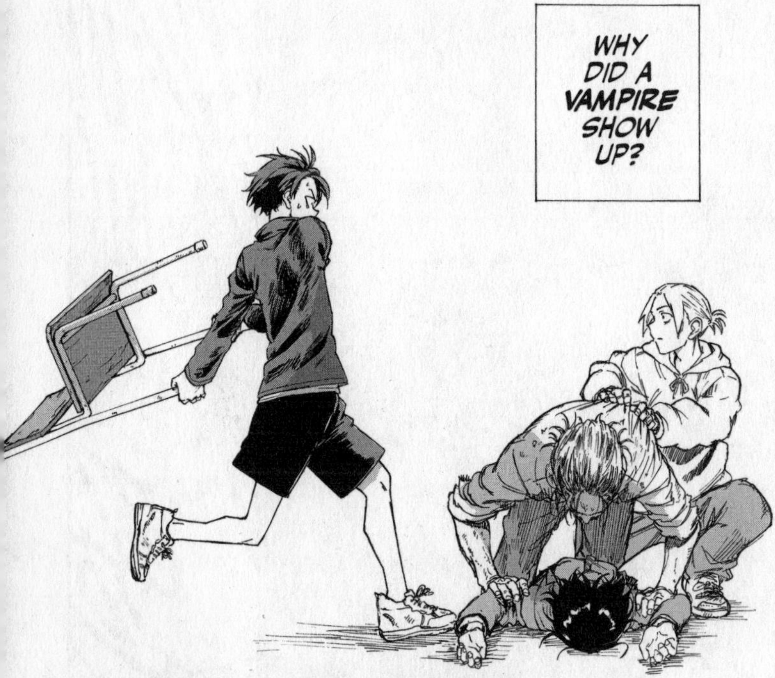
WHY DID A VAMPIRE SHOW UP?
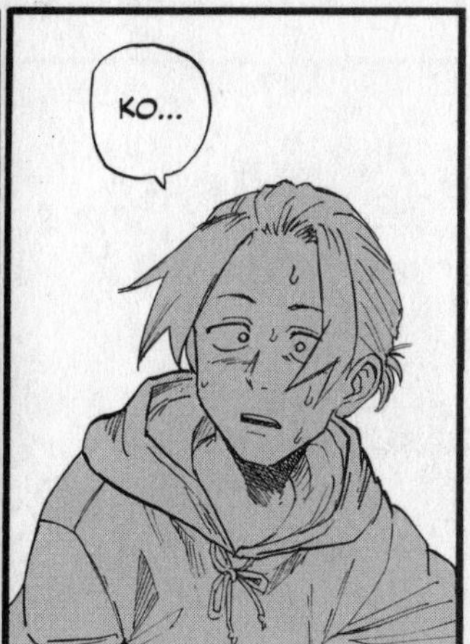
KO...
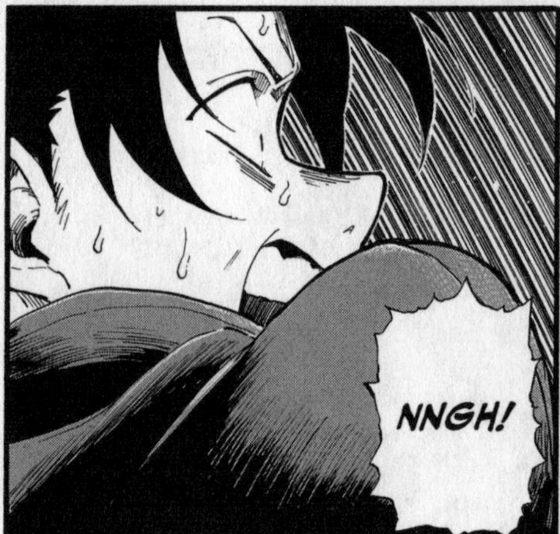
NNGH!

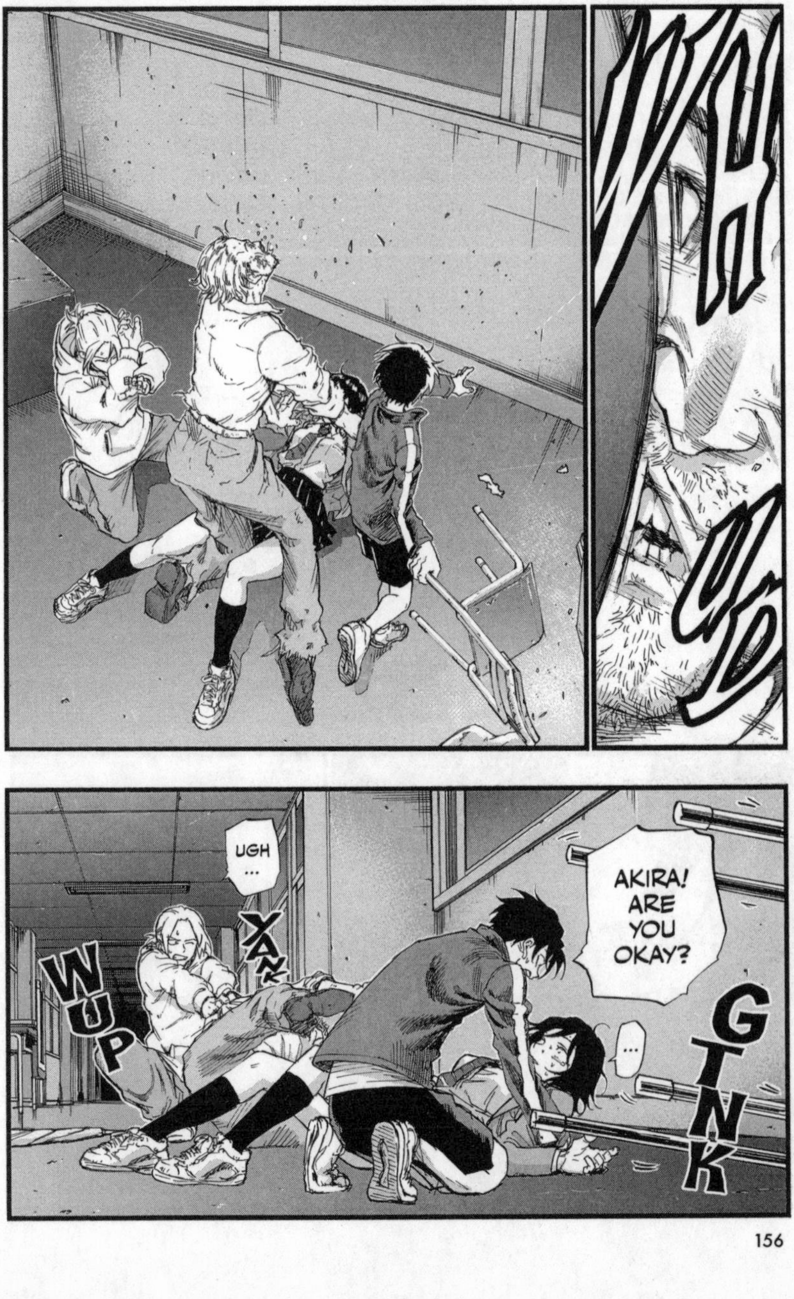
AKIRA! ARE YOU OKAY?
GINK
...
UGH ...
YANK
WUP

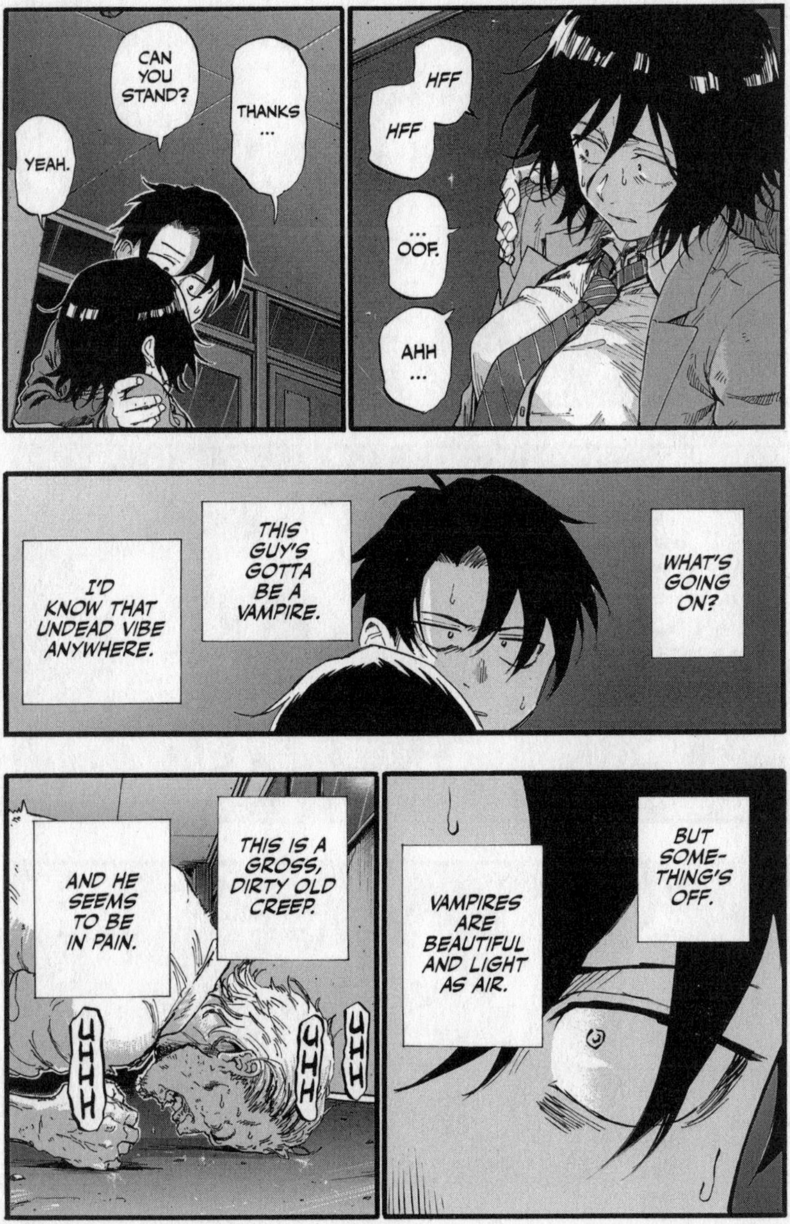
HFF
HFF
...OOF.
AHH...
CAN YOU STAND?
THANKS...
YEAH.
WHAT'S GOING ON?
THIS GUY'S GOTTA BE A VAMPIRE.
I'D KNOW THAT UNDEAD VIBE ANYWHERE.
BUT SOME-THING'S OFF.
VAMPIRES ARE BEAUTIFUL AND LIGHT AS AIR.
THIS IS A GROSS, DIRTY OLD CREEP.
AND HE SEEMS TO BE IN PAIN.
UHH
UHH
UHHH

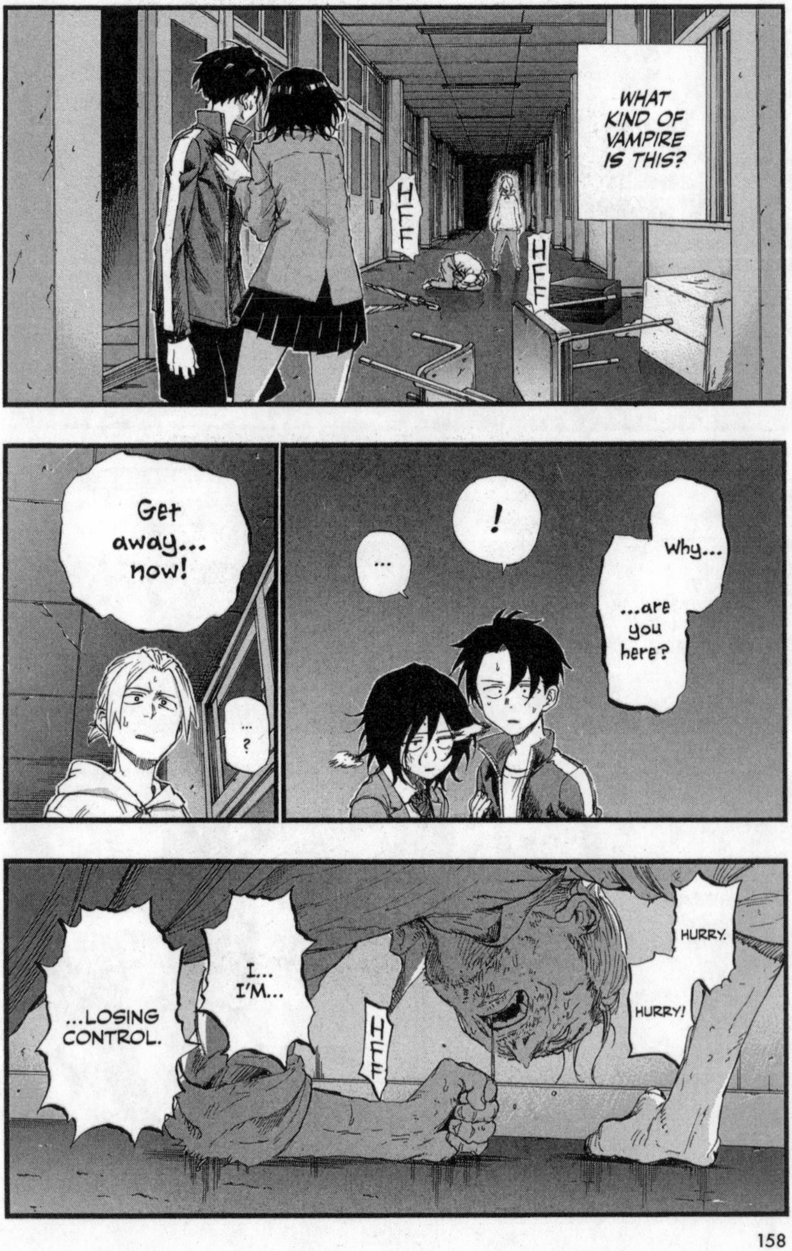
WHAT KIND OF VAMPIRE IS THIS?
HFF
HFF
Why...
...are you here?
!
...
Get away... now!
...?
HURRY.
HURRY!
HFF
I... I'M...
...LOSING CONTROL.

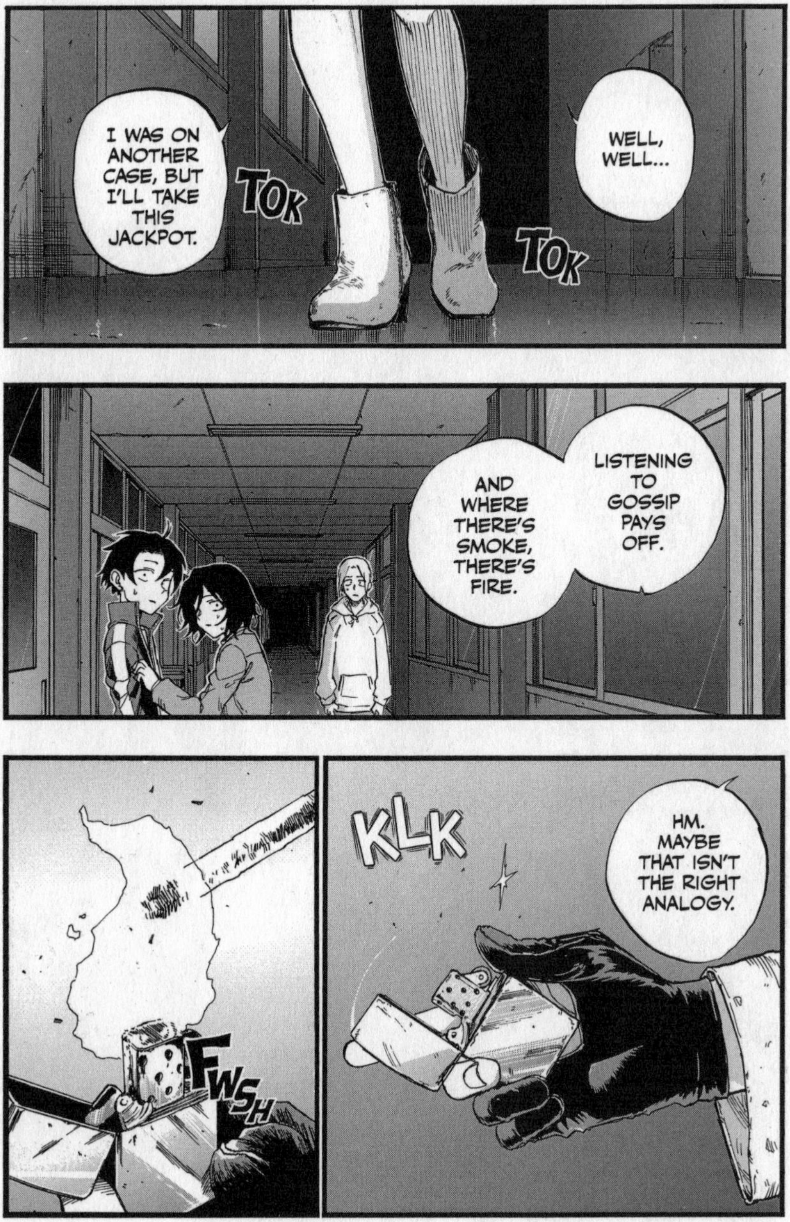
WELL, WELL...
TOK
TOK
I WAS ON ANOTHER CASE, BUT I'LL TAKE THIS JACKPOT.
LISTENING TO GOSSIP PAYS OFF.
AND WHERE THERE'S SMOKE, THERE'S FIRE.
HM. MAYBE THAT ISN'T THE RIGHT ANALOGY.
KLK
FWSH

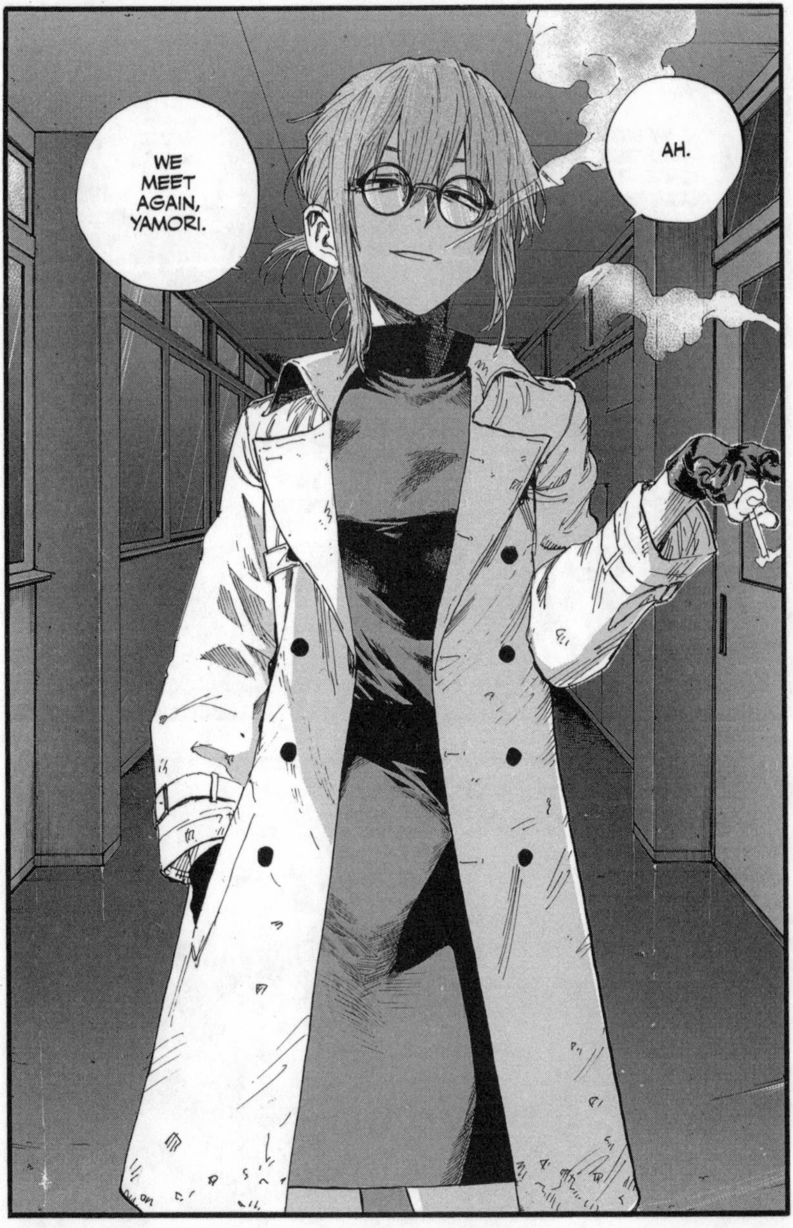
AH.
WE MEET AGAIN, YAMORI.

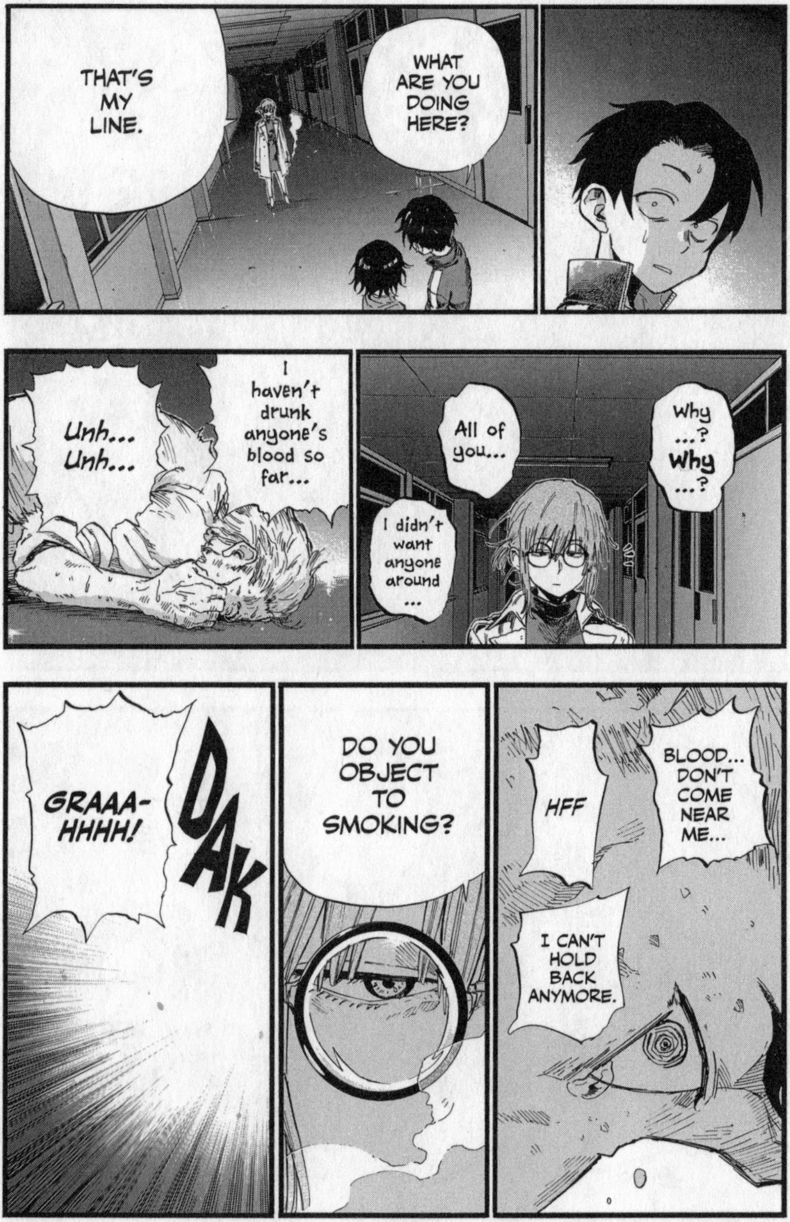
WHAT ARE YOU DOING HERE?
THAT'S MY LINE.
Why ...? Why ...?
All of you...
I didn't want anyone around ...
I haven't drunk anyone's blood so far...
Unh... Unh...
BLOOD... DON'T COME NEAR ME...
HFF
I CAN'T HOLD BACK ANYMORE.
DO YOU OBJECT TO SMOKING?
GRAAA-HHHH!
DAK

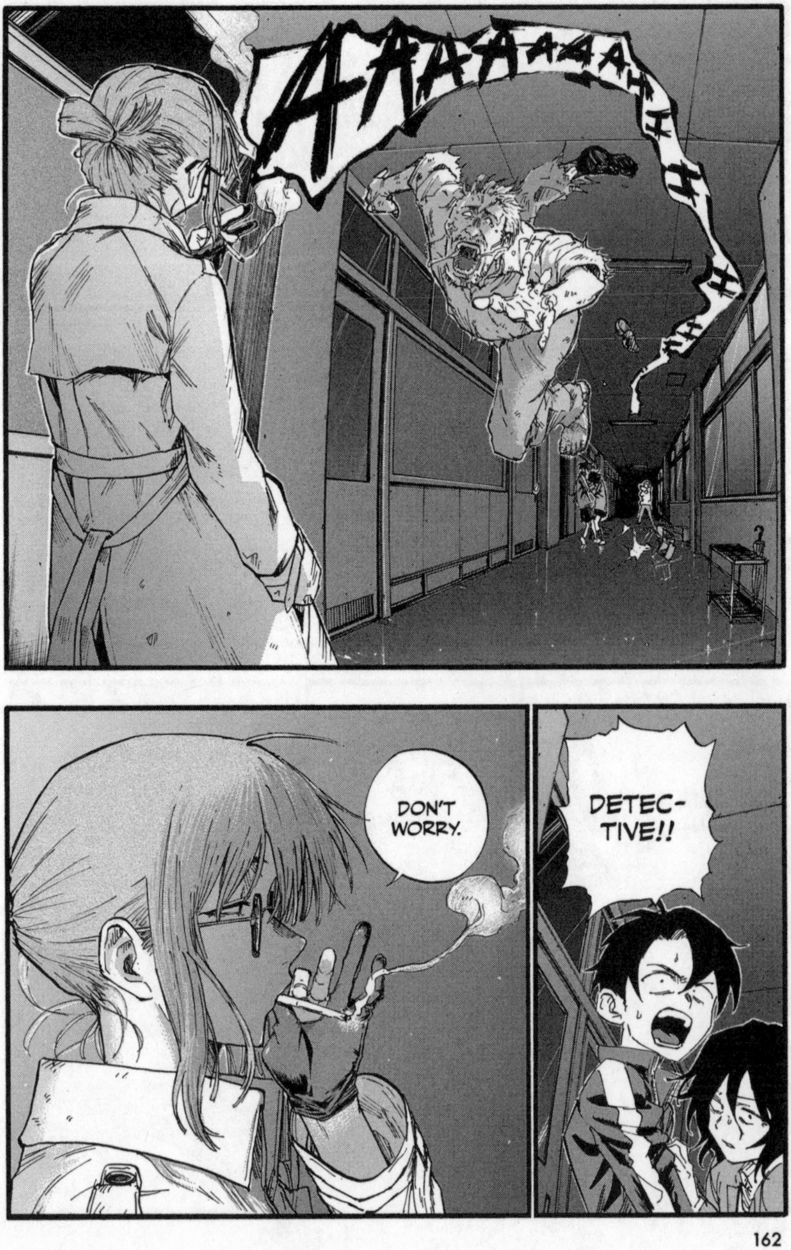
AAAAaaaAHHHHH
DETEC-
TIVE!!
DON'T
WORRY.

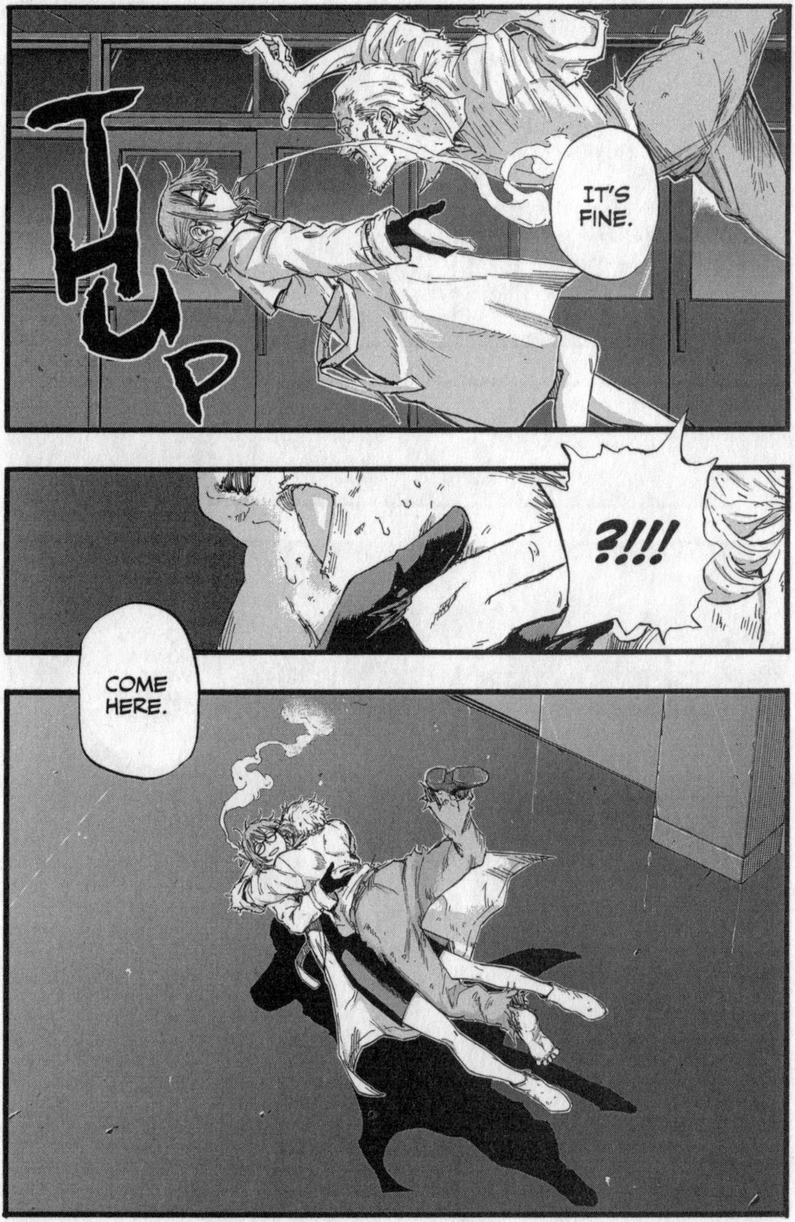
IT'S FINE.
THUP
?!!!
COME HERE.

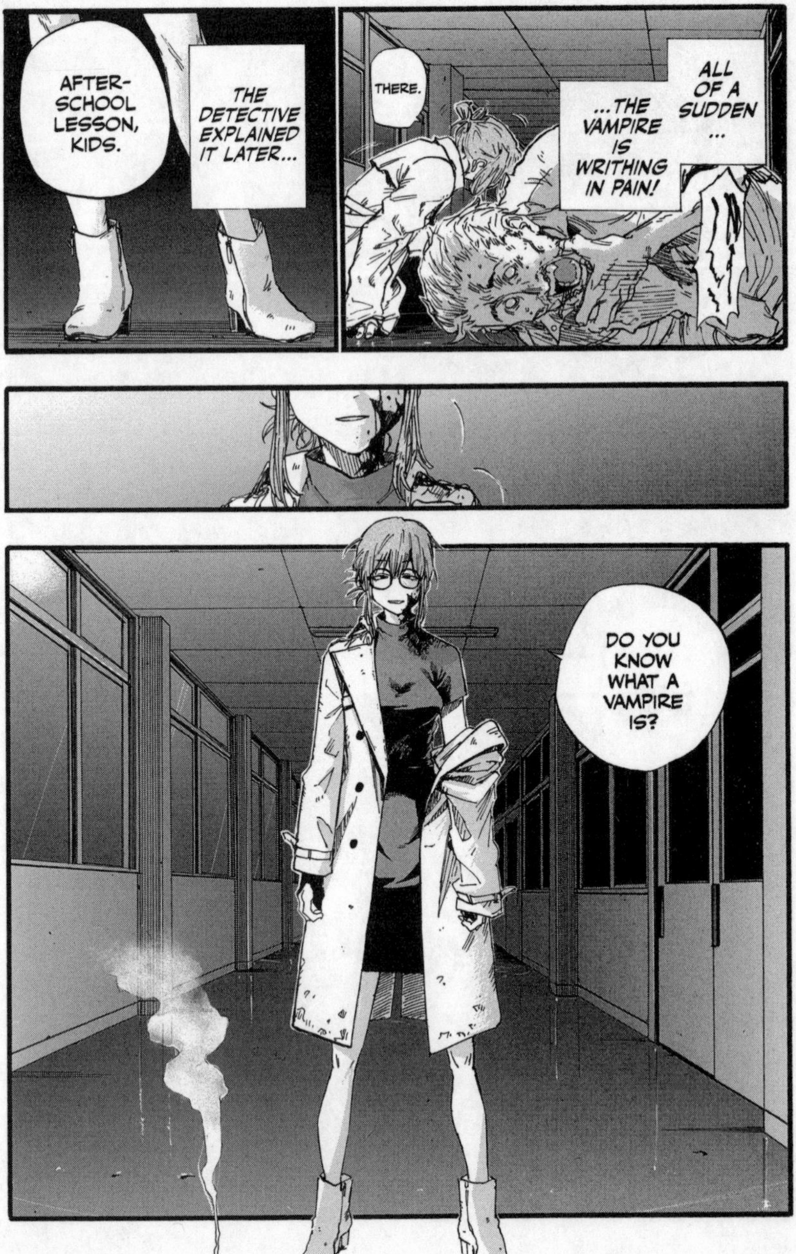
ALL OF A SUDDEN ...
...THE VAMPIRE IS WRITHING IN PAIN!
THERE.
THE DETECTIVE EXPLAINED IT LATER...
AFTER-SCHOOL LESSON, KIDS.
DO YOU KNOW WHAT A VAMPIRE IS?

NIGHT 39: YOU CAN DIE HUMAN

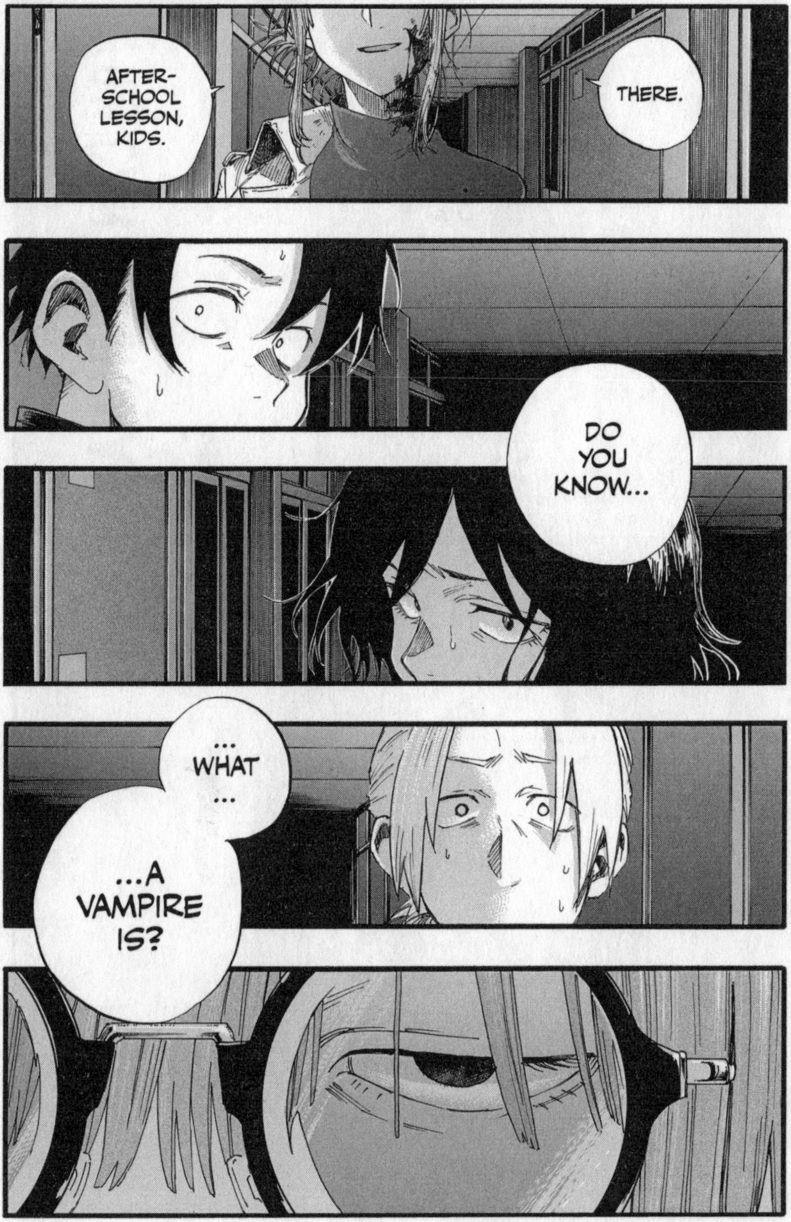
THERE.
AFTER-SCHOOL LESSON, KIDS.
DO YOU KNOW...
...WHAT...
...A VAMPIRE IS?

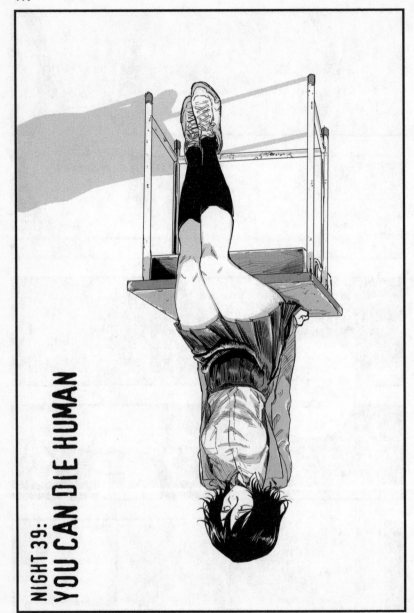

NIGHT 39:
YOU CAN DIE HUMAN

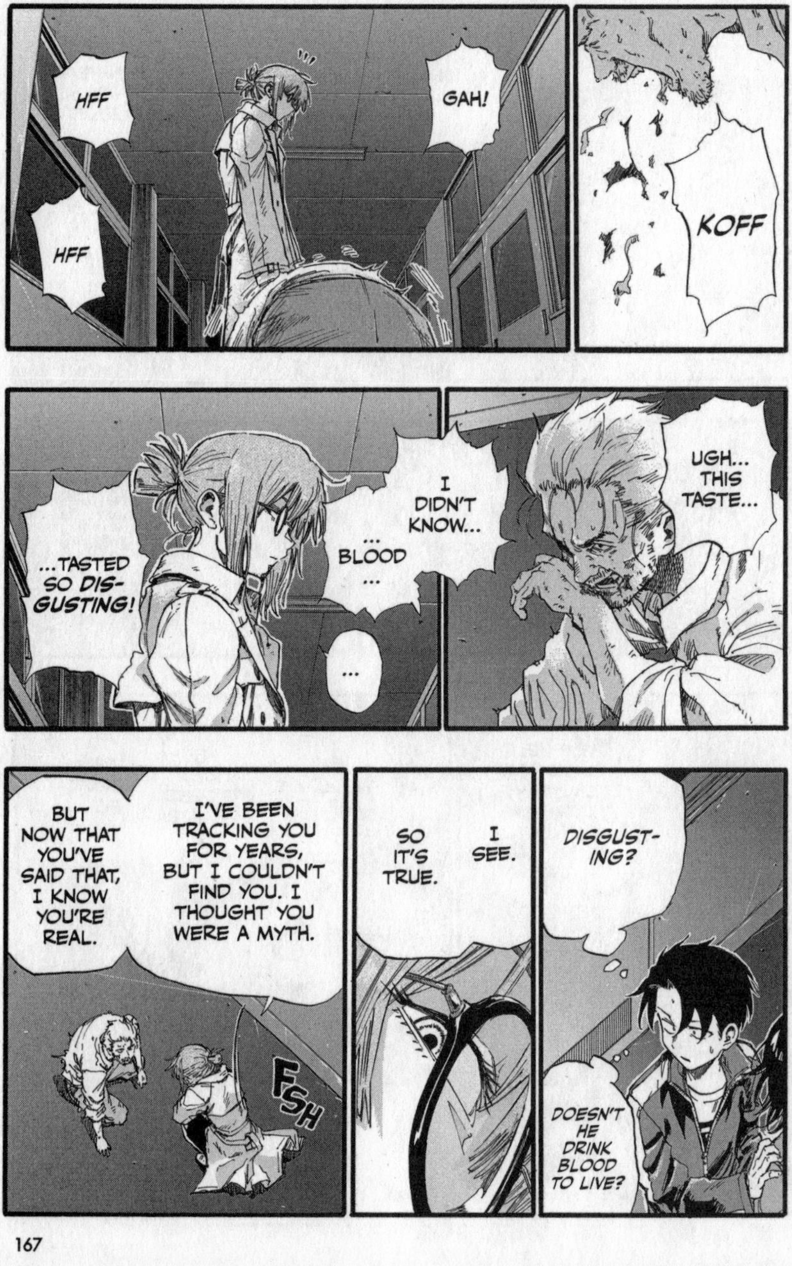
KOFF
GAH!
HFF
HFF
UGH... THIS TASTE...
I DIDN'T KNOW...
... BLOOD ...
...TASTED SO DIS-GUSTING!
...
DISGUST-ING?
DOESN'T HE DRINK BLOOD TO LIVE?
I SEE.
SO IT'S TRUE.
BUT NOW THAT YOU'VE SAID THAT, I KNOW YOU'RE REAL.
I'VE BEEN TRACKING YOU FOR YEARS, BUT I COULDN'T FIND YOU. I THOUGHT YOU WERE A MYTH.
FSH

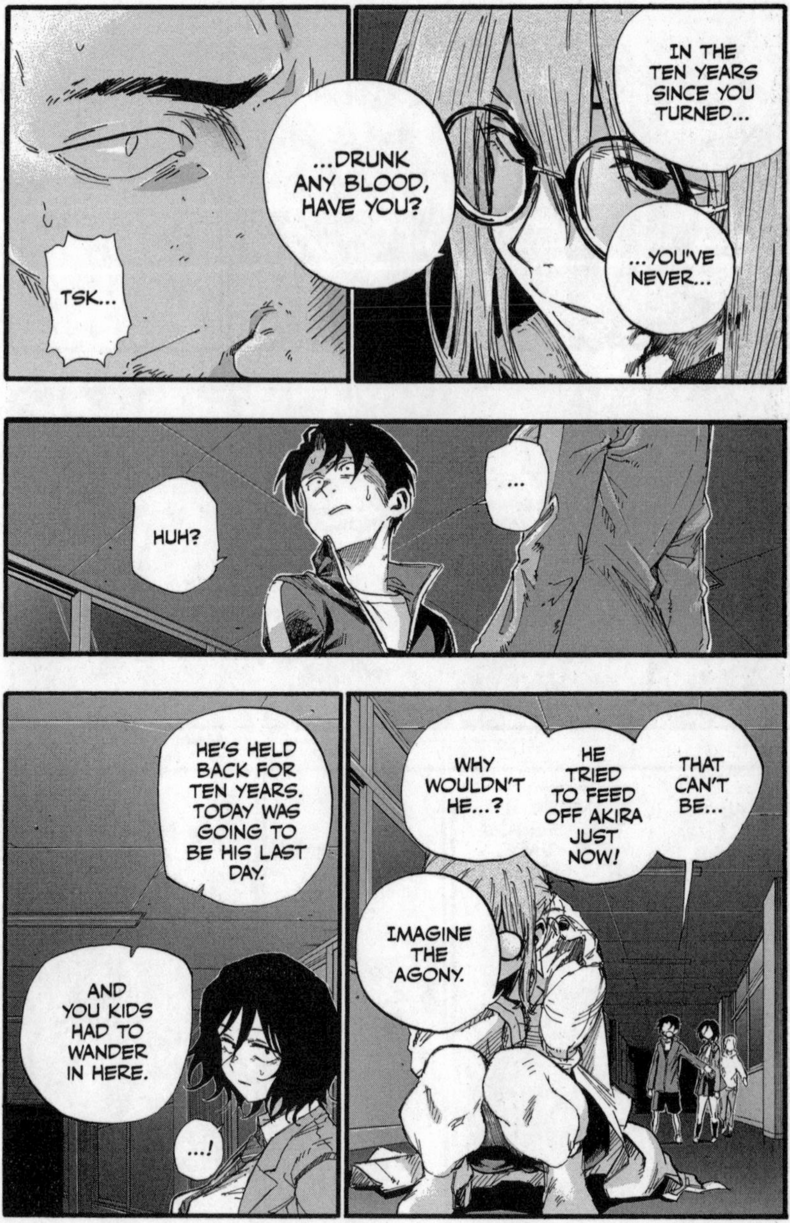
IN THE TEN YEARS SINCE YOU TURNED...
...YOU'VE NEVER...
...DRUNK ANY BLOOD, HAVE YOU?
TSK...
...
HUH?
THAT CAN'T BE...
HE TRIED TO FEED OFF AKIRA JUST NOW!
WHY WOULDN'T HE...?
IMAGINE THE AGONY.
HE'S HELD BACK FOR TEN YEARS. TODAY WAS GOING TO BE HIS LAST DAY.
AND YOU KIDS HAD TO WANDER IN HERE.
...!

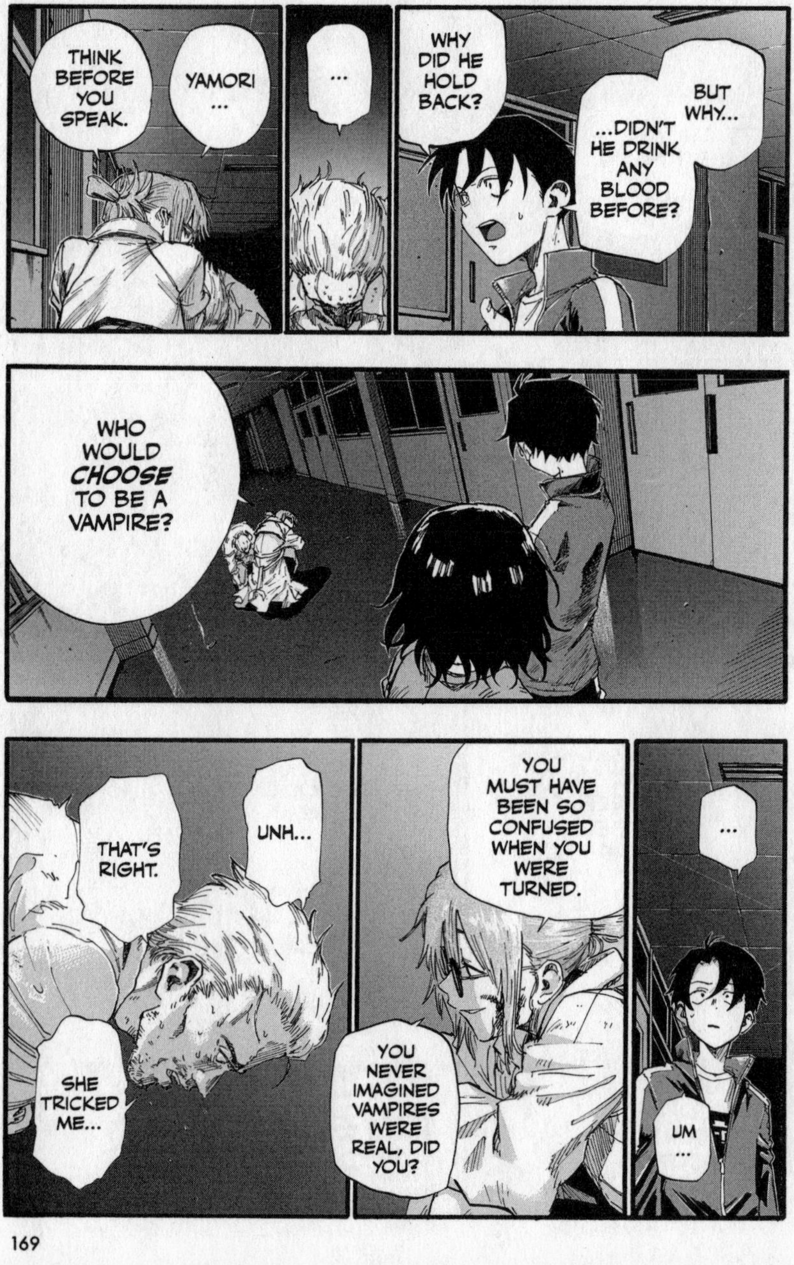
BUT WHY...
...DIDN'T HE DRINK ANY BLOOD BEFORE?
WHY DID HE HOLD BACK?
...
YAMORI ...
THINK BEFORE YOU SPEAK.
WHO WOULD ***CHOOSE*** TO BE A VAMPIRE?
...
UM ...
YOU MUST HAVE BEEN SO CONFUSED WHEN YOU WERE TURNED.
YOU NEVER IMAGINED VAMPIRES WERE REAL, DID YOU?
UNH...
THAT'S RIGHT.
SHE TRICKED ME...

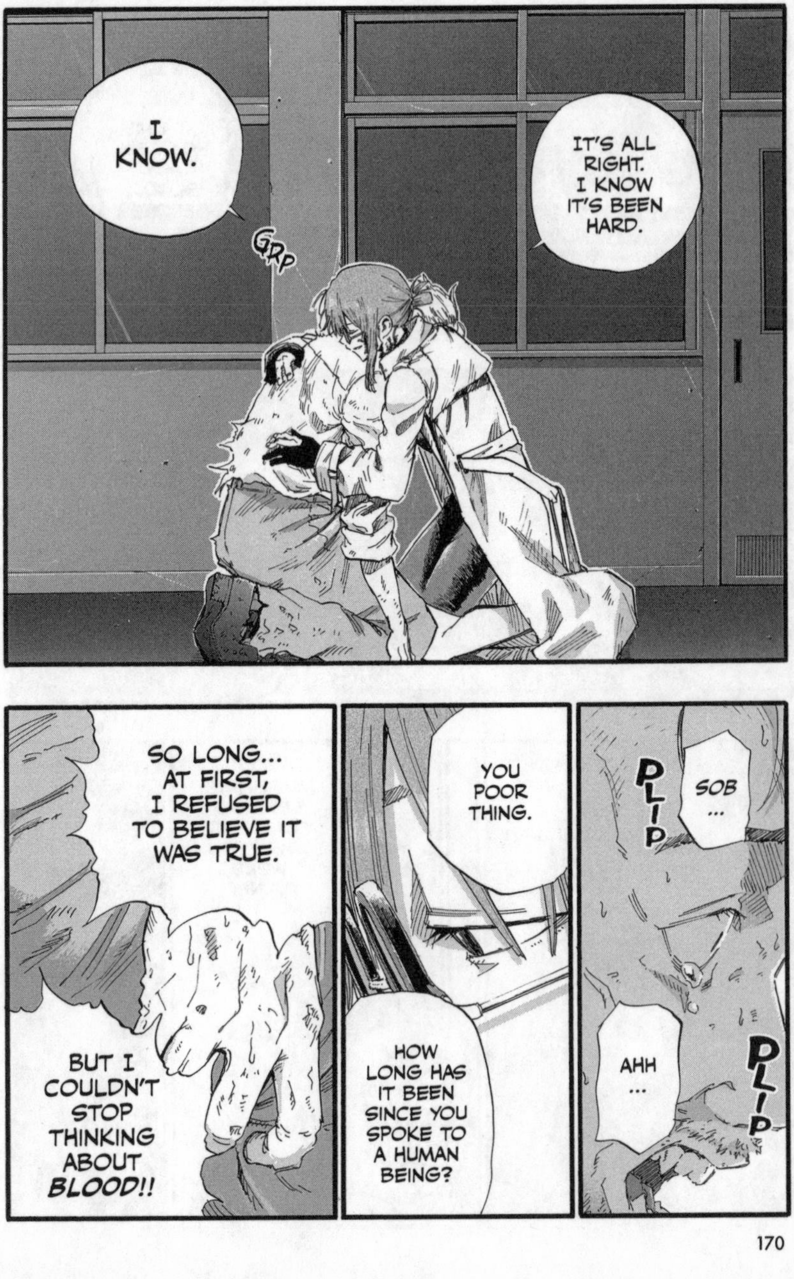
IT'S ALL RIGHT. I KNOW IT'S BEEN HARD.
GRP
I KNOW.
SOB ...
PLIP
AHH ...
PLIP
YOU POOR THING.
HOW LONG HAS IT BEEN SINCE YOU SPOKE TO A HUMAN BEING?
SO LONG... AT FIRST, I REFUSED TO BELIEVE IT WAS TRUE.
BUT I COULDN'T STOP THINKING ABOUT *BLOOD*!!

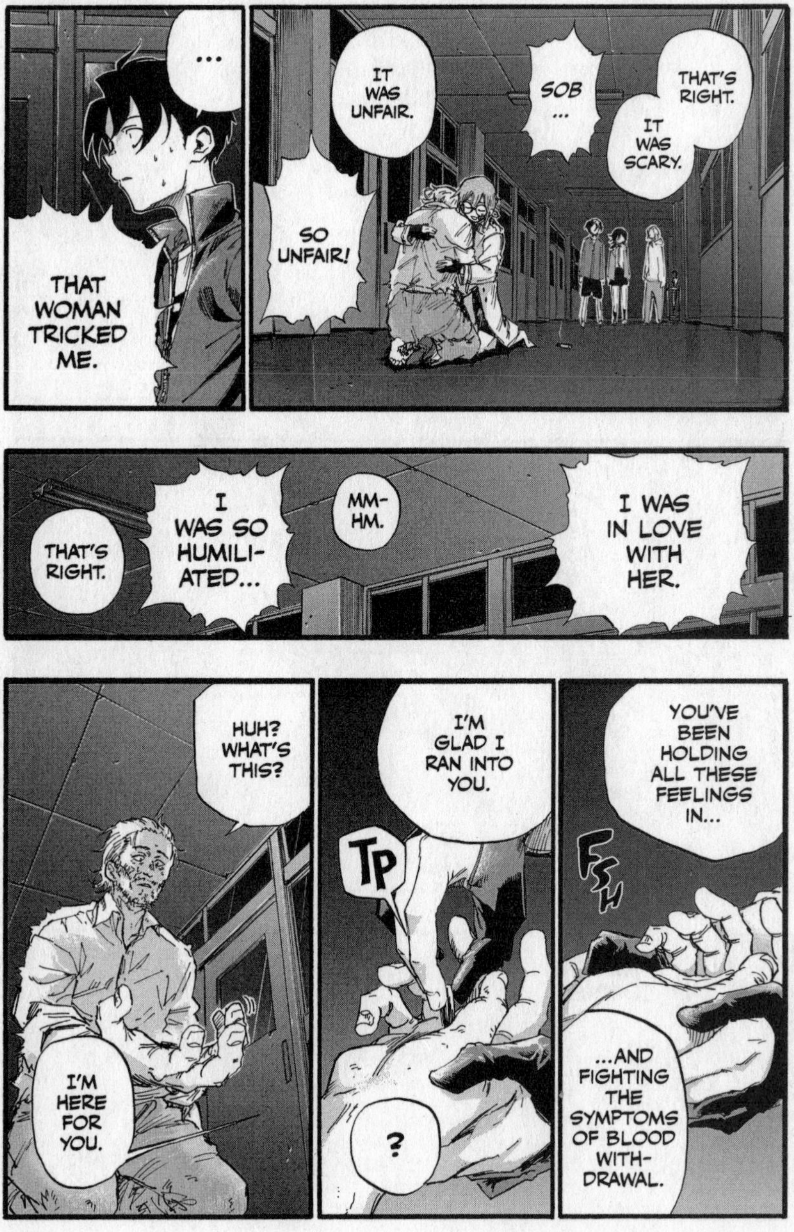
THAT'S RIGHT.
IT WAS SCARY.
SOB ...
IT WAS UNFAIR.
SO UNFAIR!
...
THAT WOMAN TRICKED ME.
I WAS IN LOVE WITH HER.
MM-HM.
I WAS SO HUMILI-ATED...
THAT'S RIGHT.
YOU'VE BEEN HOLDING ALL THESE FEELINGS IN...
FSH
...AND FIGHTING THE SYMPTOMS OF BLOOD WITH-DRAWAL.
I'M GLAD I RAN INTO YOU.
TP
?
HUH? WHAT'S THIS?
I'M HERE FOR YOU.

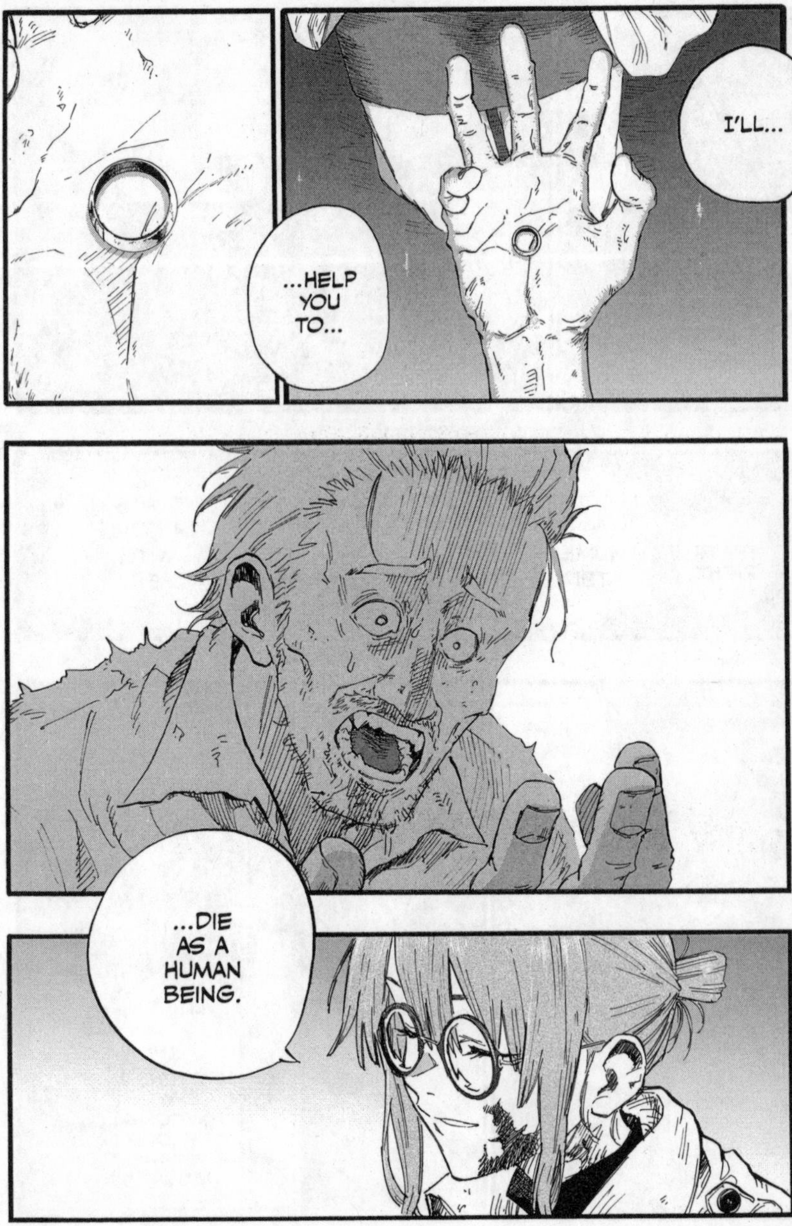
I'LL...
...HELP YOU TO...
...DIE AS A HUMAN BEING.

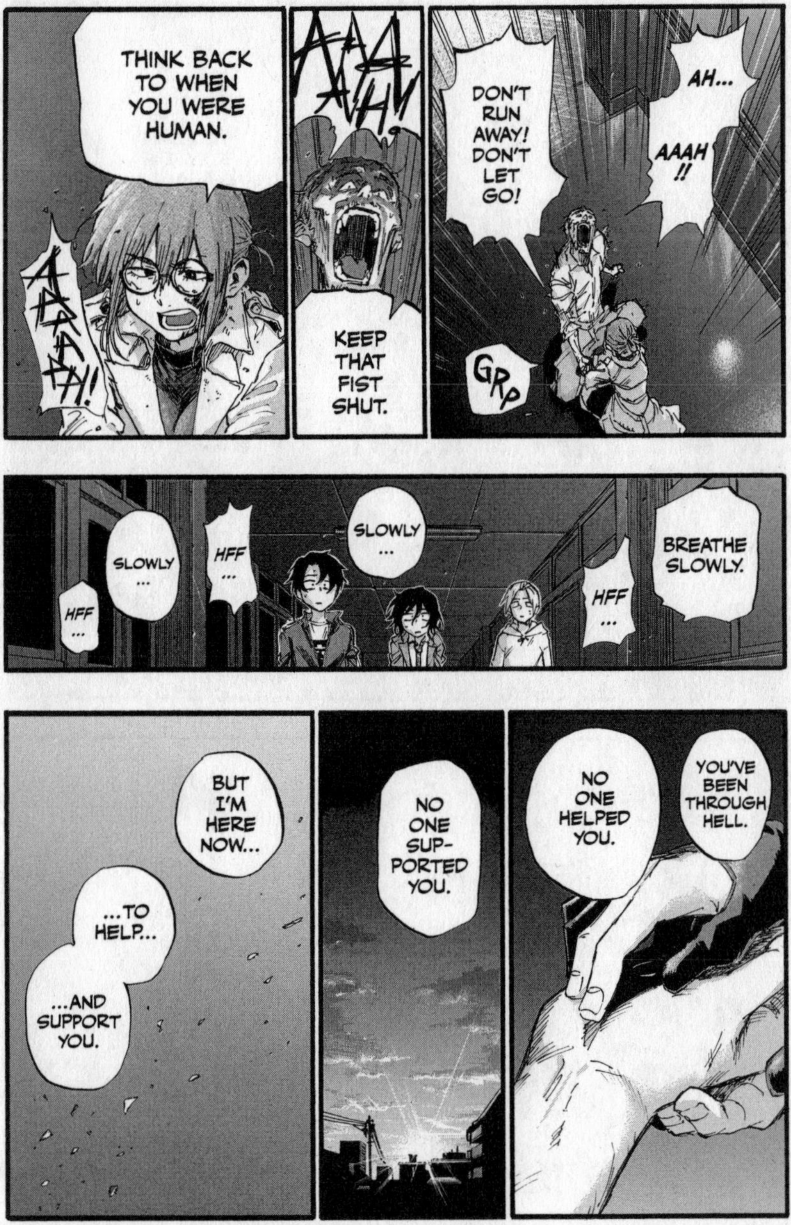
AH...
AAAH!!
DON'T RUN AWAY! DON'T LET GO!
GRP
AAAAH!
KEEP THAT FIST SHUT.
THINK BACK TO WHEN YOU WERE HUMAN.
AAAAAH!
BREATHE SLOWLY.
HFF...
SLOWLY...
HFF...
SLOWLY...
HFF...
YOU'VE BEEN THROUGH HELL.
NO ONE HELPED YOU.
NO ONE SUP-PORTED YOU.
BUT I'M HERE NOW...
...TO HELP...
...AND SUPPORT YOU.

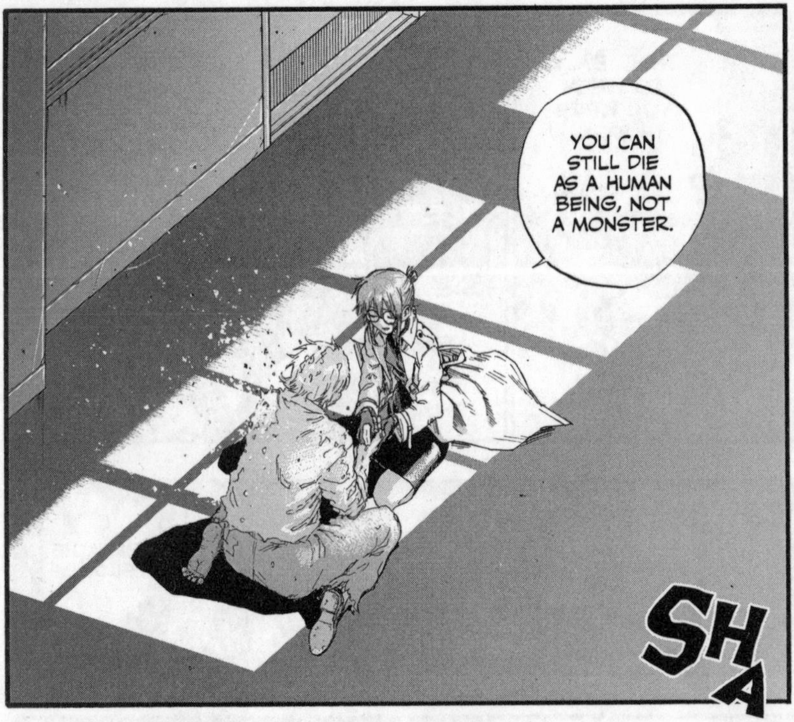
YOU CAN STILL DIE AS A HUMAN BEING, NOT A MONSTER.
SHA
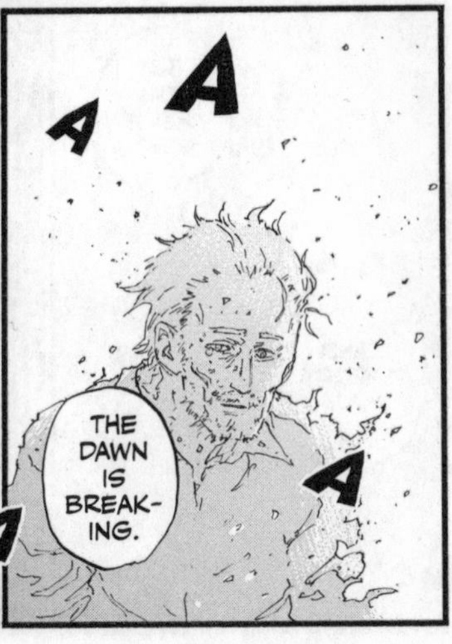
A
A
THE DAWN IS BREAK-ING.
A
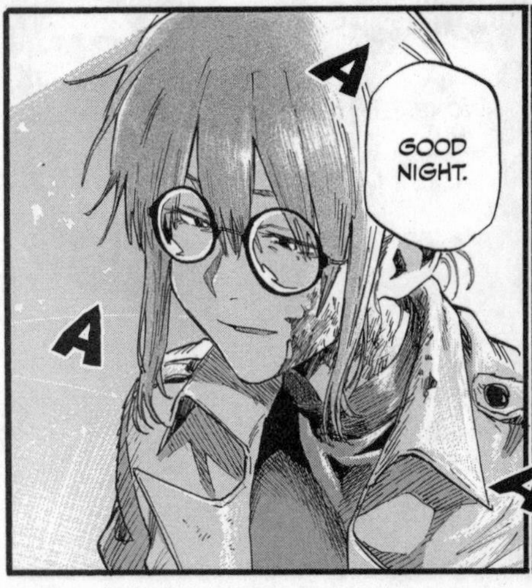
A
GOOD NIGHT.
A
A

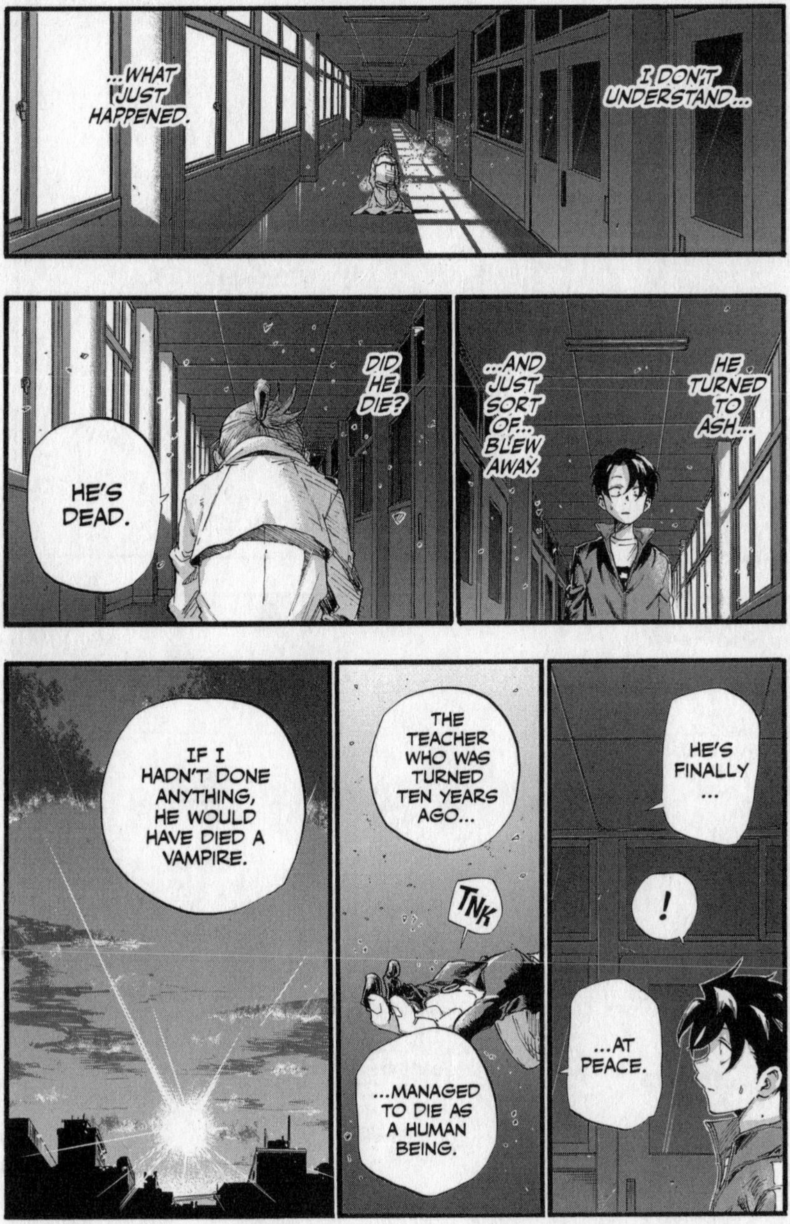
I DON'T UNDERSTAND...
...WHAT JUST HAPPENED.
HE TURNED TO ASH...
...AND JUST SORT OF... BLEW AWAY.
DID HE DIE?
HE'S DEAD.
HE'S FINALLY ...
!
...AT PEACE.
THE TEACHER WHO WAS TURNED TEN YEARS AGO...
TNK
...MANAGED TO DIE AS A HUMAN BEING.
IF I HADN'T DONE ANYTHING, HE WOULD HAVE DIED A VAMPIRE.

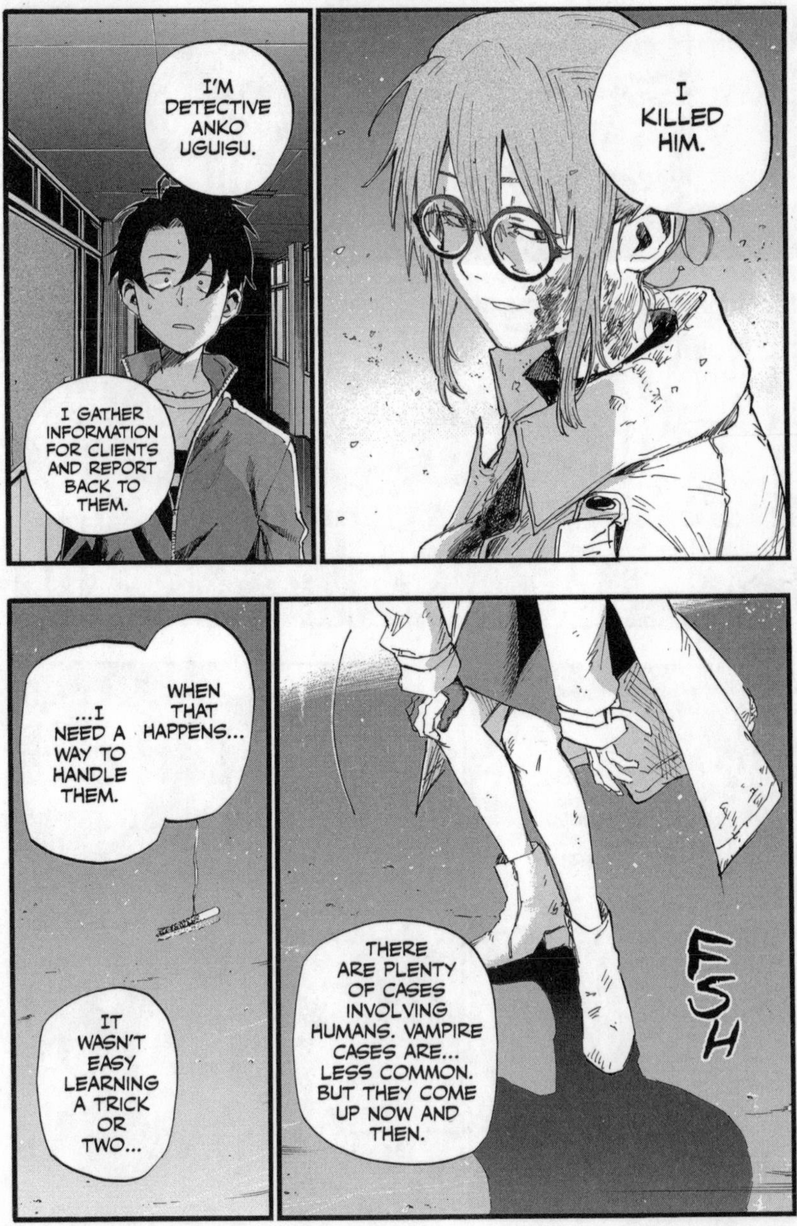
I KILLED HIM.
I'M DETECTIVE ANKO UGUISU.
I GATHER INFORMATION FOR CLIENTS AND REPORT BACK TO THEM.
FSH
THERE ARE PLENTY OF CASES INVOLVING HUMANS. VAMPIRE CASES ARE... LESS COMMON. BUT THEY COME UP NOW AND THEN.
WHEN THAT HAPPENS...
...I NEED A WAY TO HANDLE THEM.
IT WASN'T EASY LEARNING A TRICK OR TWO...

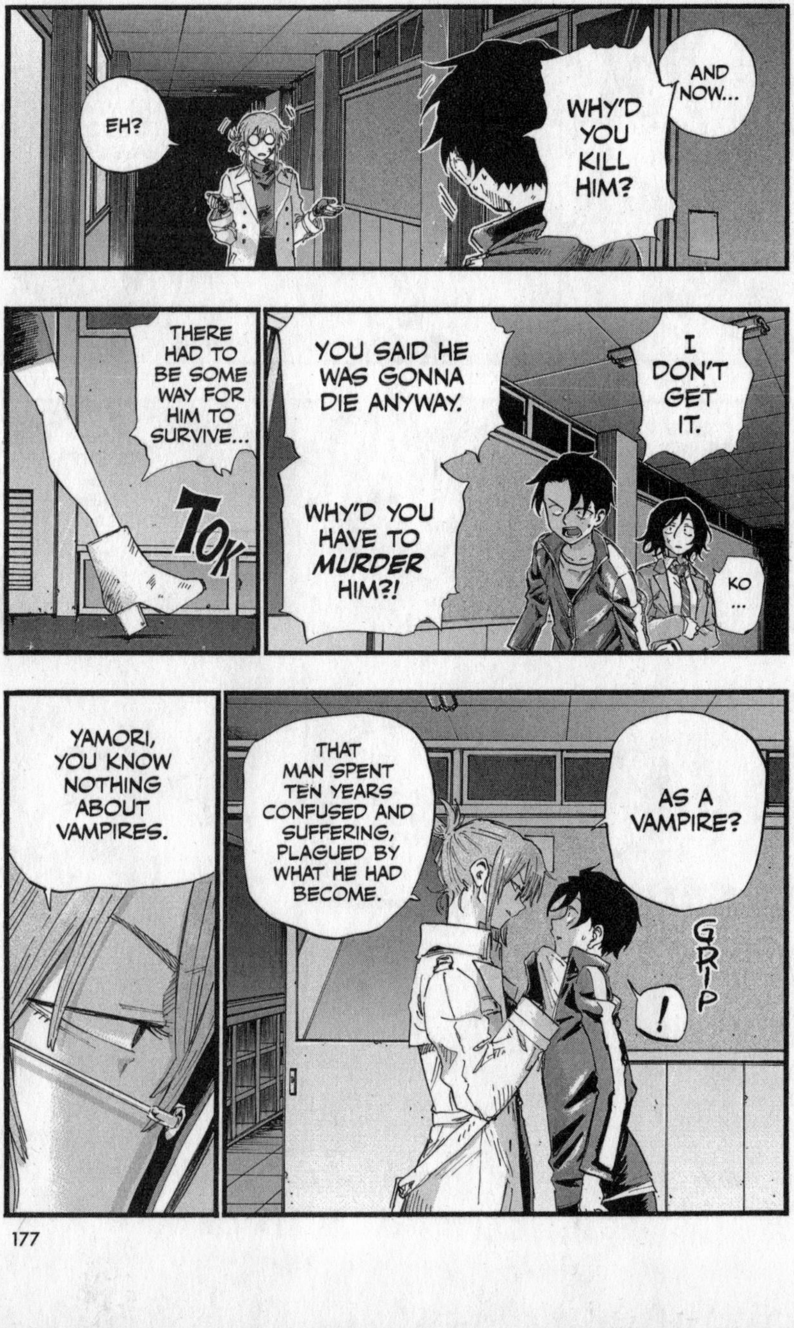
AND NOW...
WHY'D YOU KILL HIM?
EH?
I DON'T GET IT.
KO...
YOU SAID HE WAS GONNA DIE ANYWAY.
WHY'D YOU HAVE TO *MURDER* HIM?!
THERE HAD TO BE SOME WAY FOR HIM TO SURVIVE...
TOK
AS A VAMPIRE?
GRIP
!
THAT MAN SPENT TEN YEARS CONFUSED AND SUFFERING, PLAGUED BY WHAT HE HAD BECOME.
YAMORI, YOU KNOW NOTHING ABOUT VAMPIRES.

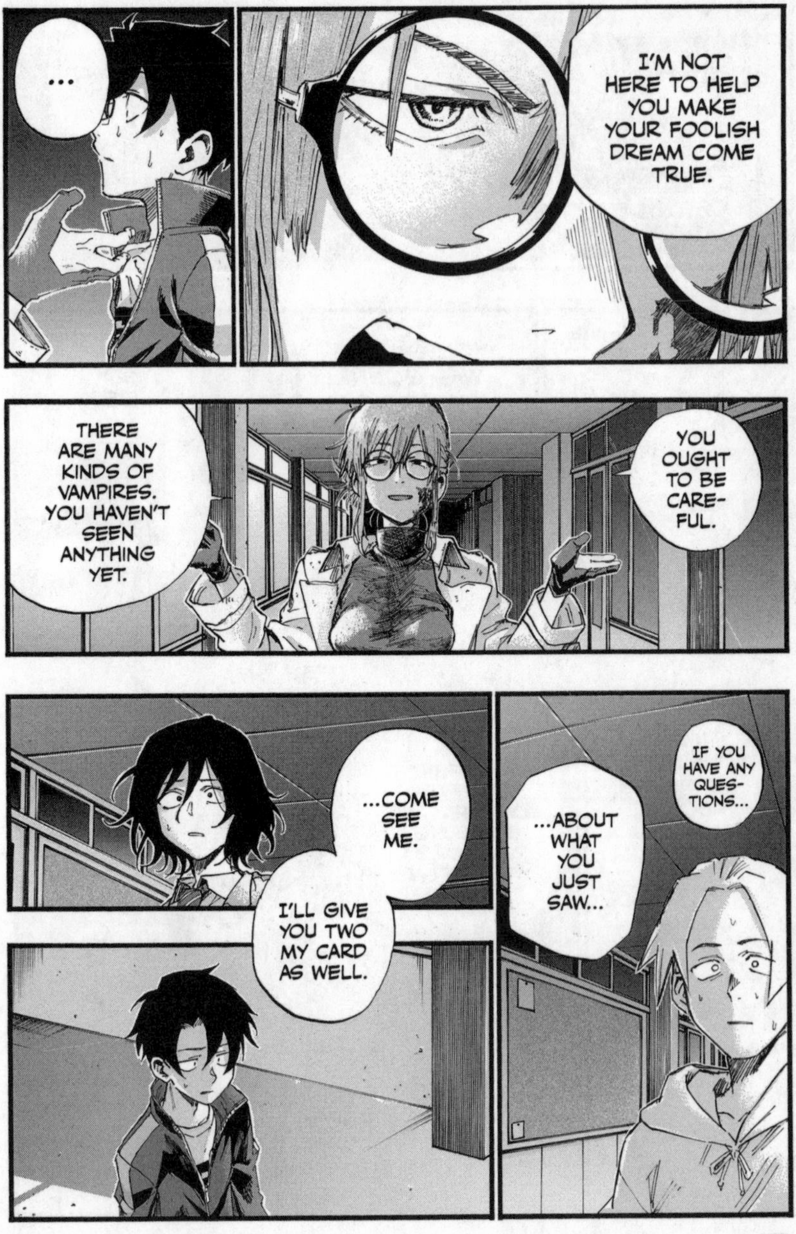
I'M NOT HERE TO HELP YOU MAKE YOUR FOOLISH DREAM COME TRUE.
...
YOU OUGHT TO BE CARE-FUL.
THERE ARE MANY KINDS OF VAMPIRES. YOU HAVEN'T SEEN ANYTHING YET.
IF YOU HAVE ANY QUES-TIONS...
...ABOUT WHAT YOU JUST SAW...
...COME SEE ME.
I'LL GIVE YOU TWO MY CARD AS WELL.

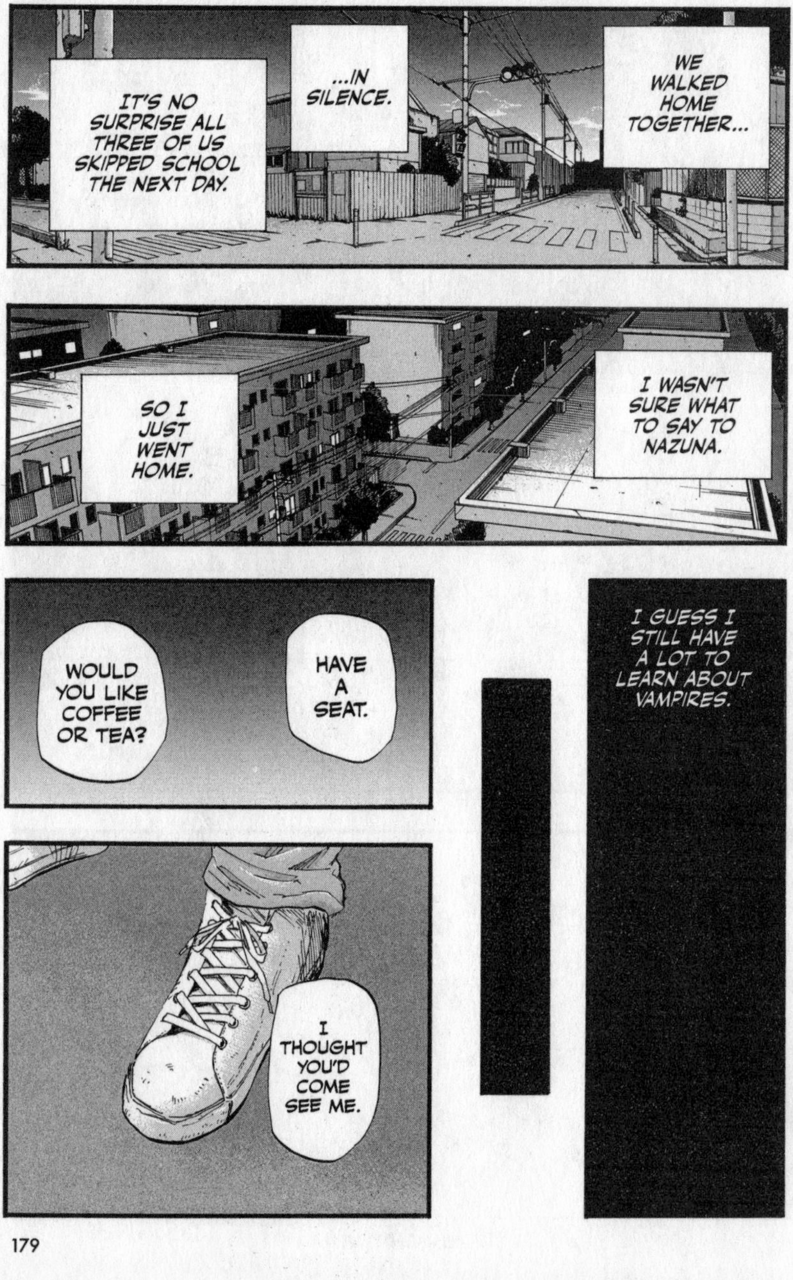
WE WALKED HOME TOGETHER...
...IN SILENCE.
IT'S NO SURPRISE ALL THREE OF US SKIPPED SCHOOL THE NEXT DAY.
I WASN'T SURE WHAT TO SAY TO NAZUNA.
SO I JUST WENT HOME.
I GUESS I STILL HAVE A LOT TO LEARN ABOUT VAMPIRES.
HAVE A SEAT.
WOULD YOU LIKE COFFEE OR TEA?
I THOUGHT YOU'D COME SEE ME.

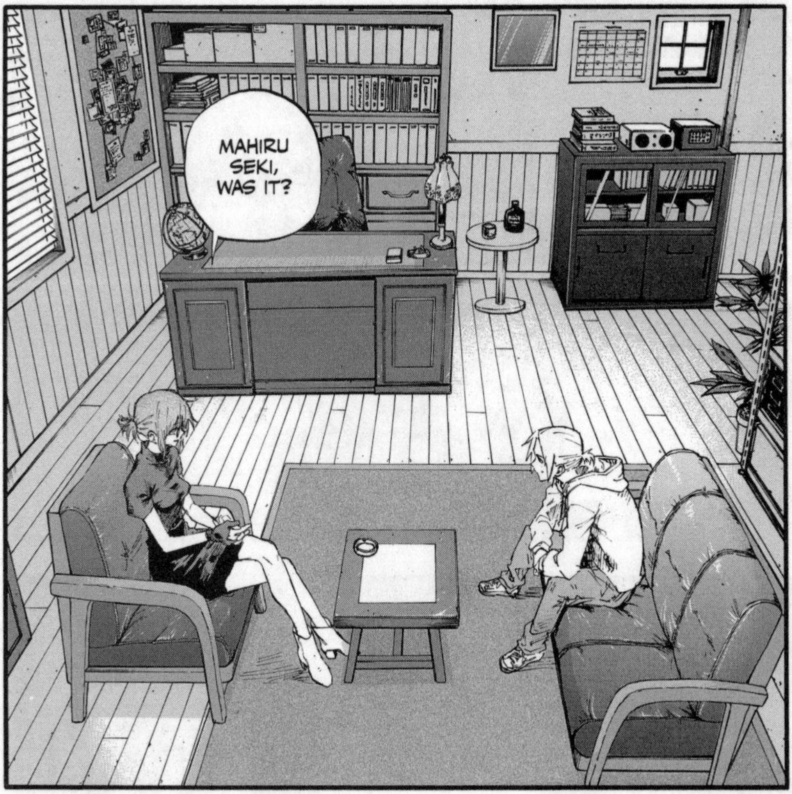
MAHIRU SEKI, WAS IT?

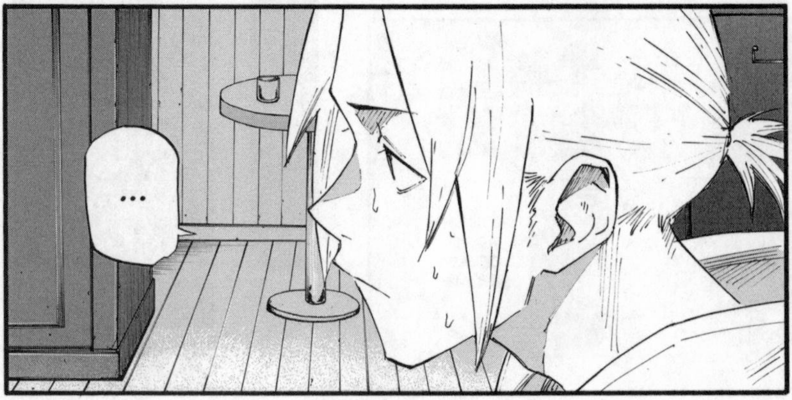
...

TO BE CONTINUED...

NIGHT 35.5: LET'S GET BACK TO THE SUBJECT

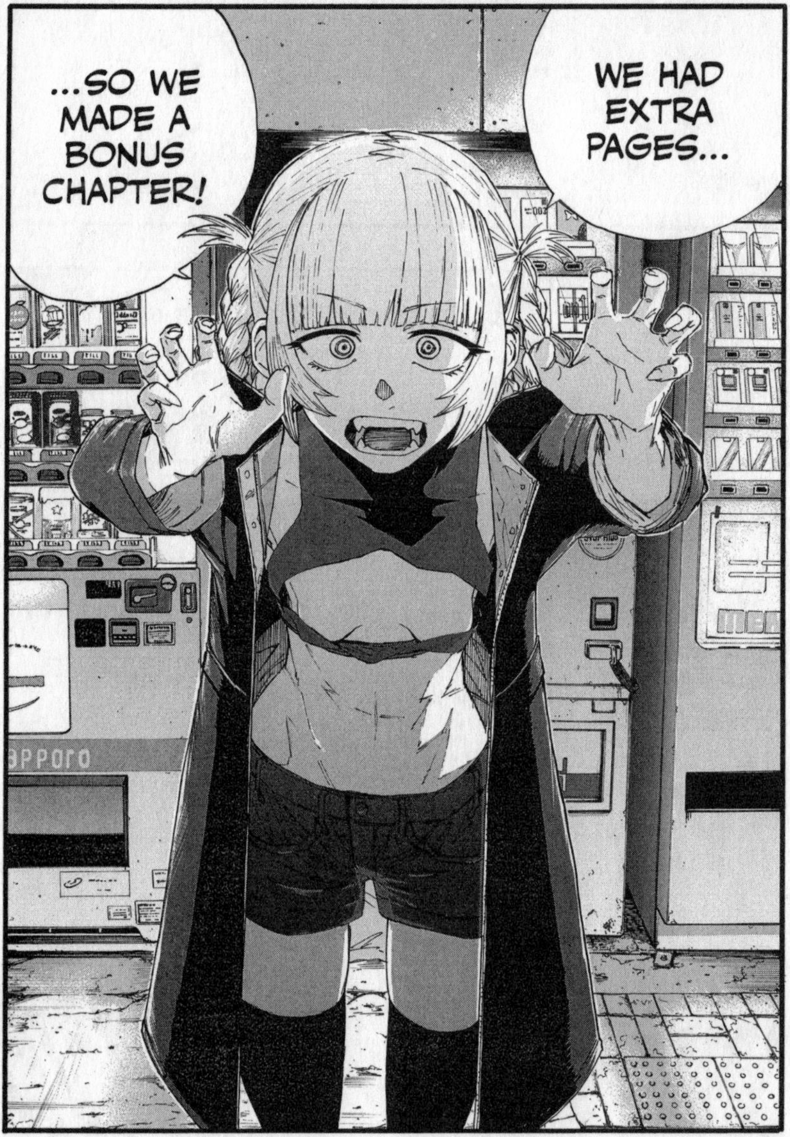
WE HAD EXTRA PAGES...
...SO WE MADE A BONUS CHAPTER!

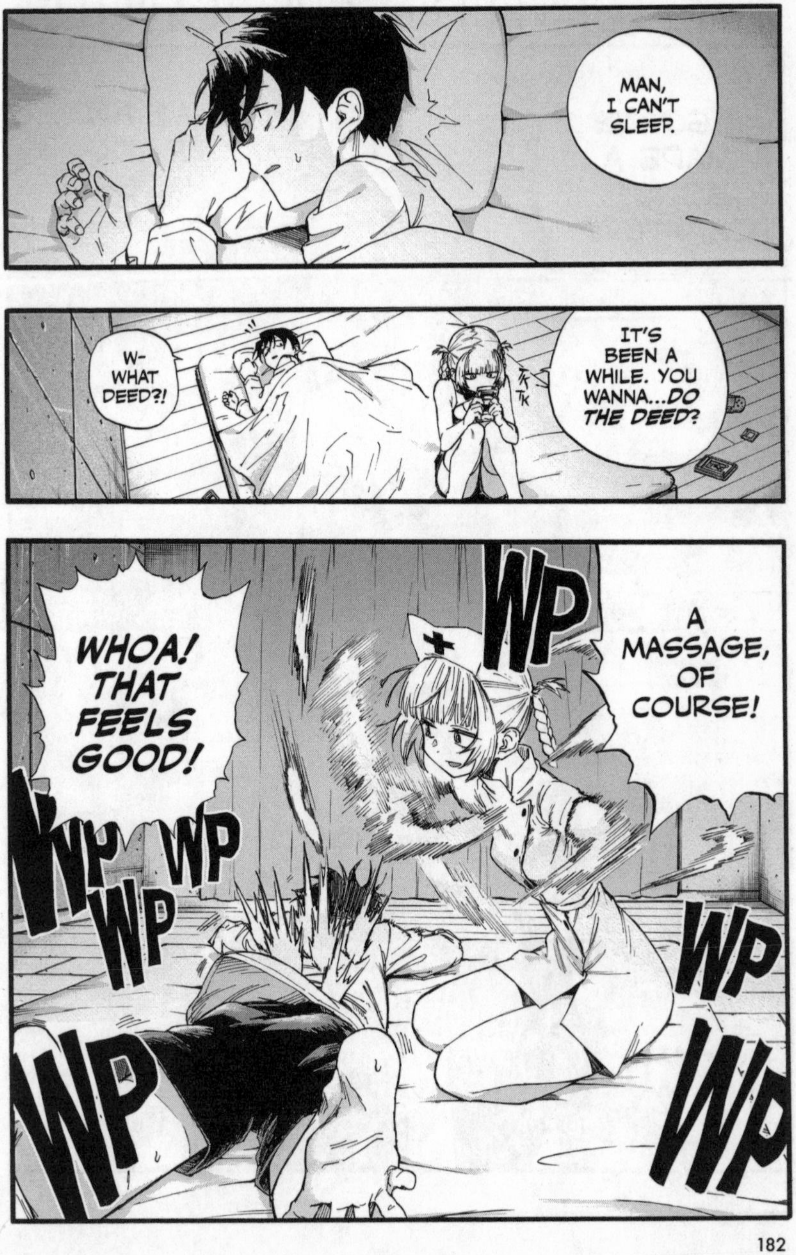
MAN, I CAN'T SLEEP.
IT'S BEEN A WHILE. YOU WANNA...*DO THE DEED?*
TK TK
W-WHAT DEED?!
WP
A MASSAGE, OF COURSE!
WHOA! THAT FEELS GOOD!
WP WP WP
WP
WP
WP

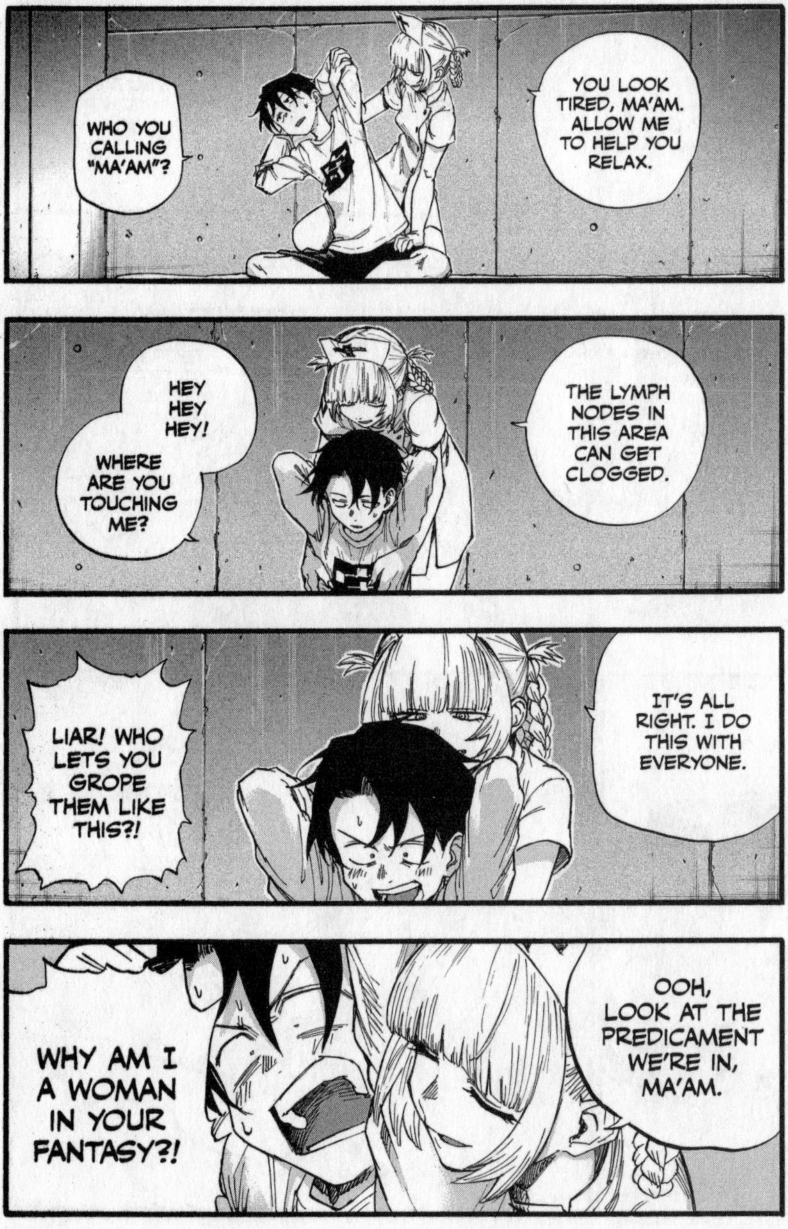
YOU LOOK TIRED, MA'AM. ALLOW ME TO HELP YOU RELAX.
WHO YOU CALLING "MA'AM"?
THE LYMPH NODES IN THIS AREA CAN GET CLOGGED.
HEY HEY HEY! WHERE ARE YOU TOUCHING ME?
IT'S ALL RIGHT. I DO THIS WITH EVERYONE.
LIAR! WHO LETS YOU GROPE THEM LIKE THIS?!
OOH, LOOK AT THE PREDICAMENT WE'RE IN, MA'AM.
WHY AM I A WOMAN IN YOUR FANTASY?!

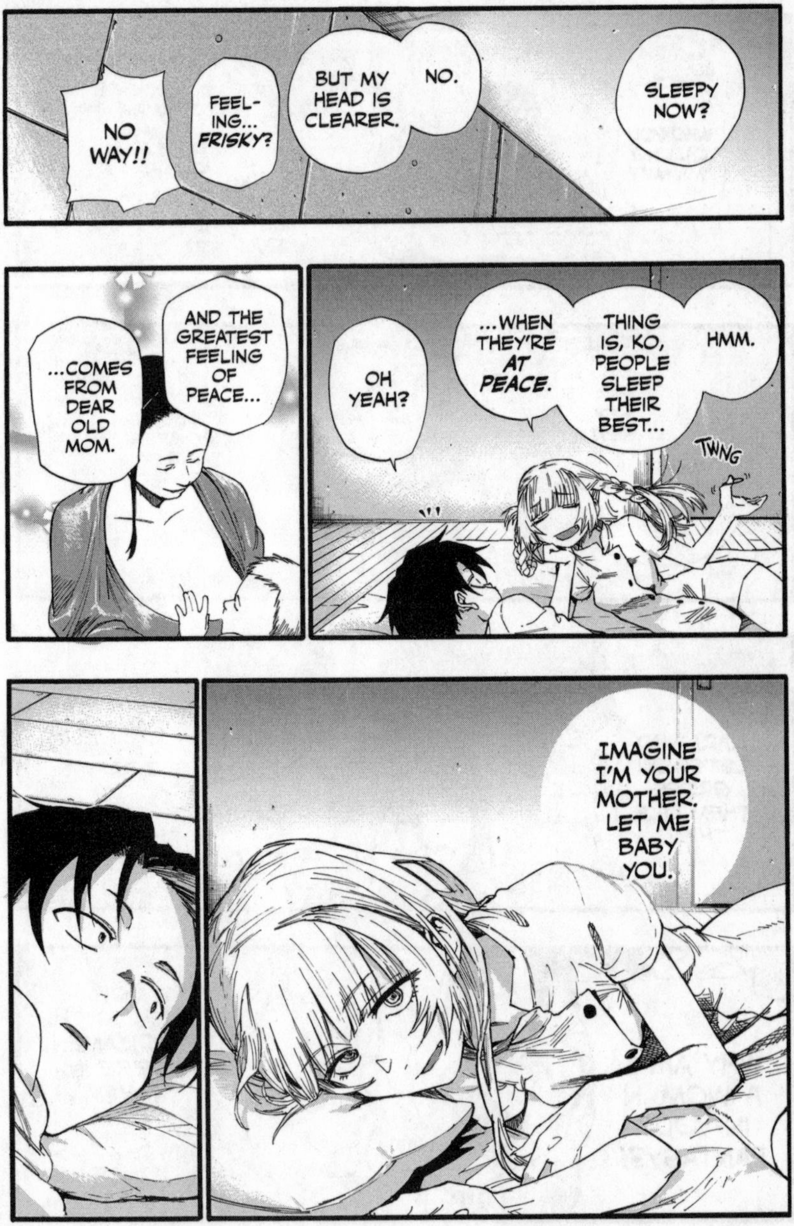
SLEEPY NOW?
NO.
BUT MY HEAD IS CLEARER.
FEEL-ING... *FRISKY*?
NO WAY!!
HMM.
THING IS, KO, PEOPLE SLEEP THEIR BEST...
...WHEN THEY'RE *AT PEACE*.
TWNG
OH YEAH?
AND THE GREATEST FEELING OF PEACE...
...COMES FROM DEAR OLD MOM.
IMAGINE I'M YOUR MOTHER. LET ME BABY YOU.

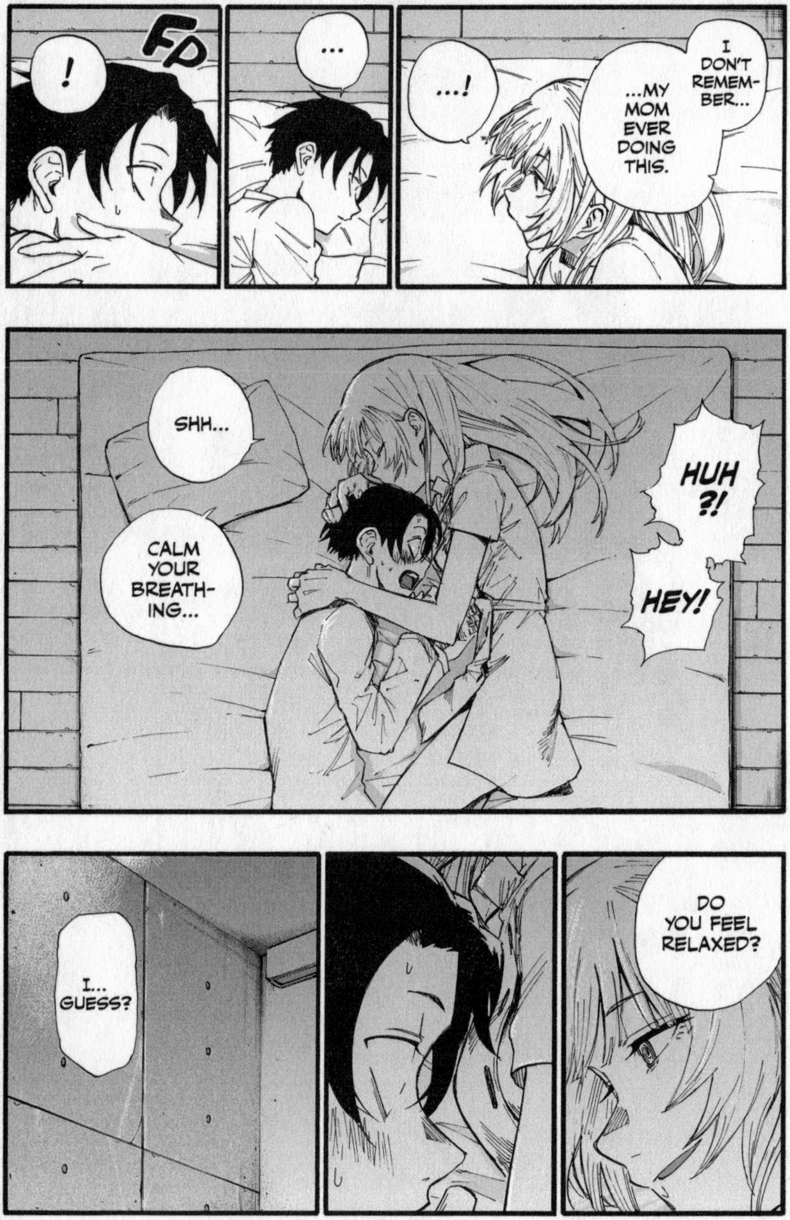
I DON'T REMEMBER...
...MY MOM EVER DOING THIS.
...!
...
!
FD
HUH?!
HEY!
SHH...
CALM YOUR BREATHING...
DO YOU FEEL RELAXED?
I... GUESS?

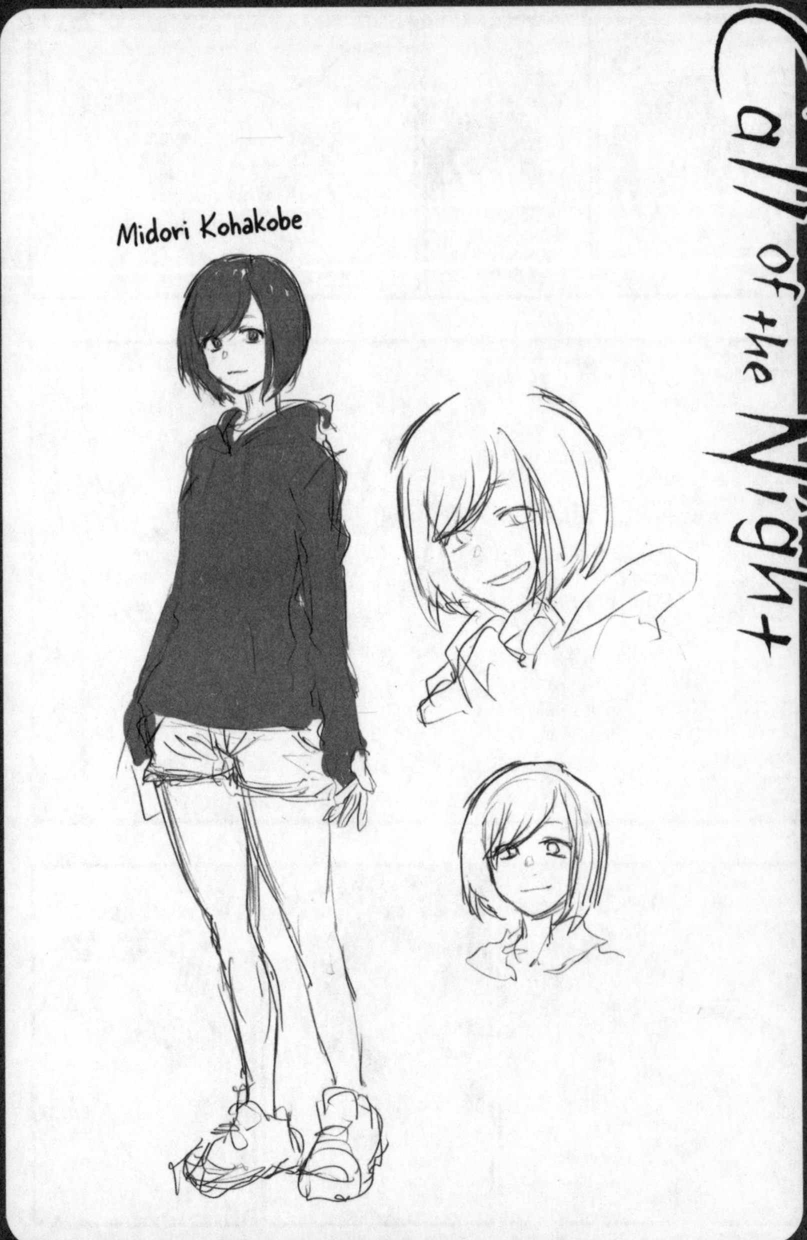
Call of the Night
Midori Kohakobe

Character Model Sheet #Midori

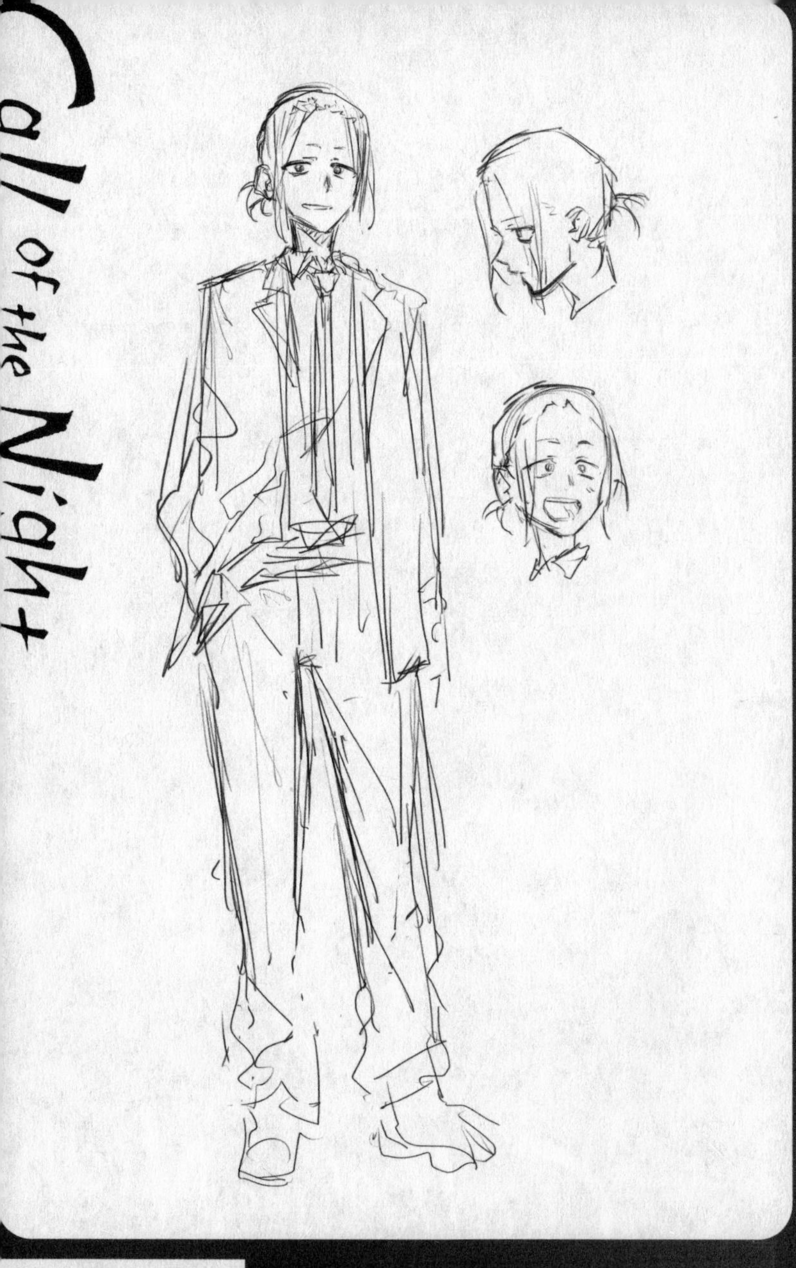
Call of the Night

acter Model Sheet #Mahiru

Call of the Night

Afterword

"I wanna draw a maid café."
That was the extent of fore-thought that went into the maid café story arc. I thought it would be fun.

This is volume 4. Thank you so much for picking it up!

I can never think of what to write in this section. I'll prob-ably get stuck for ideas in the next volume too. Considering how little content I come up with, I worry what you readers must think of me. I don't have much to say this time, either. Sorry.

See you in volume 5!

KOTOYAMA

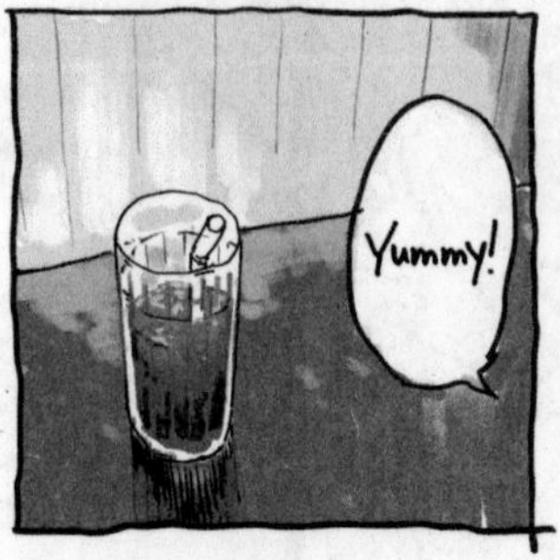
Yummy!

It's the time of year
when cold, iced black coffee
tastes especially good.

—KOTOYAMA

KOTOYAMA

In 2013, Kotoyama won the Shonen Sunday Manga College Award for *Azuma*. From 2014 to 2018, Kotoyama's title *Dagashi Kashi* ran in *Shonen Sunday* magazine. *Call of the Night* has been published in *Shonen Sunday* since 2019.

Call of the Night

⟨4⟩

SHONEN SUNDAY EDITION

Story and Art by
KOTOYAMA

Translation – **JUNKO GODA**
English Adaptation – **SHAENON K. GARRITY**
Touch-Up Art & Lettering – **ANNALIESE "ACE" CHRISTMAN**
Cover & Interior Design – **ALICE LEWIS**
Editor – **ANNETTE ROMAN**

YOFUKASHI NO UTA Vol. 4
by KOTOYAMA

Original Japanese edition published by SHOGAKUKAN.
English translation rights in the United States of America, Canada, the United Kingdom, Ireland, Australia and New Zealand arranged with SHOGAKUKAN.

Original Cover Design – Yasuhisa KAWATANI

Printed in the U.S.A.

Published by VIZ Media, LLC
P.O. Box 77010
San Francisco, CA 94107

10 9 8 7 6 5 4 3 2 1
First printing, October 2021

ratings.viz.com
RATED T+ OLDER TEEN

PARENTAL ADVISORY
CALL OF THE NIGHT is rated T+ for Older Teen and is recommended for ages 16 and up. It contains realistic violence and suggestive situations.

VIZ MEDIA
viz.com

SHONEN SUNDAY
shonensunday.com

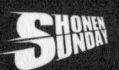

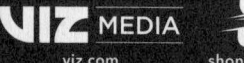

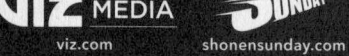

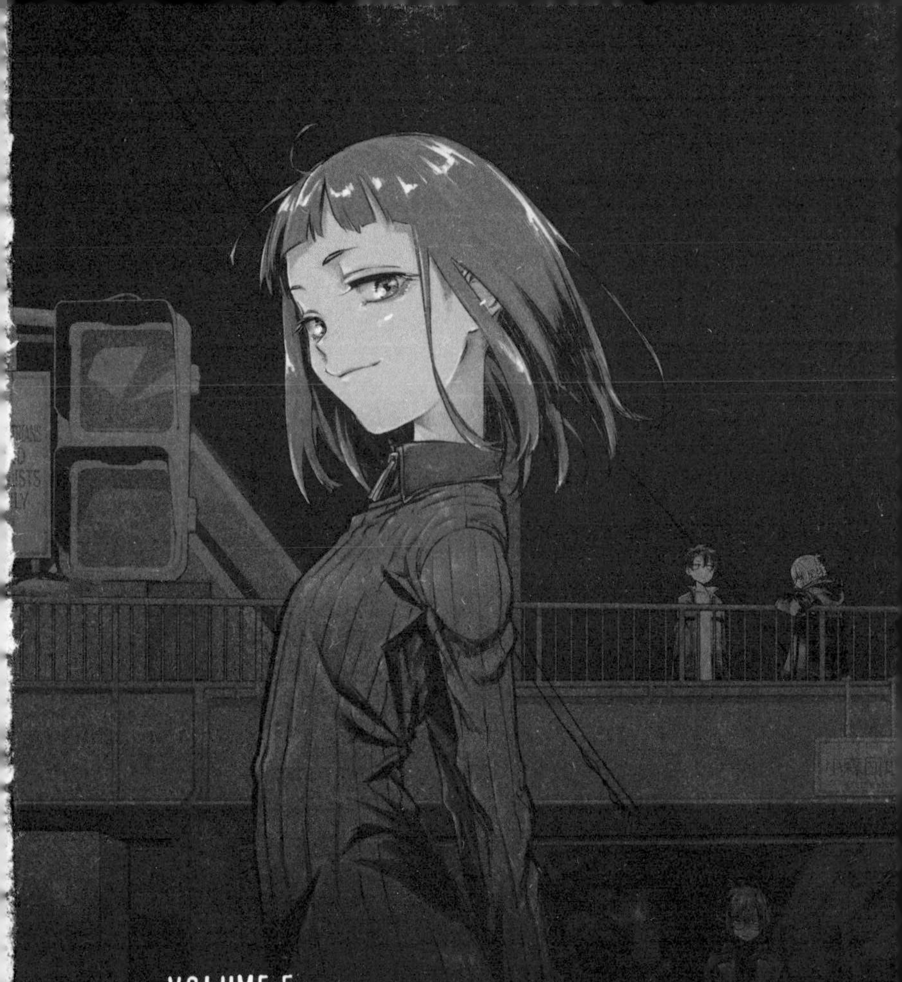

VOLUME 5

Ko seriously considers the pros and cons of becoming a vampire. But every human has a different take on it, and one of them just wants to kill them all! Then, when the police are alerted to Ko's nighttime jaunts, they start to cramp his style. Ko learns something surprising about vampire Hakka—and gets a tempting offer. Nazuna has a change of heart—but not about everything. And Ko wants to know what vampire Kiku's intentions are regarding Ko's deliciously human friend Mahiru...